Running in Good Faith?

Observant Judaism and Libertarian Politics

Cherry
Orchard
Books

Running in Good Faith?

Observant Judaism and Libertarian Politics

ALAN D. KRINSKY

BOSTON
2020

Library of Congress Control Number: 2020944465

ISBN 9781644693476 (hardback)
ISBN 9781644693483 (paperback)
ISBN 9781644693490 (adobe pdf)
ISBN 9781644693506 (epub)

Copyright © 2020 Academic Studies Press
All rights reserved.

Book design by Lapiz Digital Services.

Cover design by Ivan Grave.
Artwork by Udi Merioz, reproduced by permission.

Back cover photo by Juan Espinoza.

Published by Cherry Orchard Books, an imprint of Academic Studies
Press 1577 Beacon Street
Brookline, MA 02446, USA
press@academicstudiespress.com
www.academicstudiespress.com

To my parents,

Madelyn L. Krinsky and the late Howard B. Krinsky

Contents

Foreword *by Rabbi Arye Klapper*	vii
Preface	xi
Introduction: From Ayn Rand to Libertarianism	1
1. Freedom Versus Servitude	15
2. Ownership Versus Stewardship: The Body	39
3. Ownership Versus Stewardship: Private Property	66
4. Ownership Versus Stewardship: Taxation, Tzedakah, Charity	98
5. Government Tyranny Versus Government Protection	132
6. Individualism Versus Community	151
Conclusion: While Standing on One Foot	175
Epilogue	189
Endnotes	192
Bibliography	215
Acknowledgements	224
Index	229

Foreword

by Rabbi Aryeh Klapper

Judaism contains an astonishing number of laws—613 separate categories, each with tens, hundreds, or even thousands of sections and subsections. We are proud of the comprehensiveness of our legal system, or *halakhah*; a favorite Jewish story tells how the Khazar king was persuaded to convert by the fact that we have an extensive legal framework for restroom conduct. These people, he realized, were serious about applying religion to everything.

Libertarianism, by contrast, seeks to minimize law to the bare necessities. Every law is by definition an infringement of autonomy. At first glance, Judaism and libertarianism have radically opposed sensibilities.

But this opposition may be only seeming. Libertarianism sees human beings as free to impose any sort and number of obligations on themselves; the objection is only to imposing them on others. Moreover, some schools of libertarianism allow law to play a bigger role in smaller communities, where people have the realistic option of moving out, and where their individual voices play a much larger and more direct role in deciding what laws should be made. In other words, libertarian concerns apply to enforceable law, and especially to law that is enforced by the threat of official violence.

Much of halakhah is not law in that sense. Whole categories of Jewish law have no formal enforcement mechanism, and in fact are defined by the halakhic system to be outside the penal jurisdiction of human authorities. Moreover, the formal enforcement mechanisms of Jewish law are deliberately impractical and impracticable. For example, the only punishment listed for many violations is death, but halakhah claims capital jurisdiction only while the Sanhedrin [the highest court] is meeting in the Chamber of Hewn Stone in the Temple, and the Temple has been a ruin for two millennia, while halakhah endures. Regardless, R. Akiva and R. Tarfon stated soon after the Temple's destruction that "Had we been on the Sanhedrin, no one would ever have been executed."

For the two millennia immediately preceding 1948, Jews had very limited autonomy over themselves (and what authority they had was almost entirely local). Enforcement of Jewish law on the Jewish community was sometimes formally compelled by the non-Jewish authorities, and sometimes forbidden. Decisions about enforcement were always heavily influenced by what we might call the Jewish community's "foreign policy" rather than by concerns for domestic tranquility or individual self-actualization. It is difficult to see those decisions as derived from or reflecting any general positions about political theory.

Jews also had no authority whatever over Gentiles, and the concept of a joint Jewish-Gentile polity guided by Judaism was almost inconceivable. So the internal enforcement practices of Jewish communities have no necessary implications for evaluating the political practices of Gentile or pluralistic communities.

Given this fact, how ought Jews and Jewish communities to orient themselves in such places, particularly in the modern, secular state? Such is the question Alan Krinsky poses in this book.

Judaism does not understand its legal aspects as universally binding or applicable. Jewish law for Gentiles is formally much less expansive than that for Jews. The standard framing is that it includes only seven categories, known as the Seven Noahide Commandments, as opposed to the 613 categories for Jews. It is common and reasonable to think of the Noahide commandments as representing the bare necessities of governing relationships among human beings.

Within that framework, halakhah offers very little guidance as to how much government is necessary. For example, the commandment known as *dinim* requires the establishment of a viable criminal justice system. But for what crimes? Here is the powerful formulation of the great late nineteenth-century halakhist R. Meir Simchah of Dvinsk, in his Torah commentary *Meshekh Chokhmah* to Exodus 24:3:

> Know that Noachides are commanded regarding *dinim* (Sanhedrin 56b), and the position of the medieval authorities is that this refers to laws that appeal to human reason, but to coerce and compel regarding the statutes and commitments of Torah is justified only on the ground that "All Jews are *arevim*/guarantors for each other" (Shavuot 39a and others), so that if one transgresses, one damages their friend and their entire community, and therefore a rabbinic court is justified in coercing and judging the transgressor of the commandments of Hashem the Blessed, as without this it would be inappropriate for one person *sheyit'arev* (to mix into) another person's relationship with his Creator.

Meshekh Chokhmah's formulation seems fully consistent with a libertarian credo for Gentile society. Only laws that command rational consent may be enforced. No human society has the right to compel any human being to submit to a notion of the good that is not universally demonstrable, unless disobeying the law poses a genuine substantive threat to the wellbeing of the society. Human societies have the option of mutual religious or moral responsibility, and therefore of enforcing the law beyond libertarian limits, only when they act on the basis of a universally (within that society) acknowledged set of values.

A pluralistic society by definition does not have a universally agreed set of values. *Meshekh Chokhmah* contends that it is wrong for any group, majority or minority, to enforce its own values on a pluralistic society. In his view—which is certainly not the only Jewish voice on the issue—Judaism mandates something like a libertarian political ethos in American politics.

Certainly Judaism is not bound to any policy prescriptions advanced by a political party or movement. But it is fair and valuable to approach the question of what Judaism has to say about current policy issues with a recognition that Judaism may very well share crucial ideological ground with libertarians. Alan Krinsky does the Jewish and American publics a service by approaching such questions with that recognition. I hope his work finds broad readership and generates a great deal of productive and constructive discussion.

Preface

Can a religiously devout and observant Jew, without living a life of contradiction, uphold libertarianism—and even run in an election as a candidate championing a libertarian political platform? Would she or he necessarily violate basic religious or theological commitments? Would such an endeavor prove a betrayal of traditional Judaism? Or, perhaps, a fulfillment of it?

Initial reaction: a healthy dose of skepticism. Libertarianism, whether in terms of philosophy or political platform, remains anchored in absolute individualism and individual rights and their protection. Any version of traditional Judaism, by contrast, figures as a religion and a way of life rooted in obligation, duty, responsibility, community, and God's dominion over us and over the world (and it is not at all evident that traditional Judaism even conceptualizes the very notion of rights). How can someone who lives the latter possibly believe and represent the former?

This question and the initial, doubtful response provide not an ending, but rather a beginning, much in the way talmudic passages often do. A *sugya*, a discrete section of Talmud, unfolds as a back-and-forth, a give-and-take, a testing of hypotheses, a working out of ideas. Many such sections revolve around an effort to resolve apparent contradictions among the statements of earlier sages. A sugya might therefore unfold in the following way: The Talmud offers a possible resolution to a seeming contradiction, then rejects this proposal, and next suggests an alternate answer or resolution—repeating the process, often numerous times. Sometimes there are numerous branches: A first resolution is offered and then rejected, and then the rejection is shown not to apply, restoring the original resolution, only for an opportunity to entertain a second attempt to reject the resolution, and a dismissal of this second attempt, and so on.

Or: A resolution is offered and then rejected, then the rejection is shown not to apply and is dismissed, and yet then this dismissal is demonstrated to be mistaken, meaning the rejection of the resolution still holds. There are arguments followed by counterarguments, and should the original resolution fail to stand up, a different resolution might be offered, triggering a new cycle of argument and counterargument.

After considering the various solutions and objections and counter-objections, a sugya can conclude in a number of different ways. One approach is to recognize a disagreement and to side with one position or the other, perhaps due to the greater authority of one side over the other. Often, additional pieces of evidence will be brought to bear, possibly from other statements made by one of the original speakers in the dispute. Another approach is to demonstrate that the contradiction is merely apparent, not real. For example, two statements could refer to different cases. And such is ideal—to show that there was no contradiction among the sages. Finally, however, sometimes the Talmud lets a contradiction sit unresolved, an open puzzle. Such a talmudic section concludes with a single word: *teyku* (let it stand).

So, it is in the spirit of a talmudic sugya that we will set out to examine the question of whether or not Judaism and libertarianism exist in essential contradiction—to determine whether or not a pious Jew could, in good faith, run for office as a libertarian candidate. Our beginning will be the—at least apparent—contradiction of a libertarianism rooted in individual freedom and individual rights and a Judaism focused on community, obligation, and the service of God. Is the contradiction genuine or only seemingly so? Our approach will be to consider, in turn, a number of possible solutions to our dilemma, efforts to confirm or refute the hypothesis of fundamental contradiction. However, before we jump into such an analysis and our consideration of the compatibility or incompatibility of Judaism and libertarianism, a few caveats.

I received one of the greatest compliments of my life from my dear friend Richard (Haim) Dembo, may his memory be for a blessing, a French film director and writer. His film *La diagonale du fou* (*Dangerous Moves*) won the 1984 Oscar for Best Foreign Film, as Switzerland's entry. He and his wife, Jessica, and their son, many times welcomed me into their home while I was conducting research in Paris for my doctoral dissertation in History and the History of Science. The wonderful compliment:

Haim once told me that my French was *worth correcting*. I was by no means fluent, but neither was I a hopeless case. With the compliment, he was telling me that it was worth his time and effort to improve my French. How does this compliment become a caveat? I present here a book about Judaism and libertarianism, and although I am an expert in neither—there are many, many women and men who know much more about one or the other and no doubt a fair number who know more than me about both—I hope that my semi-fluency is worth correcting rather than dismissing outright.

What I mean to say is that I do not offer this book as a comprehensive and expert treatment of either libertarianism or Judaism, let alone both of them. Rather, I present this work as the first widely available book-length exploration of its kind, a thorough wrestling with a number of critical, thematic issues, matters of philosophy and politics.[1] My aim is to draw out ideas, to consider possible contradictions, to seek to resolve discrepancies, to raise questions. Given the breadth and depth of Judaism and libertarianism, no doubt I will have left out a number of issues others would have insisted I include. Nevertheless, I would like to think that I have made no flagrant or disastrous errors in my descriptions or interpretations. I hope what I have written remains worth correcting where appropriate.

Second caveat: In this book I seek to explore profound ideas in a readily accessible way, and any such effort requires some sacrifices for the sake of clarity and brevity. Jewish and libertarian sources are many and varied, and I make no pretension of presenting a comprehensive survey and analysis of Jewish *or* libertarian books, authors, and ideas. I will not give full voice to the varieties and complexities of Jewish or libertarian thought.

Furthermore, third caveat, neither Judaism nor libertarianism is monolithic. Indeed, as some historians, sociologists, and philosophers will explain, neither "Judaism" nor "libertarianism" is truly a *thing*. There is simply no timeless, essential Judaism or libertarianism, or of any *ism* for that matter. As my close friend, the Judaic and Religious Studies scholar Michael Satlow, explains,

> Essentialist definitions assert that there is an essence to a thing, usually marked by a set of defining characteristics. . . . Essentialist and normative

> definitions are useful for communal self-definition. . . . Such essentialist self-definitions help to reinforce group cohesion by giving its members an opportunity to unite as participants in some transcendent essence.

However,

> essentialist definitions of Judaism have more limited usefulness outside of the specific groups that use them. . . . Essentialist definitions of Judaism can never *explain* or account for the diversity of Jewish religious life, both today and through history. Those forms of Jewish life, practice, and belief that are thought to be in accord with the essentialist definition are the only data that are considered relevant, thus reinforcing the original definition.

That is, according to Satlow, it is fine for the adherent to describe herself or himself by invoking an essentialist definition, but the same proves problematic for an academic or anyone seeking to characterize from the outside, as using an essentialist approach by definition (unnecessarily and unproductively) limits the scope of description and analysis to the predetermined essential features—and this applies to other religious traditions, and presumably to other *isms*.[2]

I therefore state up front that I realize fully that one cannot speak of "Judaism" or "libertarianism" as if each is a single *thing*. If this is not obvious from the start, one need only consider the varieties of Jewish life and thought over many centuries. Across time and place, one can identify different denominations, as well as many self-identified adherents who would exclude from the Jewish community altogether many other self-identified adherents. With libertarianism too, its proponents hold many, sometimes contradictory, views. For instance, although most libertarians are pro-choice, some characterize themselves as antiabortion. More generally, some libertarians are anarchists, some are not. Yet the varieties explode far beyond this *no government* versus *minimal government* distinction, as there can be found, to name only a few, classical liberals, right-libertarians, left-libertarians, civil libertarians, minarchists, anarcho-capitalists, crypto-anarchists, geolibertarians, propertarianists, paleolibertarians, deontological libertarians, consequentialist libertarians, libertarian transhumanists, and bleeding-heart libertarians.

Given this rich diversity, I acknowledge that one really ought not to say "Judaism says . . . " or "According to libertarianism . . . " Therefore, I will seek to avoid such formulations, though in the effort of communicating ideas clearly and compactly, I will surely wind up, at least occasionally, speaking in generalities and painting with broad strokes.

In brief, I recognize both the *impossibility* and the *necessity* of speaking of Judaism and libertarianism in generalized terms. If I have anything of value to communicate with this book, let us just say that writing such a treatise remains possible only so long as we do not let an idealized perfection make speech impossible. And if Judaism and libertarianism share nothing else, they both do encourage a love of words and speech.

Returning to Satlow's distinction between those on the outside and those on the inside, it is worth noting that even if Judaism and libertarianism are not single, distinct, things, many actual human beings—as adherents, as community members—*do think of themselves* as Jews or as libertarians or as both. I take this reality seriously and see it as central to my framing of the question in terms of a committed Jew seeking to run for office as a libertarian candidate.

In further avoiding the pitfalls of essentialism, it is worth noting, as Rabbi Dr. Shlomo Dov Rosen suggested to me, that one ought to apply this lesson to individual words and not only to large concepts such as Judaism and libertarianism. Just because, for instance, one can identify and translate a particular ancient Hebrew word as meaning *freedom*, this does not entitle us to conclude that the modern American and ancient Hebrew words truly mean the same thing. Even between ancient and modern Hebrew, the same word, spelled and pronounced the same way, might bear different meanings or senses. Words that appear familiar to us today might not mean what they seem to mean.

A fourth caveat: Not only are Judaism and libertarianism not monolithic, they are not necessarily even the same sort of entities. For its adherents, Judaism is a way of life—much more than a set of theological beliefs. It can be all encompassing, turning seemingly secular and mundane acts such as eating into religious acts through the recitation of blessings and a kind of mindfulness. There are rituals and lifecycle events and often a rich communal life. As important as libertarian principles might be to someone who holds them, libertarianism remains philosophy and maybe politics, generally not a complete way of life. This is just to say that one should keep such differences in perspective. Comparing Judaism and libertarianism is not like comparing Judaism and Islam, nor is it like comparing libertarianism with socialism. In this sense, I am not asking if Judaism and libertarianism are compatible or in contradiction, but rather whether someone who is a devout Jew can also maintain, without contradiction, a set of libertarian philosophical principles and political positions. And perhaps given this difference between the sorts of things Judaism and libertarianism are, one should be neither surprised nor offended that Judaism is capitalized, whereas libertarianism is not.

In terms of the capitalization of this L-word, a fifth caveat, I am adhering to the following convention, explained to me by the libertarian economist Walter Block: use a capital L only when referring to a Libertarian Party using the word in its name, otherwise use libertarian. For the most part, I seek to discuss libertarians and libertarian ideas without pegging them to a particular political party.

And from this point, a sixth caveat: The many philosophical libertarianisms are not identical with the libertarianism of a particular political party. Indeed, I suspect that many or most individuals who identify philosophically as libertarians, who hold what they take to be libertarian principles, never register themselves as members of any libertarian political party. Certainly, few anarchist libertarians would participate in the electoral process. But many nonanarchist libertarians would object to one or more principles or claims or positions put forth in such a document as, for example, the platform of the Libertarian Party of the United States.

Why, then, is this book, beginning with its title and the first sentence of this Preface, focused on the idea of running for office as a candidate from a libertarian political party? Partly, my own professional work as a policy analyst takes place within the very practical world of politics and legislation. I analyze actual bills introduced by elected officials in a single state of the United States. I attend committee hearings and offer testimony in support or in opposition to bills. Some of these bills will be passed and signed into law. Although my work does not involve electoral campaigns, my work frequently brings me into contact with legislators, as well as with executive branch officials. In addition, a solely philosophical analysis, while no less interesting, might leave out some of the more practical matters I want to discuss. Surely I am interested in philosophical commonalities and contradictions, yet I also find fascinating the practical implications, the differences they make in our actual lives. And

I would be less than honest if I did not admit that I think the question of running for office in good faith works as a decent hook to draw in readers for a discussion of philosophical and theological questions. A more generic framing of Judaism and libertarianism as philosophies or as matters of personal belief might not achieve this to the same degree.

Also, a note about translations and transliterations. For the latter I have sought to adhere to the guidelines of the *Encyclopedia Judaica*, with exceptions made for some words commonly transliterated otherwise. Similarly, I have deferred to Anglicizations of biblical names, so Cain and Abel instead of Kayin and Hevel, and Isaac instead of Yitzchak or Yiẓḥak. For translations from the Torah, the Prophets, and the Writings (including Psalms), and from *Pirkei Avot* (*The Chapters of the Fathers*, sometimes also translated as *The Ethics of the Fathers*), I have generally relied upon publications from Koren Press. For translations from the Talmud and from post-talmudic commentators, I indicate the source of translation or note where the translation is my own; in a few cases, should a reader wish to examine it, I provide in the endnotes the original Hebrew text.

Last caveat: When writing of historically Jewish ideas and values, I will draw out some disagreements, but largely I will be writing about a more traditional Judaism (or Judaism*s*), of the texts and the ideas and the ways of life forming its foundation. I aim to explore the potential limits of expression for a religiously observant Jew (though by referring to religiously observant Jews, I do no not mean to limit my framework to avowedly Orthodox ones—after all, some Jews identifying themselves as non-Orthodox live religiously observant lives, and some Jews identifying themselves as Orthodox do not—whether in terms of ritual obligations or interpersonal obligations in Jewish law). Clearly, a secular Jew, one who perhaps identifies ethnically or culturally as Jewish, could run in good "faith" for elected office as a libertarian. I want to know, however, what such a campaign would mean for a Jew who believes that God gave the Jews the Torah, a Jew who lives her or his life in the light of this conviction and the ensuing commitments, whether those of daily life or those of ideas and theology.

Finally, why a book now about libertarianism and Judaism?

For the United States, with the electoral shocks suffered in 2016 by both major political parties, the Democrats and Republicans, and with what some would characterize as the transformation of the latter into a personality cult, the nation may prove ripe for a political realignment in the years to follow. Will disaffected, former Republicans seek out a new moderate or conservative party? Will the decades-old, though perhaps odd, Republican alliance of social and fiscal conservatives collapse? If so, the fiscal conservatives, especially those who identify as socially liberal might very well find attractive a libertarian party. If we assume for now that the United States will remain a democratic republic and not descend into authoritarianism, we may witness an opportunity unlike any other in a century or more for other political parties, such as the Libertarian Party, to capture an electorally meaningful segment of the population in future electoral cycles.

Even without any such realignment, however, the issues discussed here remain important ones. Libertarians, regardless of their own electoral potential, pose incisive questions for those on both the Left and the Right of the political spectrum. In addition to asking questions about the meaning of freedom and individualism and the nature of the state and state authority, libertarians challenge us to question when government spending of our tax dollars is necessary and effective and when it is not. Both liberals and conservatives find plenty to criticize about government priorities and spending. And libertarians also beg us to consider carefully what trade-offs we make in sacrificing liberty for security.

As Jews have long found themselves deeply involved in the political life of nations and political parties wherever such environments proved hospitable, we should not be surprised to find Jewish involvement in any ascendant third parties, a libertarian political party included.

Introduction

From Ayn Rand to Libertarianism

Where It Usually Begins

It all began when my cousin Marc gave me a copy of Jerome Tuccille's book *It Usually Begins With Ayn Rand*. That, at least, was the start of the transition—from an adolescent enamored and entranced by *The Fountainhead* and *Atlas Shrugged* and Ayn Rand's philosophy of Objectivism to a young adult drawn to libertarianism.

Listen to the intoxicating language of *The Fountainhead*:

> Throughout the centuries there were men who took first steps down new roads armed with nothing but their own vision. Their goals differed, but they all had this in common: that the step was first, the road new, the vision unborrowed, and the response they received—hatred. The great creators—the thinkers, the artists, the scientists, the inventors—stood alone against the men of their time. Every great new thought was opposed. Every great new invention was denounced. The first motor was considered foolish. The airplane was considered impossible. The power loom was considered vicious. Anesthesia was considered sinful. But the men of unborrowed vision went ahead. They fought, they suffered and they paid. But they won.[3]

I found myself swept away by Rand's confident, breathtaking prose. I too wished to join the elite ranks of visionaries, builders, creators. And I admired Howard Roark, Rand's architect-hero:

> "Do you mean to tell me that you're thinking seriously of building *that way*, when and *if* you are an architect?"
> "Yes."
> "My dear fellow, who will let you?"
> "That's not the point. The point is, who will stop me?"[4]

Is there any surprise that an adolescent, feeling alienated from the world, might embrace such soaring, powerful rhetoric, see himself or herself as one of the elite, one of Rand's men and women of vision and integrity? To be bold and accomplished, to achieve greatness—I wished to flee suburbia to realize such a dream. With Tuccille's book I discovered that I was far from alone in my teenage infatuation with the heroes of Ayn Rand's novels and with her simple, bold philosophy. As Tuccille characterizes the situation, "The young crusader in search of a cause enters the world of *The Fountainhead* or *Atlas Shrugged* . . . before long he is swept away by the rampaging prose of the author and the heroic activities of her characters." Tuccille describes the encounter in religious terms, with the adolescent seeking meaning and absolute Truth: "It is all quite heady, this stuff, when fed in massive doses to the impressionable young mind all at once. It is especially appealing to those in the process of escaping a regimented, religious background—particularly young Jews and renegade Roman Catholics, ripe for conversion to some form of religion-substitute to fill the vacuum."[5] I did grow up Jewish, though by no means in a "regimented, religious" framework. In any case, after painting this portrait of the young recruit, Tuccille then spends many chapters discussing history and politics and libertarianism in the real world. And so from my infatuation with Rand and her heroes I matured, learning something about genuine libertarian politics and philosophy.

I was not the only one to mature. I am in good company. In a 2012 *Rolling Stone* interview, President Barack Obama admitted as much about himself:

> Ayn Rand is one of those things that a lot of us, when we were 17 or 18 and feeling misunderstood, we'd pick up. Then, as we get older, we

realize that a world in which we're only thinking about ourselves and not thinking about anybody else, in which we're considering the entire project of developing ourselves as more important than our relationships to other people and making sure that everybody else has opportunity—that that's a pretty narrow vision.[6]

Like President Obama, I broke free of Rand's spell. As a first-year college student in Boston I even connected with the local chapter of the Libertarian Party—at least until ideas of cultural anthropology, language and meaning, and moral relativism shattered for some time my world, including my adolescent infatuation with Ayn Rand's purist and unambiguous fantasy (but that is another story for another time).

Libertarian: Origins of the Term

Although the ideas go back centuries—and the term or label libertarian saw some usage, at least in France, as far back as the late eighteenth century[7]—modern libertarianism as a movement and as an organized political force, at least in the United States, emerged only a few decades ago, in the 1950s and 1960s. Perhaps the first use of the term in the current, political sense, took place in 1955, with the publication of Dean Russell's short essay "Who Is a Libertarian?" In this essay, Russell (1915-1988) crisply characterizes libertarians as those who "love liberty." A libertarian, in his articulation, is someone

> who rejects the idea of using violence or the threat of violence—legal or illegal—to impose his will or viewpoint upon any peaceful person. . . . A libertarian believes that the government should protect all persons equally against external and internal aggression, but should otherwise generally leave people alone to work out their own problems and aspirations. . . . A libertarian holds that persons who make wise choices are entitled to enjoy the fruits of their wisdom, and that persons who make unwise choices have no right to demand that the government reimburse them for their folly.[8]

The publication *Ideas on Liberty* came out of the Foundation for Economic Education, an organization started by Leonard Read (1898–1983) and considered to have been perhaps the first organization to promote libertarianism as many think of it today. According to David Boaz, the executive vice president of the libertarian think tank the Cato Institute, Read identified himself as a libertarian as early as the 1950s.[9] In the essay, Russell wrote, at least speculatively, of trademarking the term libertarian. That idea might not have been entirely welcomed by anarchists, who claimed to have invoked the term a century earlier.

That present-day libertarians and anarchists might both lay claim to the label only points to the fact that once one enters the world of libertarian ideas, one quickly finds that there are many, many kinds of libertarians, as noted above, in the preface. Indeed, even such a figure as Noam Chomsky, usually considered to occupy a position on the far left of the political spectrum, has found himself associated with libertarianism:

> Actually I don't think I've ever called myself a "libertarian," because the term is too ambiguous. I do often call myself a "libertarian socialist," however.
>
> The term "libertarian" has an idiosyncratic usage in the US and Canada, reflecting, I suppose, the unusual power of business in these societies. In the European tradition, "libertarian socialism" ("socialisme libertaire") was the anti-state branch of the socialist movement: anarchism (in the European, not the US sense).
>
> I use the term in the traditional sense, not the US sense.

In terms of prominent libertarian thinkers, Chomsky sharply criticized Friedrich August von Hayek and Robert Nozick—and Ayn Rand: "Rand in my view is one of the most evil figures of modern intellectual history." Nonetheless, he recognized Milton Friedman as "an important economist" (if one he "strongly dislike[d]") and noted that he, Chomsky, shared some ideas with people at the Cato Institute, which had published him in one of their journals.[10]

Most American libertarians would characterize themselves as what many refer to as Classical Liberals, emphasizing the importance of freedom, individual rights, private property, the free market, and limited government. In the American political context, this generally places libertarians as *conservative on economic issues* and *liberal on social issues*, meaning they can find no true home in either the Republican Party or the Democratic Party. On foreign policy matters, libertarians tend to be strong noninterventionists, further away from the center than either

Democrats or Republicans. The Libertarian Party in the United States was founded in 1971, and it has run candidates in all presidential elections since. Its first party platform was adopted in 1972 and has been modified periodically since then; the current Libertarian Party Platform was revised and adopted in 2018 at the party's national convention.[11]

A Libertarian Moment?

Back in the days of my flirtation with libertarianism, during the second half of the 1980s, the Libertarian Party in the United States was still young, founded only a decade and a half earlier and still reveling in Ed Clark's 1980 run for the presidency, an election also featuring a strong Independent and third party candidate in John Anderson. Clark secured more than 900,000 votes, just over 1 percent of those cast. In 2012, Libertarian Party candidate and former New Mexico Governor Gary Johnson won more than a million votes (though just under 1 percent of all votes), and in 2016, despite running a somewhat lackluster campaign, Johnson and his running mate, former Massachusetts Governor William Weld, drew close to 4.5 million votes, over 3 percent of votes cast. Although one might have imagined that this Libertarian Party ticket would perform even better against two such unpopular main party candidates, this outcome nonetheless surpassed those of all prior tickets.

Meanwhile, Ayn Rand's books continue to sell at a rather healthy rate, in the hundreds of thousands per year more than thirty-five years after her death in 1982, at the age of seventy-seven. Former Speaker of the House and vice presidential candidate Paul Ryan was reputed to have given copies of *Atlas Shrugged* to his interns and to have made them read the over-a-thousand-page book. Former Representative Ron Paul certainly has strong libertarian leanings, embracing such thinkers as Murray Rothbard and Ayn Rand (though despite what I suspect might be a popular myth, it is my understanding that his son Senator Rand Paul's first name is short for Randall and not any sort of tribute to Ayn Rand).

More broadly, Ayn Rand's uncompromising, absolutist approach to capitalism and individualism have certainly contributed to pushing American political discourse in a libertarian direction. Such an orientation can be observed in the Tea Party and in the so-called Freedom Caucus of some Republicans in the United States House of Representatives, as well as the increasingly frequent calls to oppose *any* legislative compromise, no matter the consequences.[12]

Not only has libertarianism influenced American politics, but avowed libertarians have increasingly won political office running as Libertarian Party candidates. Across the United States at the close of 2016, Libertarians held at least 144 positions, 139 elected and 5 appointed. These office holders included 3 state legislators, 9 mayors, and more than 50 city, town, borough, and county councilors in some 36 of the 50 states. In the November 2016 elections, Libertarians fielded just over 600 candidates, including 10 for governorships, 23 for the United States Senate, and 121 in 33 states for the United States House of Representatives. The Libertarian candidate for one of Alaska's Senate seats pulled in an impressive 29 percent of the vote; another 5 Senate candidates won 3 percent or more of the votes in their races. For the 2018 elections, the number of Libertarian Party candidates rose to 833, with 54 of these elected to office. By early 2019, the Libertarian Party claimed a total of 180 elected officials, 56 of these in partisan positions, the remaining ones in nonpartisan positions.[13] The future will tell us whether or not the dozens of Libertarian mayors and city councilors and water and fire and school board officials will translate into many Libertarian Party office holders on the state or federal levels. Although Representative Justin Amash of Michigan won office as a Republican, he left the Republican Party in 2019 to become an Independent, and in April 2020 he became the first Libertarian Party member to hold office in the United States Congress. No doubt, under a system of proportional representation, rather than the winner-takes-all system throughout most of the United States, Libertarian Party candidates would win many more elected offices, at all levels of government.

Do these numbers, of candidates and office holders, bode well for Libertarian Party politics? Or, to pose the question in another way, as a noted Summer 2014 feature article in the *New York Times Magazine* asked, "Has the 'Libertarian Moment' finally arrived?"[14]

In truth, the notion of a possible "Libertarian Moment" originated a few years earlier, in a 2008 article in *Reason* magazine. Writing shortly after Barack Obama's historic election to the presidency of the United States, the authors, Nick Gillespie and Matt Welch (both of whom have served as the magazine's editor in chief), argued that freedom had *increased* during the 1960s and 1970s and since then (and despite the political darkness of the early 1970s, with Nixon's use of the government to attack his enemies, and such antilibertarian policies as freezing prices and wages, increasing tariffs, and discarding the gold standard). The authors pointed to the following pieces of evidence that such a moment had indeed arrived: gay liberation; the contraceptive pill; and free agency in sports and the arts. They celebrated the 1970s as the "Me Decade"—as a precursor in a sense to the twenty-first century as "[t]his new century of the individual, which makes the Me Decade look positively communitarian in comparison." Gillespie and Welch asserted that

> We are in fact living at the cusp of what should be called the Libertarian Moment, the dawning not of some fabled, clichéd, and loosey-goosey Age of Aquarius but a time of increasingly hyper-individualized, hyper-expanded choice over every aspect of our lives, from 401(k)s to hot and cold running coffee drinks, from life-saving pharmaceuticals to online dating services. This is now a world where it's more possible than ever to live your life on your own terms.[15]

Although one might question whether such abundance of choice brings with it greater freedom—some sociologists have contested this by pointing out the paralyzing nature of choice in modern supermarkets—or merely turns us into consumers and away from citizenship, Gillespie and Welch do marshal other evidence to support their case: the global increase in the Heritage Foundation's Index of Economic Freedom from 1995 onward; a growing consensus in favor of market economies and political freedom; increasing tolerance generated by the Internet; increasing prosperity arising out of global trade; and an increase in the number of nations ranked as free or partly free by Freedom House in 2007 as compared with 1997 and 1987. Just before the dawn of the Obama presidency, Welch and Gillespie radiated optimism about the future of freedom.

And in 2014, towards the twilight of Obama's years in the White House, did Robert Draper concur with Gillespie and Welch when he posed their question once again? Now, the latter were partisans and Draper a journalist reporting a story, so the orientations necessarily differed (Gillespie was even one of the interview subjects for Draper, who wrote that "Nick Gillespie is to libertarianism what Lou Reed is to rock 'n' roll, the quintessence of its outlaw spirit"). Despite the different purposes of the 2008 and 2014 pieces, Draper cited similar trends to those noted in the 2008 essay: gay marriage, the decriminalization of marijuana, and sentencing and prison reform becoming mainstream issues; decreasing support for United States intervention in other countries; and political momentum with the earlier Presidential candidacies of Ron Paul, and the likely candidacy of his son Rand in 2016. The author employed his portrait of Rand Paul to suggest a tension, if not a paradox, for libertarians: whether or not they can or should seek to place themselves in the mainstream of American politics—whether to remain detached and preserve some sort of purity or consistency of philosophy (though Draper shows how finding such consistency is itself no simple task) or to embrace compromise to woo Republicans and others. In the end, Draper drew a portrait of a movement and a moment and suggested that what existed in potential might not blossom, at least not at that particular juncture in history: "Our libertarian moment, in other words, might very well pass unexploited."

In 2016, during the season of presidential primaries, the pro-libertarian Cato Institute brought together—for reflection and consideration of the question "Was the 'Libertarian Moment' Wishful Thinking?"—one of the coauthors of the 2008 essay, Matt Welch, with David Boaz, as well as Ramesh Ponnuru, a senior editor at the *National Review*, and Conor Friedersdorf, a staff writer at the *Atlantic*. Without cheerleading, the participants recognized the continued phenomenon of a Libertarian Moment. Boaz went so far as to argue that the Libertarian Moment could not be isolated to recent years but extended throughout the history of the United States: "And in the sweep of history, America is a libertarian moment. Not one particular year, not one particular day, but in the scope of history, America is a libertarian moment." For Boaz, what has characterized the United States—"values such as individualism, laissez faire, anti-statism"—are atypical, across the world and across the centuries. Friedersdorf raised the issue of the mainstreaming of libertarian ideas, noting that libertarians will not find much success in a two-party system, and that as libertarian ideas gain in popularity, they will be co-opted by people who are not libertarians.[16] In terms of mainstreaming, one might also point to Ron Paul, who ran as the Libertarian Party candidate in the 1988 presidential elections and then ran again for the Republican Party nomination in both 2008 and 2012, with a fairly strong showing in the early state contests in 2012.

At least one writer has challenged such rosy characterizations of libertarian influence. Writing in the *Atlantic*, Kevin D. Williamson distinguishes between libertarian attitudes or sensibilities and libertarian policies, suggesting many more people give voice to the former than endorse the latter. He sees most Americans, after all, as supporting restrictions on free speech and increasing the minimum wage. Williamson even points to the 2016 South Carolina Republican primary, for which one poll found that 59 percent of self-identified libertarians backed the authoritarian and clearly antilibertarian winner of the primary and presidency, despite the presence of other candidates closer to libertarianism.[17] Such numbers perhaps cast doubt upon the strength of the libertarian moment, upon the success of libertarianism, whether directly or through the mainstreaming of libertarian ideas. Indeed, just how one measures success for libertarianism and libertarians is perhaps not so clear, though polls may serve as good a tool as any in this regard.

Polls of American political attitudes consistently reveal a prominent libertarian strain, far outsizing the percentage of Americans who actually vote for Libertarian Party candidates. An April 2015 Reuters/Ipsos survey of 4,770 adults concluded that 31.7 percent of those ages eighteen to twenty-nine and 12.2 percent of those ages sixty-five and older identify themselves as libertarian, with approximately 20 percent of adults of all ages self-identifying as such.[18]

A 2014 Pew Research Center poll painted a somewhat different picture, finding that only 11 percent of respondents *both* self-identified as libertarian *and* demonstrated an understanding of what libertarianism is. Furthermore, the survey did *not* find the expected large gaps between self-identified libertarians and other respondents in specific matters of policy, such as the value of government assistance, the legalization of marijuana, and how active the United States ought to be in foreign affairs. That is, individuals who self-identified as libertarian were not much more or less likely than those who did not self-identify as such to endorse or reject specific libertarian policies. Do such results—identification without understanding and agreement without identification—point towards or away from the notion of a Libertarian Moment?[19]

On the topic of the religious identification of libertarians, the nonpartisan and nonprofit Public Religion Research Institute (PRRI) appears to have found no particular association between Jews and libertarianism. According to their 2013 American Values Survey and Libertarian Orientation Scale, 7 percent of Americans can be described as consistent libertarians, with 15 percent leaning libertarian. As for religious affiliations, PRRI reports the following breakdown: 23 percent white evangelical Protestants, 27 percent white mainline Protestants, 11 percent Catholics, 4 percent other Christian, 6 percent non-Christian religious, and 27 percent unaffiliated, with 1 percent refusing to answer. Although the full report, nearly 50 pages long, refers only a single time to Jews, one might presume that Jews could be found among the 6 percent non-Christian religious, as well as among the 27 percent unaffiliated.[20] Though it might surprise many people, Jews account for less than 3 percent of the population of the United States.[21] In addition, Jews appear at least as likely as members of other religious groups to identify themselves as unaffiliated or nones.[22] Given these factors, it would not be surprising if Jews accounted for at least 3 percentage points out of the combined 33 percent of unaffiliated and non-Christian religious—thus making Jews proportionally represented, if not overrepresented, among libertarians in the PRRI survey.

For the 2016 presidential election, Jewish support for the Libertarian Party ticket of former Governors Gary Johnson and William Weld fell somewhere in the 3–4 percent range. Exit polling of 731 Jewish voters by GBA Strategies revealed a 3 percent vote, whereas the Washington Post reported a figure of 4 percent. Both are close to national support for the Libertarian ticket.[23] An August 2016 Survey of American Jewish Opinion sponsored by the American Jewish Committee offered an interesting contrast, finding only 1 percent of Jewish respondents identifying with the Libertarian Party, but 6 percent supporting, at that point in the campaign, Gary Johnson. It is possible that the difference between support of the candidate and identification with the party was due to confusion about the Libertarian Party and holding libertarian views, but more likely it was due to discontent with the other candidates in the election.[24]

Whether among Jews or more generally, perhaps one could say that a libertarian movement has succeeded to some degree in the United States, that libertarian ideas and values have gained some traction, even where the party has not. As even Williamson, a skeptic of the success of libertarian policies in contrast to attitudes, points out, "libertarianism has benefited from the fact that American elites are notably more libertarian in their views than is the median American voter."[25] For now, we have every reason to believe that libertarianism or at least the idea of libertarianism will continue to play a prominent role in American politics and in shaping national political debate. The possible collapse of the Republican Party and an accompanying realignment would make this only more likely.[26]

We also have some reason to believe that libertarianism might be making a growing contribution to national political debate in the state of Israel. In 2015, long-time Knesset member Moshe Feiglin and partners formed a new libertarian-oriented political party named Zehut, which translates as Identity. The first two items in Zehut's platform were as follows: "Opposition to coercion of all kinds: religious, antireligious, economic, cultural, or educational"; and "Maximum reduction of state intervention in the life and liberty of the citizen." Although Israel National News reported in August 2017 that the new party could win 6 of the 120 seats in the Israeli Knesset in the next elections, in the April 2019 elections the party fell one half of a percentage point short of the 3.25 percent threshold required to gain any seats. After the promises of a ministerial position and the legalization of medical marijuana, the party's membership voted to support the ruling Likud Party and not run in the September 2019 elections.

Perhaps Zehut's failure to win seats in the Knesset can be explained, in part, by the apparent diffusion of libertarian ideas within other political parties. For example, Likud is not the full name of the party; it is Likud-Liberalim Leumi, or Likud-National Liberals. Likud formed in the 1970s as an alliance of a number of parties, including the Liberal Party and Ḥerut, or the Freedom Party. All of this suggests strongly that a classic liberalism figures as part of the Likud party and ideology. In addition, the New Right (HaYamin HeḤadash) party of Naftali Bennet and Ayelet Shaked has some libertarian leanings and has at least once featured on its election slate a deputy director of the libertarian-oriented Kohelet Policy Forum.

The particularities of Israel also present unusual challenges or circumstances for libertarians. For instance, given very real security problems, few in Israel suggest ending mandatory military service. Also, in a country with a highly centralized, national education system, libertarians are more likely to advocate for simply allowing private schools to operate at all than to advocate for ending public schooling. And the very fact that Israel is a Jewish state, in part as a home and place of refuge for Jews from across the world, means that Israeli libertarians are unlikely to favor the open borders and immigration policies libertarians in the United States might support. Rather different from that of the United States, the framework for libertarianism in Israel is idiosyncratic though not inhospitable. A libertarian-leaning religious Jew in Israel might find a home in a few different political parties and not seek or need an explicitly libertarian one.[27]

The Chapters

Although in the end this book will offer an overarching argument as to the compatibility or incompatibility of libertarianism and Judaism, a good part of the fascination of the comparison lies in the consideration of the various philosophical and political ideas and arguments. And thus the division of the book into thematic chapters, each introduced with an excerpt or excerpts from the platform of the Libertarian Party of the United States. Of course, an individual could run on a libertarian platform as an independent or under the banner of another party or in a country that is not the United States, but the existing text of a formal, long-standing political party provides a handy and reasonable framework for these theme-based chapters.

Chapter 1 takes up the core topic of freedom. Is it possible to reconcile the freedom-themed account of the Exodus from Egypt with the notion of submission and service to God? Are there different kinds of liberty? Is freedom the same thing as the absence of restrictions, or is it something more than this?

Chapters 2, 3, and 4 all consider matters of ownership in Judaism and libertarianism. The second chapter asks whether or not we own ourselves? Self-ownership figures, in the eyes of many, as a fundamental libertarian concept, yet many or most Jewish thinkers assert that we do not own ourselves, that God owns us.[28] Can religiously observant Jews square these contrary views? The ownership of private property, the subject of the third chapter, also serves as a key principle in virtually all characterizations of libertarianism. And, as with the self, we can find, in Jewish thought, indications that we are stewards of property rather than owners of it. Can there be a meeting of the minds over property ownership? Following closely upon that discussion, the fourth chapter addresses taxation and government spending. Taxation, for most libertarians, raises the moral problem of coercion. And both taxation and property rights invoke the principle of the freedom to enter into contracts without such coercion. In terms of government spending, do Jewish notions of justice and *tzedakah* (often translated, or possibly mistranslated, as charity) require support for the modern welfare state, putting Judaism at odds with a libertarian focus on private, charitable giving?

In discussing coercion, the state, and morality, it is worth noting at the outset that many libertarians distinguish between *legal* wrongs and *moral* wrongs. That is, libertarians recognize many possibly immoral behaviors they nevertheless do not think should be illegal, as well as moral behaviors they do not believe should be prescribed or obligated by legislation. According to this perspective, extralegal norms and frameworks ought to and can regulate moral and immoral behavior without government involvement.

Chapter 5 entertains fundamental questions of government. What role ought government to play in our lives? Have rulers and governments historically been good for Jews? Protective of Jews or persecutors of them? What is the import of the Jewish legal concept of *dina d'malkhuta dina*, the law of the land is the law? Are Jews obligated to support, even pray for, whatever government rules over them?

The sixth and last chapter considers the individual and the community. On the surface, one might think that libertarians esteem the individual, whereas Judaism prizes community. Yet, individual dignity figures prominently in both, and as the concept of *voluntaryism* shows, by no means do libertarians reject the value of community.

In the conclusion, in contemplating the relationship between a religion-civilization dating back more than three millennia and a philosophy and movement maybe half a millennium old, we draw together the various threads and conflicts of the six chapters, to answer our opening questions. Can a religiously committed Jew, in good faith, run for electoral office on a libertarian platform? Do we find, between Judaism and libertarianism, a foundational, existential incompatibility? Or, will closer consideration reveal only a seeming discord, masking a genuine compatibility?

Chapter 1

Freedom versus Servitude

> As Libertarians, we seek a world of liberty: a world in which all individuals are sovereign over their own lives and are not forced to sacrifice their values for the benefit of others.
>
> We believe that respect for individual rights is the essential precondition for a free and prosperous world, that force and fraud must be banished from human relationships, and that only through freedom can peace and prosperity be realized.
>
> Consequently, we defend each person's right to engage in any activity that is peaceful and honest, and welcome the diversity that freedom brings. The world we seek to build is one where individuals are free to follow their own dreams in their own ways, without interference from government or any authoritarian power.
>
> – "Preamble," *Libertarian Party Platform* (2018)

Freedom figures as *the* core value of libertarianism. After all, the word *libertarianism* finds its roots in the word *liberty*. The entire libertarian approach to the world concerns the maximization and preservation of freedom and autonomy. By contrast, Judaism—at least as a traditional, religious endeavor—finds its focus in the service of God, in submission to the divine will. How, then, could a religiously observant Jew believe in submitting to God's will and at the same time embrace and promote a libertarian vision of freedom?

Libertarian Understandings of Freedom

How do libertarians understand freedom? How does the concept fit into libertarian philosophy and politics?

The "Libertarian Party Platform" begins with a preamble, which opens with these words: "As Libertarians, we seek a world of liberty: a world in which all individuals are sovereign over their own lives and are not forced to sacrifice their values for the benefit of others."[29] This one, introductory sentence speaks much to us about a libertarian understanding of freedom.

First of all, freedom requires sovereignty—and not sovereignty in general, but specifically over one's own life. The notion of sovereignty alludes to the power exercised by a king or a queen or another monarch. It is an authority which, in principle, countenances no interference, no greater authority, at least no greater *human* authority—for if there is a greater authority over me, then I am not truly sovereign. Secondly, this sovereignty extends over *my* life and *not* over the lives of others—and therefore, no one else's sovereignty extends over my life. As the libertarian writer Jason Brennan captures these two points, "We are all equally sovereign over ourselves. We are equally non-sovereign over others."[30] Third, the central means by which such sovereignty or freedom might be violated is through forced sacrifice for the sake of others. If I *choose* to make sacrifices for others, that is one thing, and perhaps at times the *moral* thing to do, yet once my sacrifice is compelled by some other power, I no longer remain free.

The preamble further extols freedom by characterizing its *instrumental* value as a catalyst for generating prosperity and peace and even diversity. This is a fascinating point, harkening back to Adam Smith and the Scottish Enlightenment and the idea that *commerce* functions as a pacifying force, bringing first prosperity and then peace to those nations allowing and encouraging it.[31] Also, in an age where we prize diversity and sometimes look to government to foster it, the *Libertarian Party Platform* makes the perhaps subtle but intriguing suggestion that greater freedom, and *not* government intervention and programs, leads to greater diversity of life and expression. Whether liberty serves the goal of diversity or the goal of prosperity, we see here that it does not exist simply as an abstract value, but can also function in a libertarian worldview as a critical foundation for a good or better world.

The core of the platform, the "Statement of Principles," discusses freedom in personal, political, and economic terms. Liberty encompasses freedom of expression, freedom of the press, and freedom to enter into contractual relationships. Finally, it is worth noting, freedom must be, or at least ought to be, accompanied by responsibility: "Individuals have the freedom and responsibility to decide what they knowingly and voluntarily consume, and what risks they accept to their own health, finances, safety, or life."[32] The implication here is that when we deny someone his or her freedom, we deny the person his or her individual responsibility. Or, perhaps, it is the other way around, that when we deny people responsibility, we deny them their liberty? Or, maybe it works in both directions? In any case, a libertarian might say that when government tells us what to do, including what we can and cannot eat, for example, we are being treated as possessing something less than full responsibility and authority over our choices, our lives, even our own bodies. In other words, we are being treated like children, who do not exercise full individual responsibility, or like infants, who do not exercise individual responsibility at all.

Of course, libertarian notions of freedom do not originate with the *Libertarian Party Platform*, but rather go back at least a few centuries, to John Locke (1632–1704), considered one of the foundational philosophers of modern libertarian thought and politics. In the second chapter of his *Second Treatise of Government*, Locke writes that "we must consider what State all Men are naturally in, and that is, *a State of perfect Freedom* to order their Actions, and dispose of their Possessions, and Persons as they think fit, within the bounds of the Law of Nature, without asking leave, or depending upon the Will of any other Man."[33] For Locke, the law of nature is reason, and reason requires us not to harm one another. In distinguishing freedom from slavery, Locke writes of "*Freedom* from Absolute, Arbitrary Power" and of not being "subject to the inconstant, uncertain, unknown, Arbitrary Will of another Man."[34] Such arbitrary power would include governments prescribing for us what we must do.

Ludwig von Mises (1881–1973), a leader of the Austrian School of economic theory and a widely influential libertarian thinker of the twentieth century, likewise sets in opposition liberty and government:

> The distinctive principle of Western social philosophy is individualism. It aims at the creation of a sphere in which the individual is free to think, to choose, and to act without being restrained by the interference of the social apparatus of coercion and oppression, the State. All the spiritual and material achievements of Western civilization were the result of the operation of this idea of liberty.[35]

Murray Rothbard (1926–1995), a student of Mises, and likewise wielding a profound influence on the development of libertarianism in the United States, emphasizes individualism, placing a special emphasis on self-ownership (this itself the topic of the next chapter) in his manifesto *For a New Liberty*:

> We are now in a position to see how the libertarian defines the concept of "freedom" or "liberty." Freedom is a condition in which a person's ownership rights in his own body and his legitimate material property are not invaded, are not aggressed against. A man who steals another man's property is invading and restricting the victim's freedom, as does the man who beats another over the head. Freedom and unrestricted property right [sic] go hand in hand.... "Slavery"—the opposite of freedom—is a condition in which the slave has little or no right of self-ownership; his person and his produce are systematically expropriated by his master by the use of violence.[36]

When Rothbard uses the word *aggressed*, he no doubt has in mind the *Non-Aggression Axiom*, perhaps as close to a central tenet as one could identify for many libertarians. David Boaz provides this compact articulation of the axiom: "No one has the right to initiate aggression against the person or property of anyone else."[37] Note that Boaz emphasizes the *initiation* of aggression, making clear that this excludes neither retribution nor punishment.

Rose Wilder Lane (1886-1968), in her book *The Discovery of Freedom*, makes the additional point that freedom cannot be taken away, by a government or by anyone. "Liberty is inalienable. I can not transfer my responsibility to anyone or anything." The implication is that it is not the job of government to provide us with our freedoms, but rather to protect what we already possess. "This fact is not recognized when individuals submit to an Authority that grants them 'freedoms.' Implicit in that plural is the belief that individuals are not free, that adult men and women must be controlled and cared for, as children are, and that, like children, they are naturally dependent and naturally obedient to an Authority that is responsible for their acts and their welfare." As Lane notes, "The Authority that grants 'a freedom' can always withdraw the grant."[38]

In brief, we see that libertarians define freedom or liberty as the ability of an individual to make choices and to *act without coercion*, whether coercion exercised by other individuals or coercion exercised by a government or its officials. Furthermore, they understand liberty as more than a founding principle or a moral right, but also as something that works, bringing about widespread peace and prosperity.

Judaism and the Service of God

Whereas freedom and slavery figure as unambiguous opposites for libertarians, one the negation of the other, in Judaism we seem to find praise for both freedom and, if not slavery, then *servitude*.

To begin, we find as one of the key themes of Rosh HaShanah, the Jewish New Year the notion of *kabbalat 'ol malkhut shamayim*, the "acceptance of the yoke of the Kingdom of Heaven," or the "receiving of the yoke of the Kingdom of Heaven." The phrase is also associated with the recitation of the Shema, Judaism's central statement of faith: "Listen, Israel, Ha-Shem (The Lord) is our God, Ha-Shem (The Lord) is One."[39] The statement is meant to be recited twice daily and even a third time before going to sleep at night. The second line of the prayer refers to God's Kingdom, providing a clear link to this "yoke of the Kingdom of Heaven." We also speak of *'ol ha-mitzvot*, the "yoke of the *mitzvot*."* Like oxen, we are yoked in our servitude of God and in the performance of God's commandments. A yoke achieves its basic function in constraining free movement. It would seem therefore that restriction functions as something of a basic theological principle in Judaism.

In *Pirkei Avot* 6:3, Rabbi Neḥunya ben HaKanna explains that "One who takes on himself the yoke of Torah will be spared the yoke of government and the yoke of worldly responsibilities, but one who throws

---

* *Mitzvot* is the plural form of *mitzvah*.

off [from himself] the yoke of Torah will bear the yoke of government and the yoke of worldly responsibilities."[40] In addition to the yokes of the mitzvot and the Kingdom of Heaven, we have here the yoke of Torah, the yoke of kingship, and the yoke of the way of the land. One interpretation, perhaps the more straightforward interpretation of this teaching, has it that one who accepts the yoke of Torah will merit not being burdened by the difficulties of government and of earning a livelihood. An alternative interpretation would be that the yoke of Torah provides a spiritual or emotional freedom from government and livelihood, though not necessarily a practical or political freedom. In this sense, accepting the yoke of Torah frees us by helping us understand what is truly important.

In any case, whether the yoke of Torah, the yoke of mitzvot, or the yoke of the Kingdom of Heaven—surely, this does not sound like liberty!

Furthermore, religiously observant Jews consider themselves 'ovdei Ha-Shem, "servants of God." Indeed, the book of Deuteronomy characterizes Judaism's greatest prophet, Moses, as an 'eved Ha-Shem, which can be translated as either "a slave of God" or "a servant of God." (Deut. 35:4) Nowhere does the Bible describe prophets or Jews in general as "free individuals."

And now a brief grammar lesson to help us better understand the language of servitude in Hebrew. The Hebrew language works on a "root" system, with groupings of generally three consonants sharing a common meaning expressed in many variations. The root for the word 'eved (servant/slave) consists of the three letters 'ayin, beyt, and dalet, and these letters, in this order, prove very important in Jewish thought, showing up in various forms. In the times of the Temples in Jerusalem, the carrying out of animal sacrifices was known as the 'avodah, the "service." In the understanding of the rabbis, prayer replaced sacrifice as the central means of service to God, and they called prayer 'avodat ha-lev, the "service of the heart." Many Jews pray three times each day and thereby undertake this service of the heart. Such Jews offer up their prayers to God, just as their ancestors offered up animal and agricultural sacrifices to God. How can people who engage in such service, or servitude—and within Judaism this is an obligatory, not a voluntary servitude—be considered truly free?[41]

This *obligatory* nature of Jewish observance ought to be emphasized, especially in the American context, where the popular notion of a *mitzvah* as a "good deed" has long held sway. Such a definition or translation is mistaken, or at least insufficient. The root letters for *mitzvot—tsadi, vav, he*—signify command or obligation. So, even though the Torah never refers to the so-called Ten Commandments as commandments, but rather as *aseret ha-devarim*, the "ten utterances," the truth is that they *are* commandments, and not as the salesman and motivational speaker Zig Ziglar perhaps first quipped, the "Ten *Suggestions*." And there are not merely ten, but according to tradition, 613 commandments, including prohibitions on performing certain activities on the Sabbath, as well as various dietary and relationship prohibitions, and also Positive Obligations to do certain things, such as honoring one's parents and enjoying the Sabbath. In light of such strictures of religion, it might seem that we cannot but conclude that any ritually observant Jewish life is lacking in freedom, that it is even perhaps a sort of subjugation or enslavement.

Taken together, the yokes and the servitude and the commandments, it might be fair to characterize traditional Judaism as fundamentally endorsing human submission to the divine will. Indeed, when God first offered the Torah to the Jews, the response was *na'aseh v'nishmah*, we will do and we will listen (Ex. 24:7). That is, the Jews agreed to submit to observance of the Torah and only then to learn and understand just what they had committed themselves to do. There is also, of course, the account of the *Akeidah*, of Abraham's bringing his son Isaac as a sacrifice to God. Now, there are a plethora of interpretations of this story, some of which argue that Abraham made a mistake, that he should have challenged the command, just as he challenged God's plan to destroy Sodom and Gomorrah. Nonetheless, Abraham's action is most frequently understood as a model of submission to the will of God.

Rabbi Joseph B. Soloveitchik (1903–1993, also known as the Rav), the intellectual leader of Modern Orthodox Judaism in the twentieth century, writes of "the awareness of a compulsory covenant, submission and acceptance of the yoke of the Kingdom of Heaven." And the individual seeking God "encounters the Inscrutable Will. This Will reveals itself to man, and instead of telling him the secrets of creation, it demands unlimited discipline and absolute submission."[42] Rabbi Aharon Lichtenstein (1933–2015), R. Soloveitchik's son-in-law and a leader of Modern Orthodox Judaism in his own right, writes that "A Jew's life is defined by being commanded. . . . Judaism is built on the notion of nullifying your will before God's, of defining your existence as being called and commanded."[43] Like R. Lichtenstein, Rabbi Shimon Gershon Rosenberg (1949–2007, known as Rav Shagar, from his initials) characterized such an orientation as central to Jewish religious observance: "As Shagar says, accepting the yoke of Heaven is 'that act around which the life of a Jew is organized.'"[44]

Judaism and Freedom

"Let My people go!" In this manner, Moses relayed God's demand of Pharaoh. The Egyptians enslaved the Hebrews, and Moses sought to secure their freedom. In this we see that liberation from slavery and tyranny and "God's identity as the liberator of slaves" rests at the foundation, the very birth, of the Jewish nation.[45] The Exodus from Egypt transformed what had been a family, and then a tribe, into a nation. This account of liberation underlies not only Jewish history, but has often served as a symbol, an example, a rallying point for enslaved and oppressed people the world over, most notably for African Americans in the struggle for civil rights in the United States. Therefore, despite what we have seen of Judaism's emphasis on service or servitude, maybe freedom is foundational for *both* libertarian and Jewish perspectives? Perhaps the two are compatible after all?

In their daily prayers, Jews recall the Exodus from Egypt, and once a year bring considerably greater focus to the event. The weeklong Passover (in Hebrew, *Pesaḥ*) holiday commemorates this departure and journey. Indeed, the Bible refers to the holiday as *zeman ḥerutenu*, the "season of our freedom." During the Passover Seder, Jews recite the text of the Haggadah, seeking not only to retell the story, but to experience it for themselves (perhaps one of the most difficult assignments in Judaism): "In each and every generation, a person is obligated to see himself as if he had left Egypt, . . . for He did not redeem only our ancestors, but also us He redeemed, as it is written 'And us He brought out from there, in order that He might bring us out, to give us the land which He swore to our ancestors.'"[46] Indeed, from the very beginning of the Haggadah, the theme of freedom is raised: "This year we are slaves; next year, may we be free people." The language used is the vernacular Aramaic, the common language of the people for whom the Haggadah was first written.

Later in the Haggadah, this liberation from slavery and servitude provides the basis for the obligation to thank and praise God:

> Therefore we are obligated to thank, to praise, to laud, to glorify, to exalt, to adorn, to bless, to elevate, and to acclaim the One who did all these miracles for us and for our ancestors, and took us out from slavery to freedom, from servitude to redemption, from sorrow to happiness, from mourning to a festival, and from darkness to great light; let us say before Him, "Halleluyah!"

The "Therefore" beginning this passage come at the end of the telling of the entire story, from humble origins to slavery to freedom—and thereby functions as a connector, linking gratitude with the liberation from slavery. The responsibility of Jews to be grateful to God is not only for creation and for life, as one might have thought, but also for this liberation.

From this pivotal passage one might also question the need to provide *two* versions of what would appear to be the same idea: "from slavery to freedom, from servitude to redemption." Why both formulations? At the Passover Seder one learns that freedom is not a simple idea, but rather a nuanced concept. A central part of the Haggadah is the elaboration of *four different* dimensions of redemption, of God leading the people to freedom: (1) "and I removed you" (*v'hotseiti*); (2) "and I rescued you" (*v'hitsalti*); (3) "and I redeemed you" (*v'ga'alti*); and (4) "and I took you" (*v'lakaḥti*). There are various, overlapping explanations of these four—as stages in a single process, as a journey, as types (including physical and spiritual), as increasing closeness to God—but the point is that freedom is not a single thing.

It is worth emphasizing that one type of servitude, generally the first of the four, includes forced labor, and we know that for libertarians forced labor is a definitive loss of freedom, the inability to control how one uses one's body. So, like libertarians, Jews celebrate the liberation from physical servitude. Finally, speaking of the physical dimension, we must note that Jews also act out their freedom throughout the Passover Seder: by reclining while eating and drinking, and by drinking four cups of wine. These are expressions of freedom and royalty—sovereignty entails living freely, as we noted earlier.

And to be clear, some of the thinkers we cited above in terms of submission to God and God's will, elaborated their thought in quite nuanced ways, seeking to integrate individual autonomy with submission to God. In one sermon, "Shagar argues that this act of submission is actually a necessary step in enabling freedom, rather than its own form of enslavement."[47] Indeed, R. Shagar appears to understand accepting the yoke of the Kingdom of Heaven as part of process of creating oneself. And R. Soloveitchik and R. Lichtenstein likewise see it, perhaps in tension with personal autonomy, as part of creating a full personality and living a complete life.[48]

We see, then, that freedom is far from an inconsequential theme in Judaism. To the contrary, it is a central theme and foundational experience. At this point, then, we cannot rule out the possibility that we will judge Judaism and libertarianism compatible, allowing our hypothetical candidate to run faithfully.

Different Kinds of Freedom

"Let My people go!" In this manner, Moses relayed God's demand of Pharaoh. And we repeat it here—because this is *not* the complete statement. Twice, in Exodus 7:16 and 7:26, the Torah tells us that God told Moses to tell Pharaoh "Send out My people, and they will serve Me." *V'ya'avduni*, and they will serve Me—the same root letters as before: *'ayin*, *beyt*, and *dalet*. As Rabbi Ezra Bick asks, "Is that merely a trading of one master for another, more exalted perhaps, but essentially the same?"[49] Did the Hebrews go from servitude to freedom, or from one servitude to another servitude? Or, is it possible to conceive of servitude to God as a kind of freedom?

To understand the notion of serving God as an act of freedom rather than one of slavery, we might first turn to a classic text by a renowned thinker, a Jew though not one hailing from a traditional, religious community: "Two Concepts of Liberty" by Isaiah Berlin (1909–1997). In this landmark essay, first published in 1958, Berlin articulates a distinction between what he names "Positive Liberty" and "Negative Liberty."[50] In brief, Negative Liberty refers to the absence of restrictions. The less others interfere in my life, the freer I am. Some describe Negative Liberty as freedom *from*, in contrast with what Berlin termed "Positive Liberty."

This latter type of freedom concerns the ability of a human to make something of his or her life and has been termed freedom *to*.

How do most of us commonly understand freedom? We generally characterize freedom as the *absence* of restrictions. If I am free, I can do absolutely anything I want. It makes sense to us, seems self-evident, to say I am *most* free when I am *least* restricted, and vice versa, that when I am most restricted, I am least free. And this sense of freedom accords with Berlin's Negative Liberty.

Proponents of Positive Liberty might argue, however, that a person could have all the Negative Liberty one could want, an absence of any and all external restrictions, but illness or poverty or depression or lack of education or something else might yet prevent this individual from acting freely, from functioning as the master of one's own life. Some would therefore posit that by providing universal health care or subsidized education or, at an even more basic level, safe sanitation and water systems, or by otherwise helping put in place the foundations for productive living, a government can help people be free, become freer. Most libertarians would, of course, question whether or not governments can actually accomplish such things effectively—and would also argue that to provide such foundations a government must violate the Negative Liberty of its citizens.

In a sense, Negative Liberty proposes no end goals, no aim for living freely; such is left to each individual. Positive Liberty, by contrast, implies at least some sort of ability to act in the world, to do something with one's life, whether as an individual or as part of a community. To many, it further implies some sort of goal, some destiny even—the fulfillment of which is an achievement of living freely. Or, in other words, Negative Liberty is solely concerned with removing external constraints from living freely, whereas Positive Liberty addresses the *means* of living freely, and possibly the ends as well.

Perhaps one might fairly describe Berlin's Positive Liberty as noble and ennobling, but is it freedom? The question is difficult—mostly because, as we have noted, both positions make some sense intuitively. We think of freedom as the absence of restrictions, as not being imprisoned by others. This often seems to us what freedom really is. And yet, if we consider someone who, while free from restrictions, nonetheless does not have the capacity—the foundations, the resources, the security—to build a life, we do not necessarily think of such a person as living a truly free life.

Another way to view Positive and Negative Liberty is through the prism of the obligations they generate. Although we do not often consider it, the flip side of a *right* is an obligation; that is, if I have a right to something, then someone else must either provide it to me or not restrict my access to it. For example, if I possess a right to emergency healthcare, this imposes a Positive Obligation upon the staff of hospital emergency departments to provide me with appropriate care, even should I lack health insurance (and presumably requires government, if not private donors or insurance companies, to subsidize such care). Generalizing Berlin's notions of positive and negative would allow us to categorize the right to emergency care as a positive right. By contrast, when I assert my right to freedom of speech, I am not imposing an obligation upon the government or upon anyone to provide me with the means of publicizing what I say. Rather, my right to free speech creates the obligation, for private individuals and government officials, to *not* interfere with my expressing myself. Such a right would be a negative right—negative in the sense that it does not require active measures on the part of anyone else, just refraining from certain actions.

As has been suggested, if Negative Liberty imposes Negative Obligations, Positive Liberty imposes Positive Obligations. Understanding Negative Liberty as my right to live my life without interference, the obligation upon everyone else is negative in the sense of requiring that people *do not* interfere, that they do nothing—it does not require them to *do* anything. Likewise, your right to Negative Liberty does not require me to do anything in an active sense, only to refrain from doing particular things, namely those things that would hinder or inhibit your freedom. This recalls the nonaggression principle noted above; when one abides by the nonaggression principle, he or she simply does nothing to interfere with someone else's liberty. When one interferes, he or she is committing an act of aggression, in violation of the principle.

What, then of a right to Positive Liberty? What does *my* right to this type of freedom require of *other* people? If you possess a right to Positive Liberty, what obligations does this impose upon me? Would I be obligated to support you, financially or otherwise, through government programs or private efforts, to help you realize your freedom? To provide you with the basic necessities of life, such as clean drinking water, food, and adequate healthcare? What about an education? How would we determine where such an obligation or set of obligations might end? Now, there may indeed be a solid argument in favor of an expansive obligation to secure the Positive Liberty of others, but this would not figure as any sort of a libertarian argument. This is not to deny that many or most libertarians understand that Negative Liberty sometimes requires positive actions or reactions and that even a minimalist government ought to protect and defend its citizens from those who would take away their liberty.

Let us consider a few examples to explain further the difference between Positive and Negative Liberty and the obligations they create. Returning to healthcare, someone might face no restrictions—no one or no government preventing her from purchasing health insurance from any companies offering it, no one or no government forcing her to purchase insurance she does not want, no one or no government telling her which doctors she can and cannot visit. However, if no company will sell her insurance due to a preexisting condition, or if she cannot afford to purchase insurance or to pay doctors and hospitals, what does all of the Negative Liberty provide for her? Wonderful in principle, not so much in practice. A libertarian might counter that forcing individuals to purchase insurance or forcing companies to sell insurance or forcing doctors to treat people at less than market value all, in effect, take away freedom from some, even if to provide freedom (or capacity) to others. And they would argue that it would be difficult to justify this stripping of freedom on moral grounds. However, so long as we live in a society where there is some sort of basic commitment not to turn individuals away from emergency care at emergency rooms, a basic commitment not to allow individuals to die for trivial reasons, such as being unable to afford an inexpensive antibiotic medication, then we have decided, by default, to force providers to provide some degree of healthcare.

Another issue: gay marriage. Many libertarians would likely say that governments should not be in the business of sanctifying marriages altogether; nevertheless, in a society where governments do sanctify and regulate marriages, many libertarians would likely agree that government ought not to restrict same-sex couples from accessing such sanctification and whatever tax and other benefits marriage might provide. But should government have the authority to force a baker to produce and sell a wedding cake for the celebration of a gay marriage, if the baker's religious convictions identify same-sex unions as sinful? Can everyone's freedom and rights be protected in such a situation? Although many libertarians might consider it *ethically* wrong for the baker to refuse to make and sell the cake, they would have a difficult time interfering—even for the seemingly noble goal of antidiscrimination—with the baker's freedom and right to enter into and to refuse to enter into contracts. Libertarians would argue that, left alone, the market will, at least in time, correct for such discrimination, and that it is not the job of government to make such corrections. Others might doubt the ability of the market to make such corrections. And although it might not be difficult in most locations to find another baker, such might not be the case for other transactions. What about a pharmacy disbursing medication? The logical consequences of the libertarian valuing of an absolute freedom to refuse to enter into contracts could very well be a return to the days when white restaurant owners refused to serve Black Americans or maintained separate seating. What if the owner of a pharmacy agreed to sell birth control to Black or Latina women but not to white women, in order to encourage the latter to have more children and to discourage the former? On what philosophical grounds could a libertarian object?

Working from Berlin's conceptualization of liberty, one would certainly identify libertarianism most strongly with the negative type. And for the most part, as we have suggested, libertarians do not place much credence in the concept of Positive Liberty. The libertarian writer and Georgetown University Professor Jason Brennan, cited above, figures as perhaps something of an exception. In his book, *Libertarianism: What Everyone Needs to Know*, Brennan writes that many libertarians acknowledge "that Negative Liberty without Positive Liberty is often of little value." This might sound shocking coming from an avowed libertarian, but Brennan stakes out a careful position, and refuses to insist that Positive Liberty is not truly a kind of liberty. According to Brennan, libertarians can agree with Marxists and socialists that Positive Liberty is genuinely a kind of freedom without therefore agreeing that governments ought to guarantee it:

> [T]he claim that positive liberty is valuable implies *nothing* about what the government should or should not do. . . . [As] a matter of historical

fact, protecting negative liberties is the most important and effective way of promoting positive liberty. The way governments best promote positive liberty is to uphold the rule of law, property rights, freedom, tolerance, and open markets.[51]

That is, Brennan acknowledges Positive Liberty without requiring any government initiative or action beyond the securing and protection of Negative Liberty.

Although, no doubt, many libertarians would still dispute Brennan's acceptance of Positive Liberty (as well as his claim that many libertarians agree with him), Brennan and his opponents would likely find themselves very much in agreement in a practical sense, in regard to actual government involvement.[52] What about in traditional Jewish thought? Do we find an embrace of both Negative Liberty and Positive Liberty? Or do we find something else or something additional?

An Enslaved Free Person? A Free Servant?

First, a brief philosophical digression: What might be the consequences of *unlimited* Negative Liberty? Above we considered the question of what use one can find in Negative Liberty when one does not possess the means to live a rich, free life. Now we consider something different: What does it mean to take Negative Liberty to its extremes and have *no* restrictions? If a person is totally free, is he or she free at all? To have no restrictions, no limitations, is this not an invitation for anarchy and chaos? Indeed, one might suppose that an anarchic freedom without limits would quickly become chaotic, violent, and far from free—as per Hobbes and his notion of life outside of society being "solitary, poor, nasty, brutish, and short."

With no anchors or standards, the completely free person risks becoming a slave to desire and to whim. Unencumbered by morality, by societal taboos and customs, by laws, a person is free to follow desire and seek pleasure without end. I am speaking philosophically here—to make a point about freedom—and I do *not* at all mean to suggest that nonreligious individuals must be or even often are slaves to their whims and desires. None of us lives absolutely freely, and empirical evidence unambiguously demonstrates that living an ostensibly religious life provides *no* guarantee against living by whim or even immorally. Indeed, the thirteenth-century giant, Rabbi Moses ben Nachman (1194–1270, also known as Nachmanides and as the Ramban), found a need to coin the term *naval b'reshut ha-Torah*: "a scoundrel with the permission of the Torah." By this he meant, for example, someone who ate only kosher food, but to gluttonous excess. Although some might find it difficult to understand, it is possible to not break a single law of the Torah and yet not be a *mentsch*, a decent and kind human being. And likewise, to live a secular life is not at all determinative of living by whim or immorally. The point, rather, is that our commonsense notions of freedom reveal something of a paradox, or at least an irony: that although fewer restrictions means greater freedom, at some point freedom can become excessive and chaotic, undermining itself.

Again, this is a philosophical point, and may make absolutely no difference in terms of a political and legal framework for freedom. In principle, therefore, an individual living under a regime of pure Negative Liberty, an ostensibly free individual, could live for all practical purposes as a servant, at least to his or her desires or appetites.

We still find ourselves with the inverse conundrum: Even if we might agree intuitively that an ostensibly free person can be enslaved to his or her passions, how can we say that someone who is avowedly a *servant* can be free? And, after all, we have already established that the Torah directs religiously observant Jews to think of themselves as servants. Can such a servant be free, let alone engage in a political campaign on a pro-freedom platform?

The fifth teaching in the fourth chapter of the talmudic tractate Gittin, concerning the laws of divorce and related matters, presents us with an unusual case: What do we do with someone who is half-free and half-slave? One wonders how an individual could end up in such a position. The Talmud explains how: an individual falls into servitude to two masters, and at some point one of the masters frees the individual while the other does not. The first suggested solution to the dilemma is that the individual alternate days, one free, one as a slave, and so on. Yet is this a tenable arrangement? The second opinion insists it is not. The male individual in this scenario has a biblical obligation to procreate—but this remains impossible to him: as he is half-slave he cannot marry a free woman, yet because he is half-free he cannot marry an enslaved woman. The conclusion is that the second master must emancipate him. (As a fascinating side note, the reasoning for this conclusion relies upon the notion or imperative of *tikkun 'olam*, as do other teachings elsewhere in this chapter. Tikkun 'olam can be translated roughly as the fixing or repair of the world, and is frequently used in our day, especially among many Jews who are not ritually observant, as a term encompassing or justifying social justice efforts. In this context, the very existence of a half-free and half-slave man who cannot fulfill his obligation to have children means there is something wrong in the world, something that needs to be repaired.)

Returning now to the problem or possibility of a servant who is free, the basic argument or claim is this: if the complete lack of restrictions leads to anarchy, any meaningful freedom requires some degree of structure. To take the claim further, one might say that structure not only *allows for* freedom but that some structural frameworks can *facilitate or cultivate* freedom—and some frameworks more than others.

Let us take the Jewish Sabbath as an example. Who is freer? The Jew who adheres to the Sabbath laws, including the prohibitions on such activities as driving, watching television, talking on the telephone, and spending money? Or, the Jew who has no Sabbath? And what about the Jew who observes something of a Sabbath, but makes exceptions when some other demands arise?

To start, the majority of those who keep the Sabbath generally experience it as freeing, especially in our days of a wired world, where many people feel naked without a charged cell phone in their hands. Instead of being enslaved to the car, the television, the telephone, and money, a person is free of these demands, perhaps even compulsions. A person is free to learn, to socialize, to spend quality time with one's family. It is time set aside, and not to be eclipsed by so many other competitors for one's attention. Furthermore, this mandated structure affects the experience of the entire week, building a rhythm, and creating a sanctuary in time, as Rabbi Abraham Joshua Heschel described it.[53] Without the Sabbath, every day can be the same. Meaningful time spent with one's spouse or children or other relatives of friends can be put off indefinitely when there is no day of rest set in the calendar. This is not to say that living a meaningful life of freedom is impossible without the Sabbath, just that this structure can help generate meaningful freedom.

This principle could be applied well beyond the Sabbath to the broad and intricate structural framework of the mitzvot, and of Jewish law—the *halakha*—which really means not "Law" but rather "Way or Path." Ideally, Jewish law does not merely enumerate dos and don'ts, but instead provides a pathway through life.

Rabbi Nathan Lopes Cardozo takes such ideas one step further, arguing that the halakhic framework can engender creativity. In arguing that Judaism can provide a structure and community within which an individual can exercise great freedom, R. Cardozo offers a fascinating analogy, comparing the musical genius of Beethoven and Bach. Which one, he wonders, was the greater composer?

> Bach was totally traditional in his approach to music. He adhered strictly to the rules of composing music as understood in his days. Nowhere in all his compositions do we find deviation from these rules. But what is most surprising is that Bach's musical output is not only unprecedented but, above all, astonishingly creative. . . . What we discover is that the self-imposed restrictions of Bach to keep to the traditional rules of composition forced him to become the author of such outstandingly innovative music that nobody after him was ever able to follow in his footsteps. It was within the "confinement of the law" that Bach burst out with unprecedented creativity. . . . Beethoven (in his later years) broke with all the accepted rules of composition. He was one of the founders of a whole new world of musical options. But it was his rejection of the conventional musical laws which made him less of a musical genius. To work within constraints and then to be utterly novel is the ultimate sign of unprecedented greatness.[54]

R. Cardozo's understanding of Bach and Beethoven shows how freedom can be found *within* the law and not simply in its absence. Although Bach might have seemed less innovative, the fact is that he worked within a stricter framework and nonetheless exhibited great creativity. Bach found freedom within structure, within a set of rules, and R. Cardozo counts this as a more masterful achievement than that of Beethoven, whose innovation took place with fewer rules and limits. Likewise, the argument continues, within the framework of Jewish law, the halakha, there is the potential for greater creativity, innovation, and even freedom than in a system without such constraints.

In this regard, the Talmud offers a telling play on words. Exodus 32:16 tells us about the first set of tablets Moses brought with him down Mount Sinai: "The tablets, they are the work of God, and the writing, it is the writing of God, engraved on the tablets." In *Pirkei Avot* 6:2, Rabbi Yehoshua ben Levi comments on the verse, considering the word "engraved," *ḥarut* in the Hebrew: "Read not *ḥarut* ('engraved') but *ḥerut* ('freedom'), for the only person who is truly free is one who occupies himself with Torah study."[55] That is, the very word we use to describe Passover as *zeman ḥerutenu*, the season or time of our freedom, appears to share a linguistic root with the word for engraving, for carving something into stone! To carve something into stone, or into one's body, indicates a kind of permanence, a binding or sorts, the seeming antithesis of freedom. R. Levi is teaching that such an engraving or binding actually generates freedom. To generalize, one might say that structure and limits can and do allow freedom to flourish.

Indeed, as John Locke himself wrote, "*the end of Law* is not to abolish or restrain, but *to preserve and enlarge Freedom*: For in all the states of created beings capable of Laws, *where there is no Law, there is no Freedom*."[56] While some libertarians promote a pure anarchism and think such a system would work, even most libertarians would agree that at least minimal structures and the rule of law are necessary for freedom, for protecting liberty, even Negative Liberty, against those who would take it away. And the entire libertarian framework is, of course, built upon the rule or limitation of not interfering with or aggressing upon the freedom of others.

In this, we see that most libertarians would likely reject a notion of freedom as the complete absence of limitations. They therefore must recognize that some sort of framework, some restrictions, if minimal ones, remain necessary for freedom to flourish. In this sense, one could say that Judaism and libertarianism find themselves in agreement on the necessity of a framework of limitations to allow for freedom; the question is more a matter of the extent of such limitations.

Might we then reason that libertarians could, in principle, accept a paradox in the relationship between freedom and servitude? Well, one might respond that there is a gaping difference between actual servitude and the minimal restrictions necessary to guarantee freedom. And Locke concludes his thoughts about law enlarging freedom by characterizing the sort of freedom he has in mind: "a *Liberty* to dispose, and order, as he lists, his Person, Actions, Possessions, and his whole Property, within the Allowance of those Laws under which he is; and therein not to be subject to the arbitrary Will of another, but freely follow his own."[57]

Nonetheless—even if Locke and others would limit the framework of government to protecting Negative Liberty and private property rights—many thinkers within the Jewish tradition (and surely outside of it, as well) would argue just this, that freedom is possible and meaningful within a set of parameters: that a servant of God can be free. That servitude and freedom are not necessarily opposites, at least not in this special context.

We might return to the question of whether or not the Hebrews merely swapped one master for another. Perhaps the answer is yes *and* no. Or rather, swapped, but not merely swapped—that the Hebrews left one master to serve *the* Master, but to serve in freedom. Or maybe to serve freely, out of their own volition?

First, although we discussed the imagery of the restraining yokes—of Torah, of mitzvot, of the Kingdom of Heaven—we never described their wearing as involuntary. Perhaps there is no contradiction over freedom and servitude when someone accepts willingly such servitude. And neither did we say that it is impossible for someone to remove these yokes. One might reasonably argue that if you believe an infinite and omnipotent God commanded you and wishes you to place such yokes upon yourself it would be folly to refuse, yet one remains free to do so. We might compare this to marriage: one can freely accept marriage and the various limitations and restrictions such a commitment entails, but one can choose this freely and one can leave it freely. Indeed, within Jewish liturgy and commentary, the metaphor of marriage is often employed to describe the relationship between God and the Jews.

Second, considering once again the themes of Passover, one might ask whether or not *redemption* is the same thing as *liberation*? Did God liberate the Jews or redeem them? And can one be redeemed without becoming free? Both terms clearly indicate removal *from* a situation of servitude or imprisonment. *To* what alternative situation, though? Liberation does not really point to any future state, it is fundamentally about shedding restrictions. To redeem someone, by contrast, suggests a reason—redeemed for or to what purpose? For example, we speak of redeeming captives or, to use a more prosaic example, redeeming coupons. We may be freeing up a little bit of money with our coupon, but redemption is not in this case liberation. In the context of the Exodus, the purpose of redemption was to serve God. On the face of it, this would seem to prove contradictory to freedom and to the compatibility of Judaism and libertarianism. Yet some would see no contradiction between being free and serving God.

Third, while we can conceive of the service of God as voluntary, certainly the Egyptian bondage of the Jews was not. Relatedly, R. Bick, who raised for us the question about trading one master for another, points out what he takes to be a critical difference between servitude of God and servitude of Pharaoh or another human being: "A slave is totally dependent on his master. The basis of his life and his destiny is in the hands of his owner. Since the master is one who has needs of his own, who needs to acquire power to achieve his goals, the slave becomes an instrument in achieving the ends of the master." A servant of God, by contrast, has a very different relationship with his or her Master:

> God has no needs that we can fill. The individual does not become an instrument for achieving the ends of God by being dependent on Him. The dependence on God is total, absolute. Everything we have, everything we want, everything we can possibly achieve, must come from Him. Avoda, service of God, is the recognition of total dependence. The dependence is so total, so absolute, precisely because God has everything, and THEREFORE, HE NEEDS NOTHING FROM US.[58]

That is, although earthly masters provide some sustenance to their servants or slaves, they also expect and demand and extract something, labor or otherwise, in return. Although God might command us, God needs nothing from us, and this fact cannot but alter the entire dynamic of servitude. Now, not everyone agrees on this theological point, that God needs nothing from human beings, but given this axiom, R. Bick's logic does seem to follow—at least that there might be a difference between serving a master who needs things and extracts them and serving a master who requires nothing. In this sense, a person is not simply exchanging one master for another. Even so, even if serving a master with no needs is something different, is this difference necessarily freedom in contrast to slavery? Or is it merely a different kind of servitude?

R. Soloveitchik presents yet another twist on the Exodus and the notion of Passover's freedom. The Paschal sacrifice was critical to the Exodus itself and to the observance of Passover through to the times of the Temples in Jerusalem. One thing distinguishing the sacrifice of the lamb is that it cannot be brought by an individual. Rather, it is brought by a *ḥavura*, a group of people. This joining together was integral to the experience of freedom. The Passover sacrifice figured as the centerpiece of a meal devoted to solidarity and community and mutual responsibility. This familial and communal framework for freedom is intriguing, and not necessarily foreign to most libertarian thinking, given the framework of individuals gathering together freely in voluntary associations (a topic to be discussed in a later chapter).[59] Additionally, although we might find sensible the notion of achieving at least Positive Liberty in community and in cooperation, there always remains the danger that communal "freedom" transmogrifies into a kind of fascism, and a substantial loss of freedom. This becomes amplified yet further should the members of one community come to see the freedom of other communities as threatening, as incompatible with their own freedom, in which case war or subjugation can come to be seen as a means of securing the liberty of my group at the expense of the liberty of another group or other groups.

Finally, the late Israeli scientist and thinker Yeshayahu Leibowitz (1903–1994), someone with at least libertarian leanings, offers a different understanding—a challenging and possibly problematic understanding—to reconcile servitude and freedom:

> The claim that a man who accepts the authority of the Halakhah is in bondage is only too familiar. . . . If the world possesses constant regularity, man is subordinate to the entire system of natural reality, which includes not only his body but his soul. He is subject to it both physiologically and psychologically. Under these circumstances, what is man's freedom? Willing acceptance of a way of life which does not derive from human nature implies the emancipation of man from the bondage of raw nature.

Leibowitz is arguing here that to live and act in *accord* with the natural world and with human nature is to live in a kind of servitude, to the way things are "naturally." Only if one goes beyond human nature and beyond the natural world does she or he become free: "The only way man can break the bonds of nature is by cleaving to God; by acting in compliance with the divine will rather than in accordance with the human will." Human will and desire remain part of the natural world. "The true meaning of the Talmudic adage 'None but he who busies himself with the Torah is free' is that he is free from the bondage of nature because he lives a life which is contrary to nature, both nature in general and human nature in particular." In this way Leibowitz seeks to square the circle of servitude under God as freedom.[60]

Also, in line with the thinking of Leibowitz, it is worth noting that although faith and reason are often contrasted, this is not necessarily the case in thought and practice. Submission to God need not be an abandonment of rationality. Rather, doing so can be and can be experienced by the adherent as a rational choice, whether in response to intellectual arguments or as a conscious commitment to a community and its traditions.

Human Slavery/Servitude in the Bible and Talmud

We cannot complete our review of liberty and slavery without acknowledging the fact that the Bible and Talmud view as legal some types of human slavery or servitude. There are at least two responses to contextualize the situation.[61]

First, Maimonides championed a view that distinguishes between Torah-commanded and Torah-tolerated. This approach posits that the Torah was given and received in a particular time and place and that some changes would have proven too radical to make the covenant acceptable or perhaps even comprehensible to the recipients. Therefore, God allowed the continuation of certain undesirable practices, with the ultimate goal of allowing them to phase out. For example, although it might have been preferable to outlaw animal sacrifice, the practice was too ingrained among the nations of the time, so the Torah at least banned human sacrifice—and eventually prayer, as the service of the heart, came to replace animal sacrifice. Likewise, slavery was a widespread practice and therefore tolerated, but eventually ended within Judaism, and centuries prior to efforts to eliminate it in the Western world.[62]

Secondly, given some ambiguity in the translation of *'avodah* as both slavery and servitude, it is possible that most of what we find in the

Bible and Talmud are types of indentured servitude, where individuals sell their labor to pay off a debt. According to the Bible scholar Joshua Berman, "Though the word *'ebed* is often translated as 'slave,' in fact no distinct and exclusive term for 'slave' exists. *'Ebed* means a servant, a subordinate, an official, but does not connote ownership of the person, and does not indicate the duration of the status." Berman explains that "an Israelite can hire out only years of service, not his person."[63] In general, we are not necessarily talking about an endless slavery without end and without rights. Indeed, rabbinic law carefully circumscribed the practice. The rules served so much to protect the dignity and life of the servant that we are told in the talmudic tractate Kiddushin that "Whoever purchases a Hebrew servant purchases for himself a master."[64]

Exclusive or Overlapping Ideas of Liberty?

In the end, it is difficult to imagine that most libertarians could accept, as a general model for society, a more expansive Jewish view encompassing both Negative and Positive Liberty. And yet, so long as a Jewish perspective does not exclude, but rather encompasses, a libertarian sensibility, then the two are not quite incompatible. That is, nothing in Jewish theology or religion rejects a libertarian notion of freedom. And furthermore, so long as a Judaism does not impose its notions of Positive Liberty upon others, through government intervention or otherwise, then it is not at all clear we have a contradiction in practice. In actual political governance, practitioners of traditional Judaisms would not necessarily reject a polity based upon a libertarian view of freedom. In brief, it would seem that we have found space for a religiously observant Jew to run for office as a libertarian candidate, and without betraying any convictions.

We have also established that most libertarians would agree that some sort of at least minimal legal structure is necessary to preserve liberty. How much or how little of a framework is necessary—this is a matter of discussion and debate. And, no doubt, this discussion and debate is of interest to libertarians and religiously observant Jews alike.

Such a discussion does not end here. For what does freedom mean if we do not own ourselves, own our physical bodies? The at least apparent disagreement, between libertarianism and Judaism, over this very question is what we turn to in the next chapter.

Chapter 2

Ownership versus Stewardship: The Body

> Individuals own their bodies and have rights over them that other individuals, groups, and governments may not violate. Individuals have the freedom and responsibility to decide what they knowingly and voluntarily consume, and what risks they accept to their own health, finances, safety, or life.
> – Section 1.1 "Self-Ownership," *Libertarian Party Platform* (2018)

In the fifth chapter of the second book of his *Two Treatises of Government*, John Locke declares simply that "every Man has a *Property* in his own *Person*."[1] That is, we own our bodies.

Indeed, if *I* do not own my body, then who does? Can another human being own my body? Can a government own it? And furthermore, what does it even mean to *own* a body? Does such ownership entail the right to use it as one wishes? To sell it? Even to dispose of it? What do libertarian and Jewish sources have to say about these matters?

Conflicting Jewish and libertarian perspectives on ownership of our material bodies would appear to strike at the very foundation of our identities, at the very center of our lived, physical experience. If nowhere else, it would seem that libertarian and Judaic traditions are irreconcilable over the ownership of our bodies, of our selves. For many, perhaps most, self-identifying libertarians, one of the basic, definitional principles of libertarianism is self-ownership—by contrast, it would seem to be common knowledge among religious Jews that we do *not* own our bodies, but that God owns them, entrusting them to us for our years on this earth and charging us with stewardship over them. If true, this distinction would appear to cleave an unbridgeable rift between Judaism and libertarianism, demonstrating unequivocally the fundamental incompatibility of the two.

If true.

As we learned in the previous chapter, first appearances often prove deceptive. Jewish sources on this matter are not as unambiguous as many would assume, and libertarian texts are not as unified as many would expect. This chapter will first outline a libertarian principle of self-ownership and then examine traditional Jewish sources concerning the ownership status of the self. Are the orientations so alien to each other that a religiously observant Jew would be unable to embrace and voice support for self-ownership?

Self-Ownership of the Body in Libertarian Thought

By proclaiming that we have property in our own persons, Locke provided the foundation for modern libertarian understandings and justifications of self-ownership. Locke expounded further: "This no Body has any Right to but himself. The *Labour* of his Body, and the *Work* of his Hands, we may say, are properly his."[2] In short, we own ourselves and that which we produce.

The very first subsection of the *Libertarian Party Platform* addresses this central principle—that we own our bodies, that we can make decisions regarding our bodies, and that others remain prohibited from violating these rights.[3] The entire first section of the platform is devoted to personal liberty, and of its nine paragraphs, that of self-ownership comes at the beginning, suggesting its necessity for the eight that follow: expression and communication, privacy, personal relationships, abortion, parental rights, crime and justice, the death penalty, and self-defense.

Indeed, in his broad survey *The Libertarian Mind*, David Boaz roots *all* rights and liberty in the principle of self-ownership:

> Because every person owns himself, his body and his mind, he has the right to life.... The right to self-ownership leads immediately to the right to liberty; indeed, we may say that "right to life" and "right to liberty" are just two ways of expressing the same point. If individuals own themselves,

and have both the right and the obligation to take the actions necessary for their survival and flourishing, then they must enjoy freedom of thought and action.[4]

Murray Rothbard likewise identifies self-ownership as fundamental, calling it a "universal right" and the "primary axiom" for a libertarian.[5]

As Rothbard and others point out, we do not find ourselves with a promising set of alternatives should we reject the principle of self-ownership. At least so long as we retain some notion of ownership. Likely the real issue for Rothbard is control, whether or not one employs the language of self-ownership. That is, if I do not own myself and possess the accompanying rights and control over my body, then someone else could at least try to exercise such rights and control. Using the rhetoric of self-ownership, if each person does *not* own himself or herself, then we must say that some person or persons own other people, or possibly that in some collectivist sense we all own a very tiny bit of each other. With billions of individuals on the planet, the latter remains impracticable. And the former—that some people can own other people—requires us to say and accept what strikes most of us as repellent: that some human beings are, in effect, less than fully human and do not deserve the rights due to other people.[6]

When we discuss ownership of persons, we cannot avoid the analogy of ownership of physical property (the focus of the next chapter). In this sense, as Rothbard notes, echoing Locke, a physical assault against a person can be characterized as a type of *property* crime; if I have property in myself, then anyone who assaults me is violating my property rights. And what are property rights in regard to physical property? The prerogative to *make use* of such property—though also, it would seem, to trade it, sell it, or destroy it. Libertarians disagree over the extent to which such rights over physical property might apply to ownership of our own bodies or persons, yet the essential point remains: they reject the idea that some individuals should possess the latitude to wield such rights over and against other individuals. This, simply put, is slavery. Therefore, unless we wish to grant some people the right to own or enslave other people, one might reasonably conclude we must accept a libertarian notion of self-ownership.

Where libertarians take pause and disagree over self-ownership, it is over its extent, and whether *any* limitations exist—and just how far to take the analogy with ownership of other sorts of physical property. This disagreement manifests itself in debates over the right to kill oneself and over whether or not one could sell himself or herself into slavery. With a physical object I own, I am free to destroy or dispose of it. Therefore, according to a principle of self-ownership fully analogous to property ownership, I ought to be able to dispose of the body that is my property. To deny this would seem to be a serious challenge to or limitation upon my self-ownership rights. Others contest, however, that the action of suicide makes nonsense of all other principles, of liberty and even of self-ownership itself. Not that libertarians would *outlaw* suicide or necessarily oppose physician-assisted suicide for terminally ill individuals suffering severe pain, but they still might see suicide in principle as a *moral* wrong. As for selling oneself, libertarians clearly endorse free contracting in selling one's labor to another. And most libertarians oppose the criminalization of prostitution, thereby allowing individuals to sell their bodies in some sense. The problem and the paradox, as with the case of suicide, is that if one were free to sell oneself into servitude permanently, one would be exercising the right of self-ownership to strip oneself of that very right. If self-ownership figures as an absolute value, then maintaining both of these at the same time becomes impossible: one could not deny someone the right to sell oneself permanently, yet that someone could not do so, because there would be a loss of self-ownership. In these regards, even some libertarians suggest at least philosophical limits to the principle of self-ownership.[7]

Of course, most societies and polities do not embrace a principle of *full* self-ownership. The widespread practice of compulsory national service, in the military or otherwise, betrays a recognition that states do exercise control over the bodies of individuals. And thus the near-universal libertarian opposition to military drafts or mandatory service of any sort. For compulsory service requires coercion of individuals and their physical bodies.

Coercion—or, rather, its rejection—truly figures at the center of the principle of self-ownership, as well as the nonaggression principle discussed in the previous chapter, and indeed libertarianism as a whole. Murray Rothbard explains that "[t]he right to self-ownership asserts the absolute right of each man, by virtue of his (or her) being a human being, to 'own' his or her own body; that is, to control that body free of coercive interference. . . . [to] think, learn, value, and choose his or her ends and means in order to survive and flourish, . . . without being hampered and restricted by coercive molestation."[8] And so, many or most libertarians firmly embrace the idea of self-ownership. But what about religiously oriented Jews? It would at least appear that Judaism has long rejected this idea.

Ownership and Stewardship of the Body in Jewish Thought

In our day, the notion that God owns our physical bodies and that we serve as guardians or stewards of them strikes most religiously observant Jews as self-evident, as a basic and simple principle of Judaism, as an idea we might give voice to confidently and unselfconsciously.

As Yeshiva University's Rabbi Dr. J. David Bleich states the matter in his book *Judaism and Healing: Halakhic Perspectives*, "Judaism recognizes divine proprietorship over all objects of creation, including the human body." R. Bleich, one of the foremost contemporary authorities and writers on Jewish law and medical ethics, with six volumes of *Contemporary Halakhic Problems* among his many publications, writes concerning suicide as follows:

> Jewish teaching with regard to suicide is rooted in the concept that man does not enjoy proprietary rights with regard to his body or his life. God, as the Author of life, entrusts the human body to the stewardship of man for preservation and safekeeping but retains to Himself title to life. Accordingly, man's life is not his to dispose of at will.[9]

It appears that in R. Bleich's understanding, the Jewish tradition remains unambiguous on the issue of ownership and stewardship of the body.

Indeed, other writers echo R. Bleich in their articulation of and certainty regarding these principles. Rabbi Alfred Cohen, founder, editor, and frequent contributor to the *Journal of Halacha and Contemporary Society*, contrasts the Jewish view of body ownership with what he describes as the "accepted wisdom" of the Western world, namely that women have full latitude over their own bodies in regard to pregnancy, sterilization, and abortion. While recognizing that denying such a notion might appear to threaten advances in recognizing the dignity of not only women, but also older people and those with disabilities (and after all, I would be remiss not to point out that many women have suffered greatly due to men exercising power over women's bodies, and that something similar would apply in other circumstances), R. Cohen nonetheless rejects the accepted wisdom: "But this is not the approach of Jewish thinking, not for women and not for men."[10] That is, R. Cohen does not at all mean to suggest that Judaism rejects the rights of women in favor of the historical norm of men maintaining such control. Rather, in his understanding, neither women *nor* men own their bodies or each other's bodies.

In a 1973 essay entitled "Bodies Belong to Whom?" Bar Ilan University president and later chancellor Rabbi Dr. Emanuel Rackman (1910–2008) argues against the practice of active euthanasia.[11] "The gift of life that we enjoy is from God," he writes. "Our bodies, without which life is impossible, are from Him too. According to Judaism I am only the custodian of my physical self. I may not mutilate myself any more than I may mutilate that which belongs to someone else." Because we do not own our bodies, R. Rackman reasons, "the mere thought that a moral problem may be resolved on the assumption that my body belongs to me and I am the sole judge of what should happen to it is repugnant to Judaism."[12] He therefore rejects, as immoral, permitting a doctor to play an active role in causing a person's death. Indeed, he clearly disagrees with any attempt to ground or root moral choices in the principle of self-ownership.

Rabbi Dr. Immanuel Jakobovits (1921–1999), a pioneering Jewish medical ethicist and once the Chief Rabbi of the United Hebrew Congregations of Great Britain and the Commonwealth, does not (perhaps surprisingly) address the issue in his several-hundred-page, trailblazing 1959 book *Jewish Medical Ethics*, though he does elsewhere: "Man is not the owner of his body but merely its custodian, charged to preserve it from any physical harm and to promote its health where this has been impaired."[13] The obligations incurred by this custodial status clearly override, for R. Jakobovits, the right of an individual to do whatever he or she wants with his or her body.

Rabbi Eliezer Waldenburg (1915–2006, also known as the Tzitz Eliezer) served as the premiere rabbinic author of responsa on medical cases in the twentieth century, particularly in Israel. That is, the Tzitz Eliezer was the go-to authority for practical questions from doctors and others, even concerning patients undergoing medical treatment. According to Alan Jotkowitz, the Tzitz Eliezer argued that "based on the principle that a person's soul belongs not to him but to God," individuals and families do not possess the authority to make the decision of whether or not to try to extend a life, and that a person cannot even injure herself or himself because "a person does not have ownership over their body."[14]

Rabbi Moshe Feinstein (1895–1986, also known as Rav Moshe), who lived on New York's Lower East Side and was perhaps the most widely respected American Orthodox rabbinic decisor from the 1950s until his death, addressed the issue of self-ownership in an interesting way. As context, it is important to note that individual cases can include specific details that might result in different rulings on situations appearing remarkably similar (such would certainly apply to the decisions of the Tzitz Eliezer), and it is also important to note that Jewish medical ethics often distinguishes between removing or stopping treatment and not starting new treatment; the former, in contrast to the latter, can more clearly be viewed as actively hastening someone's death. Rav Moshe, as he was commonly known, appears to have held a position along these lines, though not all rabbinic authorities would necessarily have agreed with him. In at least one case of a patient near death he argued that the mental or physical trauma caused by forcing someone to begin new and unwanted treatment, in this case connecting the patient to an intravenous feeding device, could actually cause death to occur more quickly. In a different case, R. Moshe ruled that a quite ill individual could choose to undergo a very risky treatment, even one with a greater than 50 percent likelihood of a fatal outcome—if success meant a significant increase in quality and length of life. According to Daniel Sinclair, R. Moshe based this ruling in the idea of God's ownership of human beings, asserting that "'people become the owners of their bodies with respect to improving the quality of their lives,' and, in effect, God transfers His title in that patient's life to him."[15]

Finally, Rabbi Yisrael Meir Kagan (1838–1933, also known as the Chofetz Chaim) wrote that human beings and everything in the world belong to God. Discussing the laws of the Sabbath and the obligation to observe them, he wrote that "Since God is Creator of all, He is therefore

Master over all, and we are His servants and are obligated to do His will and to serve Him with our entire body, soul and resources—for all belongs to Him."[16] Whereas these words came from the third of six volumes of his work the *Mishnah Berurah*, there is also a story told about him as the Chofetz Chaim, which means lover of life: If a doctor instructs a person to quit smoking, presumably due to the damaging health effects, the person becomes obligated to quit. The Chofetz Chaim asked, "How may a slave choose to do as he pleases if he belongs to his master?"[17]

Within the Orthodox Jewish world, at least, we therefore find a near consensus that we do not own ourselves. Outside of the Orthodox Jewish world, both non-Orthodox and academic writers have expressed comparable characterizations of the traditional Jewish view of stewardship and ownership of the body. In a summary article on Jewish bioethics, Professor Dena S. Davis states in simple terms that "Judaism teaches that because our bodies were created by God, they are owned by God and loaned to us; therefore it is our obligation to care for them." Davis does, however, go on to explain that many Reform Jews reject the idea of God's ownership in favor of personal autonomy and self-determination, including in the area of medical ethics.[18]

Rabbi Elliott Dorff, a bioethicist and a leading contemporary figure in the movement of Conservative Judaism, similarly explains the traditional outlook:

> The Rabbis assumed that human bodies were God's property, which he leased for the duration of one's life. If a person were to rent an apartment, he or she would not have the right to destroy it, but would have the responsibility to take reasonable care of it. In the same way, because a person's body was on loan, one did not have the right to destroy it by suicide, but rather had the responsibility to take care of it.[19]

Note that both Davis and R. Dorff point specifically to the principle of God's ownership to *explain* various prohibitions against harming oneself, as well as obligations to take care of oneself. That is, God's ownership of our bodies is viewed not only as a fact or principle, but also serves to justify or ground other principles, an issue we will return to below.

In one innovative and thoughtful essay, Adam Goodkind, at the time a college student, reflects on our relationship to our bodies. He articulates the paradox that quite often we perceive and experience our own bodies as being, in some deep way, separate from ourselves; especially during adolescence, one's body can very much feel like something outside of one's full control.[20] University of California-Berkeley law professor Meir Dan-Cohen's more scholarly investigation of a similar notion examines the very language we use to talk about ourselves and our bodies. According to Dan-Cohen, our ownership of objects "resembles our relationship to our body; in both cases ownership is grounded in the use of the personal pronouns *I* and *me* to allude to the respective items, and is revealed by the similar role that the possessive pronouns *my* and *mine* play in our body-talk and in our property-talk."[21] That is, we use similar language when referring to our bodies and to objects we own, and this parallel helps explain why we could think that we own our bodies. Dan-Cohen's philosophical investigation raises many other issues, including the relationship of the body to the self, and indeed whether or not they are the same thing. In any case, both Dan-Cohen and Goodkind suggest reasons why we might experience our bodies as objects outside of ourselves; the difference is that for Dan-Cohen this turns the body into an object open to ownership, whereas for Goodkind the body becomes something foreign, something that is not fully part of one's true self. Therefore, although he acknowledges not seeing himself as religiously observant, Goodkind nevertheless embraces the traditional view of our bodies being gifts from God. And he notes that regardless of whether or not one accepts this theological perspective, he agrees "that our bodies are not wholly ours; they are, in a very real sense, on loan" for the duration of our lives.[22]

Clearly, the notion of God's ownership, along with human stewardship, of our physical bodies carries widespread acceptance in Judaism. Yet where did this idea originate? In which basic sources of the Jewish tradition do we find this? Is the principle stated simply in the Torah or the Mishnah, Judaism's written and oral laws, respectively? In fact, grounding the principle in early, fundamental Jewish sources is neither straightforward nor unambiguous. The basic sources are not clear, and the commentators are far from unanimous.

One would think to begin with the five books of Moses, the Written Torah. Yet here one will not find any direct statements about who owns us. There are verses confirming God's ownership of the entire world, but not of human bodies specifically. There is no simple, clear statement to the effect that the Lord your God has given you your body on loan, for safekeeping, to be returned at a future date. The Oral Torah, consisting of the Mishnah and the talmudic commentary upon it, likewise reveals no explicit statement of God's ownership of our bodies. At least, I am unaware of any later commentator referencing such an assertion—and commentators certainly would cite such proof if available. Where, then, ought one to look, if not to the Written and Oral Torah?

Shylock's Pound of Flesh

When addressing the topic of self-ownership, contemporary Jewish writers generally point first and foremost to Rabbi Shlomo Yosef Zevin (1888–1978), the founder and chief editor of the *Encyclopedia Talmudit* and the most widely recognized advocate of what the Center for Modern Torah Leadership's Rabbi Aryeh Klapper has termed the "Divine Ownership Theory." In a famous essay "The Case of Shylock," R. Zevin seeks to determine whether or not, according to Jewish law, Shakespeare's Jewish character from *The Merchant of Venice* possesses the right to claim a pound of another's flesh?! Whether or not Shylock can assert such a right depends upon whether or not a person *owns* his or her flesh, and self-ownership therefore figures as the pivotal issue in the matter.[23]

R. Zevin makes the argument that Shylock has no right to demand a pound of flesh from Antonio for defaulting on a loan, and furthermore, that any such transaction would be null and void—all because a person does not truly own his or her body and therefore has no right to dispose of it, just as a person possesses no right to dispose of the money or the property or a life *belonging to someone else*. In brief, if I do not have the right to claim a pound of *your* flesh, I possess no more a right to sell or dispose of a pound of my own. R. Zevin invokes a number of arguments and authorities to establish his case that we do not own our bodies.

The first of these, Rabbi Shneur Zalman of Liadi (1745–1812, also known as the Ba'al HaTanya), the founder and first leader of the Hasidic Chabad-Lubavitch community, states that even if someone gives another person permission to strike him or her, this other person remains prohibited from doing so. Although the prohibition against injuring *oneself* is clearly articulated in the traditional sources, why should it be forbidden to hurt *someone else* when he or she grants explicit permission? R.

Zevin quotes R. Shneur Zalman as asserting that a person has no such authority over his or her own body to allow this—and yet at the same time, R. Zevin recognizes that such a principle is not established explicitly anywhere in the classical sources.

R. Zevin must therefore identify a textual foundation for R. Shneur Zalman's assertion. He finds this in TB Sanhedrin 84b. The law here allows a son to bloodlet his own father for the purpose of healing. Yet if a father can simply grant his son permission to "hurt" him, why does the Talmud need to invoke healing as the justification? Why is not enough to say the father can give permission regardless of the reason? Furthermore, we have no grounds to suppose that I can harm anyone who grants me permission, with the lone exception of my parents. Permission alone must therefore prove ineffective in allowing the bloodletting. We know that the son can harm his father by drawing blood, but we also know that it is not the father's *permission* that allows for this—so there must be another reason. For R. Zevin this reason must be the healing. There is no right to give permission to harm, because we do not own ourselves, but the need for healing does allow this to take place, even for a son treating his father.

Rabbi Moshe ben Maimon (1135–1204, also known as the Rambam and probably best known as Maimonides), offers perhaps a stronger foundation for R. Zevin's position. In the first chapter of the Laws of the Murderer from his *Mishneh Torah*, Maimonides discusses the case of the "blood redeemer," one who is obligated to avenge the murder of a relative by killing the murderer. What if the murderer offers the court money to *not* go through with the execution, and moreover the blood redeemer agrees to this? Can the killer pay to avoid punishment? Maimonides rules that the court *cannot* take any amount of money for this. Why not? In the fourth law of the first chapter he explains to us as follows: "That the soul [*nefesh*] of the one murdered is not a possession [*kinyan*] of the blood redeemer, but rather a possession of the Holy One, Blessed Be He, as it says, 'You shall not take ransom for the soul of a murderer.'" Now, at first this reasoning might seem odd—Maimonides appears to be discussing the soul of the victim, and yet the proof he brings from the book of Numbers (35:3) refers to the soul of the murderer. Perhaps, then, Maimonides sought only to make the point that no soul can be ransomed, neither murderer nor murdered. Basically, to accept the offer, even with the permission of the blood redeemer, would be in a sense to take money in exchange for the life of the victim. Even though the blood redeemer possesses an obligation to avenge the life of the relative, the relative's life was never his possession, but belonged to God! R. Zevin concludes from this argument that we do not own ourselves.

Maimonides uses the language of kinyan in making his point. What is a kinyan and why is the notion important here? In Modern Hebrew, the verb *liknot* means to purchase. In biblical and in talmudic and other rabbinic texts, the concept seems to have a somewhat broader scope, meaning to acquire or to possess, or perhaps to acquire *and therefore* possess. So, for example, the word is used in the very first blessing of the central prayer of Jewish ritual, the *'amida*: God is described as *koneh ha-kol*. In Modern Hebrew, one might translate this as *purchases everything*. Of course, God does not purchase anything, so we are better off translating it as *possesses everything*. Some translate *koneh* here as *creates*, perhaps linking the notions of creation, acquisition, and possession. This language finds its first appearance in the fourteenth chapter of Genesis, where God is twice described as *Koneh shamayim va-aretz*, or the One Who possesses the heavens and the earth. We can learn from the expression *koneh ha-kol* at least two things: one, that God acquires or possesses *everything* (and everything must include human beings); and two, that God's acquisition is, in essence, a necessary consequence of the act of creating; God acquires by creating, and from this we might also understand that human ownership of things can be achieved through a creative act of building or producing. Returning to the argument, if we, along with the entirety of creation, are acquisitions of God, and God owns us, how could we possibly own ourselves? Given the links between creation and ownership, if the concept of kinyan does not match precisely the more modern and libertarian notion of ownership, there no doubt remains a reasonable likeness.

R. Zevin points to two other authorities to bolster his position. Rabbi Joseph ben Meir HaLevi ibn Migash, called the Ri Migash (1077–1141), was a teacher of the father of Maimonides and the author of many responsa, answers to questions posed to him on matters of Jewish law. In one of these, the Ri Migash makes an argument that might strike us—living in a world of myriad popular diets—as rather strange. The questioner asks him about the case of someone who plans to move to the land of Israel and makes a vow to abstain (except during the Sabbath) from meat and wine until he goes ahead and moves to Israel. The Ri Migash responds that such a person is a sinner against God and the Torah, and sins every day he continues with this vow, because he is endangering himself—and such is prohibited. He notes that harming oneself is prohibited just as harming someone else is prohibited, and further makes the point that a person is not permitted to incriminate oneself in a case where the death penalty is at issue, though self-incrimination is permissible for monetary matters. A later authority, Rabbi David ben Solomon ibn (Abi) Zimra (c.1479–1573, also called the Radbaz), echoes the argument about self-incrimination, pointing to a verse in the eighteenth chapter of Ezekiel where God speaks through the prophesizing of Ezekiel: "Behold, all souls [*nefashot*] are Mine; like the soul of the father, so the soul of the son; behold, the soul that sins, it shall die." (Ezek. 18:4)

With these arguments and sources, and especially with the weighty authority of Maimonides seemingly on his side, R. Zevin would appear to have a strong case. And yet, can we not imagine ways in which we *do* seem to own our bodies? Just turning to the issue of the blood redeemer, if the redeemer and court do *not* own the life of the victim for the purposes of sale or ransom, then how can one say the court has any permission to execute the murderer in the first place? Indeed, if we do not own our bodies, then how can *any* killing or even injuring—*even in self-defense*—be permitted?!

Rabbi Shaul Yisraeli (1909–1995) raises just such problems in his critique of R. Zevin's position. If R. Zevin is cited by most commentators today for his defense of the Divine Ownership Theory, R. Yisraeli is almost always cited in tandem with and in opposition to him.[24] After all, as R. Yisraeli explains, Jewish law clearly permits killing in self-defense and furthermore permits killing in warfare, even the accidental killing of noncombatants. If we in no way own ourselves, then none of these would be allowed. At the least, therefore, we might say that God's ownership of our bodies comes with limitations. As human beings we must, at a minimum, *share* in the ownership of our bodies. In this way, we would become partners with God. Perhaps we have no permission to commit suicide not because we do not own ourselves fully, but rather because we have no right to give up God's share—and there is no means of giving up our own share without at the same time giving up God's share.

Returning to R. Zevin, he actually employs related logic in asserting and explaining the responsibility to save someone who has attempted or is attempting to commit suicide. He compares this to the responsibility to return a lost object to someone. In general, someone who finds a lost object bears an obligation to return it. In the case of a deliberately lost object, however, the one who finds it is *not* obligated to return it. This would seem to imply that there would be no responsibility to rescue someone who sets out deliberately to kill herself or himself! R. Zevin argues that because we do not own ourselves, the potential suicide has no right to commit such an act. That is, trying to commit suicide is not akin to deliberately losing an object, because the individual has no right to lose himself or herself. R. Klapper counters that applying the very concept of the obligation to return lost objects demonstrates that we *do* in some sense own ourselves, because if saving someone is akin to returning a lost object, clearly we are "returning" the person to himself or herself. In any case, regardless of the matter of suicide, someone who kills in self-defense is not liable for murder and judicial execution, because the attacker has given up God's share, if without divine permission.

R. Yisraeli is able to invoke Maimonides *against* R. Zevin, and with a neighboring textual source. Where R. Zevin looks to the first chapter of the Laws of the Murderer, R. Yisraeli points us to the very next chapter. In the fourth law of the second chapter, Maimonides clearly delineates the authority of both the religious court to return a verdict and sentence of capital punishment and the king to carry out executions where the court fails to do so. And, after all, in prohibiting the acceptance of ransom, even the law cited by R. Zevin acknowledges the court's right and responsibility to carry out the death penalty. Again, if we do not own our bodies to any degree, then all killing ought to be prohibited, including judicially ordained capital punishment.

R. Yisraeli also turns the Radbaz against R. Zevin. He explains that the Radbaz does recognize that it is permissible to kill in self-defense. And despite saying that a person's nefesh belongs to God, the Radbaz emerges in R. Yisraeli's view as a supporter of shared ownership, with God and people as partners. How so? In killing in self-defense, it would seem that the aggressor has forfeited the right to life—yet we know the aggressor has no right to do so. The earthly court cannot convict the one acting in self-defense. However, at least in the case where the defender could have warded off the aggressor with less than deadly force, the heavenly court can hand down judgment, inasmuch as the aggressor had no permission to forfeit God's share of his or her nefesh. Following this logic, the Radbaz can conclude that self-incrimination in a capital case must remain ineffective, because the self-incriminator, like the aggressor in the other case, has no authority to forfeit the divine ownership share in the nefesh.

Undergirding R. Yisraeli's entire argument is a focus on the notion, also articulated by Maimonides, of *dina d'malkhuta dina*, which basically means that the law of the land is the law (this is a crucial concept to which we will return in a later chapter). Jewish law accords a certain degree of respect for the laws of the government, wherever one lives. According to some, this submission to secular law extends to both civil and criminal matters. For R. Yisraeli, likely following contract theory, the laws of the state, and even international law, depend upon the agreement of the governed. As such, in human society, we appear to have longstanding agreement granting kings and other governors the power to execute, and for soldiers to kill during war.

R. Yisraeli employs his argument about *dina d'malkhuta dina* to suggest that R. Shneur Zalman, R. Zevin's foundational source, does not truly mean what he appears to say—and precisely where R. Zevin quotes him to frame his argument—that we have no authority over ourselves. According to R. Yisraeli, R. Shneur Zalman is merely exercising a sort of poetic license by rewording the Talmud's injunction against self-wounding into a phrasing that suggests we have no authority whatsoever over ourselves. R. Yisraeli insists that the R. Shneur Zalman does accept Maimonides's understanding of *dina d'malkhuta dina*.

Nonetheless, at least one noted descendant of R. Shneur Zalman of Liadi takes his ancestor literally. Rabbi Menachem Mendel Schneerson (1902–1994), the seventh rebbe and leader of the Hasidic Chabad-Lubavitch community, articulates this forcefully in a 1969 letter. Referencing the *Tanya*, the book from which R. Shneur Zalman earned his *nom de plume*, R. Schneerson cites a passage in which his ancestor does not actually use the language of property and ownership. Rather, in the beginning of the second chapter, R. Shneur Zalman refers to the soul as *chelek Ha-Elohim,* as a *part* of God. He derives this from the biblical verse of God blowing into Adam's nostrils the *nishmat ḥayyim*, the soul of life. Furthermore, this first Lubavitcher Rebbe uses strong language to indicate that he does *not* read or mean this *metaphorically*; in his view, the soul truly is a part of God. R. Schneerson writes that "not only is the Neshama [i.e., the soul] . . . but also the body of a Jew is sacred and is the property of G-d, while the Jew is no more than a guardian of it."[25] Therefore, R. Schneerson's language of ownership would appear to be a logical inference that if something is a part of you, you own it—and in this case we are referring to God, not to a human being. His addition to his predecessor's assertion is that the logic applies not only to the immaterial soul, but to the physical body as well. He then echoes what we have already seen, explaining that this notion underlies various obligations and prohibitions relating to the body, referring to rare exceptions—for autopsies, for instance—as permissible *only* due to "the Owner's will," meaning the will of God, the Owner.

By moving from the soul to the body, R. Schneerson here extends, in a nontrivial way, any notion penned by his predecessor. Until now, we have not done much to distinguish just what is being owned here. The body? The soul? Both? Something else? The *guf* is the physical body, and R. Schneerson explicitly includes the guf as under God's ownership. The *neshama* has different connotations but is most easily defined as the soul. There is a third term, one we have referred to already: the nefesh. The nefesh is sometimes understood as the soul, or at least a dimension of it, yet is probably best characterized as the "life force." Animals also possess it. And the prohibition upon Jews over consuming the blood of kosher animals relies upon a notion of the blood being or carrying the life force. The nefesh is something immaterial yet at the very same time intimately bound up with the materiality of our bodies. There does not appear to be any reason why ownership of neshama, nefesh, and guf must be the same, either all owned by God, all owned by human beings, or all shared. However, for all practical purposes, insofar as we discuss the political and policy differences and similarities between Judaism and libertarianism, we seem to have in mind the guf and the nefesh, the body and the life force. In this regard, R. Schneerson's explicit mention of the ownership of the body is neither surprising nor inappropriate.

At the end of the debate between Rabbis Zevin and Yisraeli, we would have difficulty declaring R. Zevin the undisputed victor. R. Yisraeli appears to have marshalled enough reasonable sources to support a contrary position, one of *shared ownership*, despite the fact that a majority of Jewish thinkers today seem to hold by the Divine Ownership Theory and furthermore consider it a basic, indisputable, and self-evidently obvious theological principle.

Beyond Absolute Self-Ownership: Alternative Explanations

The debate does not end there. We began our discussion of Jewish thought with a promising argument that we do not own our bodies, and now see that perhaps this very argument is not quite as compelling as we might have thought at first. Perhaps, however, neither side is correct? Is there a third Jewish view, or multiple alternative Jewish views, as to whether or not we own our bodies?

Just to be clear and fair, despite the fact that there appears to be within today's Jewish world a near consensus that we do not own ourselves, some of the key summaries of the matter do recognize the lack of uniformity of opinion. Rabbi Dr. Avraham Steinberg, in his definitive opus, the three-volume *Encyclopedia of Jewish Medical Ethics*, notes both the pro- and anti-divine ownership theories:

> The other fundamental principle upon which the concept of informed consent is based is the *ownership rights over one's body*. This principle is also not simply and generally accepted in *halakhah*. Some Rabbis rule that a person has no ownership rights at all over his body. Other Rabbis rule that one cannot totally negate ownership over one's body and that a person has partial rights over his body in partnership with the Holy One, Blessed be He.[26]

A section on "Ownership Rights Over One's Body" in *The Oxford Handbook of Judaism and Economics* similarly points to differences of opinion on the matter, including the dispute between Rabbis Zevin and Yisraeli. The *Handbook* explains that the contemporary authority Rabbi Zalman Nechemia Goldberg (b. 1932) argues for a position of limited ownership rights; just as the Jewish owner of a Canaanite slave cannot do to the enslaved individual *anything* the owner wants, such as removing a limb, so too an individual cannot do anything he or she wants with or to his or her own body.[27]

Perhaps the most important and simple third side in the dispute is that we just do not appear to require the Divine Ownership Theory to explain the various injunctions and prescriptions concerning the body in Jewish law. Earlier we noted how various writers and authorities have asserted that God's ownership of us figured as *the* reason for obligations and prohibitions, such as caring for oneself and not harming others. Yet it is not entirely clear why the two need linking. For, after all, we have recourse to other principles that do the job without needing to insist on divine ownership. That is, we can ground all these various prohibitions and obligations in at least one other principle: *the sanctity of life created in the divine image*. This notion has a clear textual basis—we learn in the book of Genesis that humans are created *b'tselem Elohim*, in the image of God. Later on, the twenty-fourth chapter of Leviticus situates the laws of murder and maiming within the broader context of sanctity, including the sanctity of God, the priests, and the Tabernacle (the desert precursor to the Temple in Jerusalem). This suggests that human life has value in itself—that murder and maiming, suicide and self-injury, may be prohibited not as a violation of God's ownership rights, but rather over this basic value and sanctity. Furthermore, the fact that Jewish law interprets "an eye for an eye" as requiring monetary compensation for injury would seem to suggest we do own our bodies—otherwise why would a person be entitled to compensation for the loss of a limb? It would seem, then, that these ideas are enough to explain and justify prohibitions and obligations concerning the body without requiring one to invoke the responsibilities incumbent upon a guardian or trustee—and therefore apply whether or not we own ourselves.

And there are yet other principles that might suffice without requiring the invocation of divine ownership. One might ground the rules about self-harm and self-protection in recognizing an offense in destroying God's creations or even in failing to sustain God's creations. One could also understand the prohibition of self-injury and suicide as merely special cases of the general prohibition of injuring or killing a person. After all, we do not condemn murder and assault or identify them as simply wrong just because the murderer or assailant does not *own* the victim or the victim's limbs! Such actions are prohibited in their own right. Of course, in the end, it might not matter in any practical sense—the same obligations and prohibitions remain, regardless of the basis. As

R. Steinberg notes, "However, even according to this view [i.e., against the Divine Ownership Theory], a person has no right to bring harm to his body by refusing sound medical treatment."[28]

Indeed, one of the perennial caveats about Jewish law is that in most cases reasons do not ultimately decide the case. That is to say, while the reasons are not *un*important, the facts of the laws, their being binding upon us, are not dependent upon our discussion of or conclusions about the reasons. Sometimes, we do not understand the reasons at all, but a law remains in place nonetheless. In our case, for example, suicide is forbidden—whether or not we own our bodies. Self-defense is permitted—whether or not we own our bodies. Indeed, as R. Klapper has noted, whether we are owners of our bodies or stewards of our bodies, we find ourselves possessing certain rights and responsibilities. It would appear that these rules largely remain the same regardless of ownership status.

One final possibility remains: that we have been asking the wrong question all along, that we have made a conceptual error. That is, perhaps the Hebrew scriptures, and even the rabbis of the Talmud, had no concept of self-ownership? If we could ask Moses or Rabbi Akiva whether we own our bodies or own ourselves in some other way, would they proffer ready answers or would they offer confused looks, uncertain how to respond to such a nonsensical question? Perhaps we are seeking to impose our modern notions of ownership where they do not fit? Certainly, there was a concept of ownership in the Talmud, but maybe being self-owned was not a characteristic applicable to the human body or soul in the sense we think of it today?[29]

This might become clearer if we consider a couple of examples of conceptual errors. For example, we speak of religion as if it is a thing, an objective thing, rather than a linguistic, sociological, and analytical tool. But have people always looked at what we today call Judaism and thought of it as a religion? Or, the ancients had no conception of the credit card, let alone the different types of such cards. Prior to the discoveries and insights of Lister, Koch, and Pasteur in the nineteenth century, no one had conceptualized the germ theory of disease as we know it—so to ask how the rabbis of the Talmud grappled with the germ theory would prove nonsensical. It might seem evident that our forefathers and foremothers recognized a notion of self-ownership, but perhaps we project onto them our own conceptions of the world.

Self-Ownership of the Body in Libertarian Thought: An Absolute Value?

Having cast serious doubt upon the claim that within Jewish thought there is but a single approach to self-ownership, what about within libertarianism? Earlier we considered the *Libertarian Party Platform* and other libertarian voices, and the position in favor of self-ownership seemed firmly set. Only with the tricky and paradoxical matters of suicide and selling oneself into permanent slavery did we encounter a problem. But are there examples demonstrating that not all libertarians believe in absolute self-ownership?

One stark case shatters the unitary, absolutist position: children. Children pose a serious problem for the principle of self-ownership. Do children, particularly infants, own themselves? At least in any meaningful way? If self-ownership is a fundamental right and principle, then children should own themselves. And yet, whether we are speaking theoretically or practically, parents and other adults routinely violate such self-ownership—and if they did not, infants could not survive. Perhaps one could argue that given the inability of infants to survive on their own, the seeming "violation" of their self-ownership is not the same sort of coercion we would see in violating an adult's self-ownership? In any case, the *Libertarian Party Platform* has this to say about parents and children: "Parents, or other guardians, have the right to raise their children according to their own standards and beliefs, provided that the rights of children to be free from abuse and neglect are also protected."

Childhood does not figure as the only challenge to absolute self-ownership. Initially, we might suspect that libertarians would wholeheartedly oppose mandatory vaccinations and immunizations as violations of both the self-ownership and the nonaggression principles. After all, to require or force someone to have a substance injected into his or her body would appear to be some sort of assault upon the person. And yet, not all libertarians oppose mandatory vaccinations. On what grounds? Herd immunity. Anti-vaccine activists like to argue that their decisions not to vaccinate their children should have no impact on those who do choose to do so, so why force them? If vaccines truly work, the thinking goes, then those who get them will be protected and those not getting them will pose no threat to the vaccinated. Medical science and epidemiology teach us otherwise. Vaccinations are not a hundred percent effective, and when too few people receive vaccinations against a disease, the disease-causing organism is able to maintain a reservoir of hosts and continues to spread more easily. However, when the vast majority of a population—the "herd"—does achieve immunity through vaccination or exposure, then the disease organism faces a much more difficult path in thriving and spreading. If too many refuse vaccinations, herd immunity will not be achieved, therefore endangering not only those who remain unvaccinated by choice, but also those who were vaccinated but for whom the vaccination did not take hold, and in addition for those individuals who cannot receive any vaccination due to their being immune-compromised. This science and reasoning together undergird support for a pro-mandatory vaccination position among some libertarians. For, if my failure to have my children vaccinated reduces herd immunity and endangers others, then this refusal, this nonaction, can be understood as a kind of assault itself, a violation of the nonaggression principle.

The argument from herd immunity resonates among Jewish thinkers as well. There is a positive obligation to care for oneself, whether as a steward or an owner of one's body—and this obligation would appear to require getting medically recommended immunizations. It is true, despite the lack of foundation in Jewish law for an anti-vaccine position, such views have spread in recent years among some Orthodox groups, resulting in serious outbreaks of measles and whooping cough. This phenomenon most likely figures as part of a more general distrust of scientific, medical, and political authority and not as a traditional, religious stance.

So, largely anti-regulatory libertarians have grounds to support mandatory immunization laws—but what about other things we put into our bodies? Should the government and the law care about illicit drugs, as well as pharmaceuticals and foods? What might libertarians have to say about the legalization of marijuana, heroin, cocaine, and other such substances? The regulation of the contents of nutritional supplements and what their producers claim as benefits? The inspection of slaughterhouses and food manufacturers, and other measures to protect the safety of the food supply? Laws mandating the labeling of food products and restaurant offerings? And finally, restrictions on "unhealthy" foods, such as attempted bans on soft drinks above a certain size?

Clearly, libertarians overwhelmingly oppose the criminalization of illicit drugs. Even if such substances are bad or problematic, libertarians do not see it as the proper role of government to police such use. Individuals should have the right to consume potentially destructive substances, so long as doing so does not itself cause harm to other people. In this sense, these are victimless crimes. It is not at all clear that there is any Jewish position on this matter, beyond the general obligation to obey the laws of the land, whether or not those laws criminalize the use of illicit drugs. Certainly, as we have seen, there do exist Jewish prohibitions on harming oneself, and so use of some or all such drugs might be prohibited by Jewish law, but this says nothing about what the secular law ought to be. Similar logic, for libertarianism and Judaism, respectively, would apply to efforts to ban or legally limit the consumption of what some experts would characterize as unhealthy foods.

It seems likely that this logic would apply yet again to the case of labeling laws. Even if most people would agree that more information is better for the consumer, it is not so clear that most libertarians would support legal mandates to provide such nutritional details, nor that Jewish law would have a strong position one way or the other. For libertarians, at least, if consumers prefer informational labeling of products, then the market will respond to this demand.

When we turn to the actual content and processing of foods and pharmaceuticals, the issues become more complicated. For libertarians, the question is whether the market itself can prevent adulteration and fraud, or whether instead preemptive government regulations and interventions are necessary? There is the practical question of whether or not such government regulation has proven effective, for instance in protecting the public from E. coli, salmonella, and other foodborne illnesses, which kill hundreds or thousands of Americans each year—and if ineffective, is this because regulation does not work, or because it is too weak? The problem with laws punishing fraud *after* the fact is that great harm will have already been done—and human experience tells us that people will commit fraud and adulterate products so long as they can make a quick profit, and so long as the risk of capture and punishment is not great. Thus, although libertarians tend to express skepticism over government regulation, some might argue that with foodstuffs and pharmaceuticals, the dangers simply remain too great not to anticipate fraud and try to identify it before harm is done. Nevertheless, some libertarians will insist that at least in the long run, the market will prove more effective than government regulation in punishing and rooting out such fraud.

Even in the seemingly unambiguous matter of conscription—of mandatory military or other government service—libertarian views do not reveal uniformity. With conscription, a government declares its right or ability to control the bodies of its citizens, to tell people where to go and what to do, usually for a period of one to three years. Conscription is the forceful control of one's body, by the government, and as such one would imagine it universally reviled among libertarians. Does it not strike at the entire notion of self-ownership, making the principle meaningless? Although the logic here appears solid, one must remember that the primary purpose of government for libertarians remains the protection of people and the defense of their freedoms and rights. Given the reality of threats from those people, whether domestic or foreign, who would do others harm, it is not inconceivable that even a minimalist libertarian government could or would require some sort of service, or at least a draft in time of war. True, preference would lean towards an all-volunteer army, but at least one writer articulates a minority position in seeking to make a coherent libertarian case for conscription. Pointing particularly to the Swiss case, a relatively free and wealthy and peaceful state, Pascal-Emmanuel Gobry argues that, "Switzerland's history shows its freedom is intimately bound up with its centuries-long tradition of military service, just like Switzerland's prosperity is linked to its low taxes." Gobry also finds "strikingly ahistorical" the libertarian argument against military service: "Up until late in the 20th century, it was seen as self-evident that freedom is ultimately secured by force of arms, and that private citizens' duty to freedom was to be able to defend that freedom."[30] And although Americans have not been subject to a military draft since the Vietnam War and are not accustomed to mandatory, national service, in Israel and in most European countries and in many countries around the globe, national service (military or otherwise) figures as a critical and normal part of the life experience of many or most citizens. Admittedly Gobry's position remains rare among libertarians, but the strongly libertarian Cato Institute did allow the argument a hearing in its online journal and forum *Cato Unbound.*

Abortion figures as perhaps the most controversial and bitter moral-political issue dividing Americans. In seeking to understand libertarian—and Jewish—positions on the topic, we might think our task straightforward. If so, we would be mistaken. On the surface, we might have thought that libertarians, as strong supporters of individual rights, would universally declare themselves pro-choice, expressing wariness of most or all legal restrictions on the procedure. And we might have anticipated a variety of Jewish positions, with most Jews similarly pro-choice, and maybe the Orthodox taking up a more religiously conservative stance in favor of significant restrictions, if not a ban. As we have come to expect, the reality proves somewhat different.

Most libertarians do, indeed, oppose restrictions on the right of a woman to elect to have an abortion. After all, women own their bodies, and the government has no place telling them what to do with them. How is it, then, that a noticeable minority of libertarians either identify as pro-life or support some abortion restrictions? As fraught as the term "pro-life" has become, it hints at an answer. If a fetus is a life, a human life, a person in its own right, then it enjoys the same rights and protections, including government protections, due to any other person. From the viewpoint of this minority of libertarians, abortion is an illegitimate assault on a living person. For Christians who identify as libertarians, this makes sense, but some non-Christian, even atheist libertarians find the reasoning compelling—they simply do not view the abortion issue in terms of the mother's self-ownership; and if the fetus does not figure as part of the body a woman owns, then the self-ownership principle would not apply. No doubt recognizing the disagreement among libertarians, the *Libertarian Party Platform* does not endorse any restrictions, a pro-choice position in practice, yet neither does it embrace wholeheartedly a pro-choice philosophy: "Recognizing that abortion is a sensitive issue and that people can hold good-faith views on all sides, we believe that government should be kept out of the matter, leaving the question to each person for their conscientious consideration."[31]

If the libertarian approach has proven more nuanced than we expected, the Jewish orientation might actually prove less so. To start, it is not at all clear that the pro-choice leaning of most American Jews has any connection with Jewish tradition. More likely, this position developed as part of a broader, liberal outlook. And the relatively recent phenomenon of some Orthodox Jews siding with Catholic and Evangelical Christians to make abortion wholly illegal is just that—a relatively recent phenomenon, likely driven by a wider cultural rejection of modern society.

According to the most common and straightforward understanding of Jewish law, once a fetus becomes viable, it achieves a degree of personhood, independent from the mother. Abortion in such a situation is akin to murder, except in cases where the fetus poses a threat to the mother. The rabbis of the Talmud characterized such a fetus as a *rodef*, a pursuer, and as in any situation where one person seeks to kill another person, the latter can employ self-defense, even to kill the pursuer (at least so long as self-defense cannot be achieved by lesser means). This certainly applies where a woman's life is in clear biological danger, but in some cases might be applied where the danger is of a more traumatic, psychological sort. According to the Tzitz Eliezer, the esteemed decisor of Jewish law, the latitude is far from narrow: "If there is a danger to the mother from continuing the pregnancy, one should permit abortion without hesitation. Also, if her health is poor and to cure her or to relieve her from great pain it is necessary to abort the fetus, even if she is not in actual danger, there is room to permit it, based on the halachic authority's evaluation of the situation."[32]

In brief, then, the mainstream interpretation of Jewish law undergirds the fact that Orthodox Jewish leaders have traditionally opposed abortion bans, seeking in this way to preserve legal space for abortions when permitted or even necessitated by Jewish law.[33]

The Candidate?

It would appear that one cannot neatly separate libertarian and Jewish notions of ownership of the body. On the one hand, libertarians recognize limitations to self-ownership, at least in the case of children, and on the other hand, we can find legitimate Jewish views rejecting complete divine ownership of our bodies. As we have learned, the Divine Ownership Theory, although perhaps a common or commonsense and widely accepted notion among Jews today, is one genuine position within Judaism, but not the only such position, and its foundation in traditional sources may not figure quite as strongly as many would think; a principle of shared ownership may find as much or more support in the sources.

Whether we own our bodies or not impacts a range of political and ethical matters—and yet, we might also realize that views of self-ownership do not map directly or easily onto the specific political positions one holds on such matters. Interestingly, as we have observed, differences over the principle of divine ownership, its acceptance or rejection among Jews, does not necessarily lead to different and opposing political and ethical positions; for example, suicide remain forbidden regardless, and abortion remains permitted in certain cases regardless. It may indeed be possible for a religiously observant Jew to agree with various stands as advocated in the *Libertarian Party Platform* or something similar, and still not maintain an absolutist position about self-ownership.

It is even the case that John Locke, widely acknowledged as the source for the libertarian notion of self-ownership, demonstrated some ambiguity in the matter. The very same John Locke who wrote that "every Man has a *Property* in his own *Person*" also penned the following words:

> For Men being all the Workmanship of one Omnipotent, and infinitely wise Maker; All the Servants of one Sovereign Master, sent into the World by his order and about his business, they are his Property, whose Workmanship they are, made to last during his, not one anothers Pleasure.[34]

Therefore, according to the very expositor and primary source for the theory of self-ownership, we truly are servants of God and the property of God, and we are required to preserve ourselves and others. As Locke summarizes, basing himself on reason as a law of nature, "no Man can, by agreement, pass over to another that which he hath not in himself, a Power over his own Life."

Still, could our hypothetical candidate support wholeheartedly the view on self-ownership presented in section 1.1 of the *Libertarian Party Platform*, that "Individuals own their bodies and have rights over them that other individuals, groups, and governments may not violate"?

In the end, traditional Jewish thought and law do not permit complete autonomy or authority over one's body, whatever the reason, whether we own our bodies in full, in part, or not at all. Is this a fundamental difference, prohibiting the full compatibility of libertarianism and Judaism? Would the theological rejection of complete self-ownership prevent a traditionally religious Jew from running for office as a candidate of a libertarian party? Or, would the lack of dogmatic Jewish positions combined with the variety in libertarian views on practical, political issues mean that such a candidacy could be mounted in good faith? Given all of the dimensions and doubts, it does not seem unreasonable that one should hold open the possibility that a good-faith run for office could take place.

Chapter 3

Ownership versus Stewardship: Private Property

> As respect for property rights is fundamental to maintaining a free and prosperous society, it follows that the freedom to contract to obtain, retain, profit from, manage, or dispose of one's property must also be upheld. Libertarians would free property owners from government restrictions on their rights to control and enjoy their property, as long as their choices do not harm or infringe on the rights of others. Eminent domain, civil asset forfeiture, governmental limits on profits, governmental production mandates, and governmental controls on prices of goods and services (including wages, rents, and interest) are abridgements of such fundamental rights. For voluntary dealings among private entities, parties should be free to choose with whom they trade and set whatever trade terms are mutually agreeable.
> – Section 2.1 "Property and Contract,"
> *Libertarian Party Platform* (2018)

Whether or not one owns oneself, can a person own property? Just as with the body, so too with property in Judaism: a strong presumption that we cannot truly own land or other physical, material items, that everything belongs to God, and that while on this earth we are stewards of God's property. And this would seem to stand in opposition to views widely held by libertarians, who place a prime value on private property, valuing it as fundamental to dignity, prosperity, and freedom. How could a religiously observant Jew campaign as a libertarian candidate, promoting private property and free market capitalism, when Judaism brings into question the entire notion of property ownership?

Libertarian Notions of Property Ownership

The 2018 *Libertarian Party Platform* uses the word *freedom* eleven times and *liberty* nine times, whereas it invokes the word *property* fifteen times. Alongside the right to life and the right to liberty of speech and action, the right to property is identified as one of three fundamental, individual rights not to be infringed upon by government: "Government force must be limited to the protection of the rights of individuals to life, liberty, and property, and governments must never be permitted to violate these rights. Laws should be limited in their application to violations of the rights of others through force or fraud, or to deliberate actions that place others involuntarily at significant risk of harm." Such protection entails a rejection of "all government interference with private property, such as confiscation, nationalization, and eminent domain" while promoting support for "the prohibition of robbery, trespass, fraud, and misrepresentation."[1]

This means that governments should never employ force to take the property, including money, of its citizens. Indeed, the platform finds the use of force permissible in only a single case: "The only legitimate use of force is in defense of individual rights—life, liberty, and justly acquired property—against aggression." Not only should the government refrain from interfering with property rights, it ought to protect them: "The only proper role of government in the economic realm is to protect property rights, adjudicate disputes, and provide a legal framework in which voluntary trade is protected. All efforts by government to redistribute wealth, or to control or manage trade, are improper in a free society."[2] In the next chapter, we will return to this issue of government redistribution of wealth through taxation and spending; for the moment our concern remains with the ownership of property.

As with freedom, libertarians view property ownership not simply as *philosophically* good but as *practically* good as well, as a generator of prosperity and peace and even environmental protection. In the words of the libertarian writer and educator Tom G. Palmer, "Well-defined, legally secure, and transferrable property rights form the foundation for voluntary cooperation, widespread prosperity, progress, and peace."[3]

The libertarian emphasis on property ownership goes back at least to John Locke. And Locke's notion of property ownership finds its grounding in his notion of self-ownership. Let us explain how the two are linked. According to Locke, God or Nature gave to humanity all property in common, without any private ownership. How, then, could commonly held property become privately owned property? Locke offers the following logic:

(1) Human beings have ownership in their own persons.
(2) Humans therefore own the labor of their bodies.
(3) When humans mix their labor with what nature provides, they thereby join what was part of the commonly held property to something of their own and thus make it their own property.[4]

The blending of my labor (which I own) with ownerless property or natural resources produces a new entity of which my labor figures as an essential contribution. This concoction of owned labor and ownerless property becomes property I now own. Given abundant natural resources and property, this situation might remain unproblematic. At least so long as there remains enough from the commonly held property for others to use their labor to transform into their property and so long as individuals take no more than what they need, then Locke envisions no difficulties, and also no need for the consent of others. "He by his Labour does, as it were, inclose it from the Common."[5] Locke applies this logic both to landed and other property, not only to what the earth produces and to what animals produce, but to land itself.

Locke does recognize that an unequal distribution of property exists in the world, and that the acquisition of land or other property does not occur simply through the application of labor to the commons:

> [I]t is plain, that Men have agreed to disproportionate and unequal Possession of the Earth, they having by a tacit and voluntary consent found out a way, how a man may fairly possess more land than he himself can use the product of, by receiving in exchange for the overplus, Gold

and Silver, which may be hoarded up without injury to any one, these metals not spoileing or decaying in the hands of the possessor.

For Locke, money itself came into use through "mutual consent."[6]

Consent proves critical for Locke. First of all, an individual's property cannot be taken without that person's permission. And secondly, Locke locates the central purpose of government in protecting this arrangement: "For the preservation of Property being the end of Government, and that for which Men enter into Society, it necessarily supposes and requires, that the People should *have Property*, without which they must be suppos'd to lose that by entring into Society, which was the end for which they entered into it, too gross an absurdity for any Man to own."[7] That is, Locke finds it nonsensical that people would become part of a society and create a government to protect their property rights, only for that very government to deny those rights and take their property.

Locke here suggests something not at all obvious at first glance: perhaps property ownership has *no* meaning at all unless a person's right to her or his property is secure? That is, if another individual, or even the government, can remove property from my possession without my agreement, then there remains little sense to speak of it as being or ever having been *my* property: "For I have truly no *Property* in that which another can by right take from me, when he pleases, against my consent."[8] Nonetheless, the libertarian writer Jason Brennan does insist that the right to property cannot be truly absolute, offering the example of someone stepping onto another's private property to avoid being killed by an out-of-control car wielded by a drunk driver. If property rights were absolute, then a person would need to forfeit his or her life rather than escape the car by trespassing. Outside of such emergency situations, however, libertarians would generally argue that property rights must be sacrosanct. To them, it makes little sense for individuals to *sort of* have property rights. Indeed, Brennan concurs with Locke in this regard: "If people can't count on their property rights, they can't make stable long-term plans. If people know their property rights can be overridden whenever society deems it useful to do so, they then cannot trust the property system anymore."[9]

At the outset of this chapter, we suggested that parallels exist between self-ownership and the ownership of property. David Boaz explicitly connects these two notions: "Libertarians believe that the right to self-ownership means that individuals must have the right to acquire and exchange property in order to fulfill their needs and desires. To feed ourselves, or provide shelter for our families, or open a business, we must make use of property."[10] For Boaz, like Locke, property rights are a natural, logical, and necessary extension of the ownership of the self. To have no right to own property would make owning oneself meaningless—and although Boaz does not make the comparison here, we realize that those who are enslaved own neither property nor themselves. Boaz goes so far as to equate property rights with *human* rights. If I cannot own property, as well as make use of property (and not only or particularly landed property) with some security, then I am lacking something in my human rights, according to Boaz.[11]

Likewise, Murray Rothbard argues that the liberal *celebration of human rights* and simultaneous *rejection of property rights* makes little sense. In his explanation, liberals accept ownership of the self but not of things. "If a man has the right to self-ownership, to the control of his life, then in the real world he must also have the right to sustain his life by grappling with and transforming resources; he must be able to own the ground and the resources on which he stands and which he must use."[12] Although, contra Rothbard and Boaz, some sort of cooperative ownership of resources might be at least philosophically reasonable—that we could sustain our lives without owning any personal property—admittedly this might not work well in practice, as least not on a large scale, such as that of nation states, as perhaps history has demonstrated.

John Hospers, author of the 1971 book *Libertarianism: A Political Philosophy for Tomorrow*, seeks to disabuse us further of our misunderstanding of property rights. The right to own property is not simply the right to own land, and it is even more than the right to own things. "The right of property is not the right to just *take* it from others, for this would interfere with *their* property rights. It is rather the right to work for it, to obtain noncoercively, the money or services which you can present in voluntary exchange."[13] Property rights are *not*, we might say, fundamentally about greed and ownership and growing wealthier and wealthier at the expense of others. For libertarians, property rights undergird a humane system of interaction and flourishing, a system absent of coercion and fraud. Hospers suggests that the right to property is inextricably bound up with the rights to liberty, to life, and to speech. If I cannot be secure in my property, if people can freely enter my home or the government can confiscate my belongings, then I cannot plan for the future. I would not be truly free to live my life, and my very life would remain perennially in peril.[14]

As for free speech—something many of us might have imagined an even more fundamental right than that of owning private property—both Hospers and Rothbard argue with some persuasion that free speech *depends upon* property rights (making the latter more fundamental) and is limited by it, that without the latter we cannot possess the former. They aver that there is no absolute right to free speech—for instance, to demand that a newspaper or media company provide me with an outlet (i.e., their properties) to say what I want. They both point out that we misunderstand the notion of why it is forbidden to yell "Fire!" in a crowded theater. This is not in any sense a limitation upon or compromising of one's free speech rights. Indeed, it is not a freedom of expression issue at all. Rather, it is a matter of property rights. I and others have purchased tickets and entered onto the theater owner's property. The property belongs to her, and in a way, the purchase of a ticket is the acquisition of a property right in the viewing of a film or performance. Whether explicitly or implicitly, there is a contract, a sale, an understanding of what has been sold and purchased. My yelling "Fire!" (or the owner's yelling "Fire!") when there is no fire defrauds the patrons of their property, that to which the tickets entitle them; my yelling "Fire!" also infringes upon the property rights of the owner.[15]

In brief, one might argue that property exceeds in importance even freedom in much libertarian thought. Do property rights have any similar or otherwise essential value in traditional Jewish thought or practice? Or, is this notion a foreign one?

Jewish Ideas Against Property Ownership

In the book of Deuteronomy, Moses tells the people "Behold, to Adonoy Our God [belong] the heavens and the heavens of the heavens, the land, and all that is in it." (Deut. 10:14) From this statement it would indeed appear that God owns everything, both our material world and the nonmaterial world. And if our entire world belongs to God, then how can humans own *any* of it?

In Genesis, God tells the first human beings that they "have dominion over the fish of the sea, and over the fowl of the air, and over every living thing that creepeth upon the earth." (Gen. 1:28) Two verses earlier, when God first announces the plan to create the human being in the image of God, the scope of this dominion includes not only birds, fish, and creeping things, but also cattle and "all of the land." (Gen. 1:26) The question here is what is meant by "dominion"—does this mean that God gave to humans ownership or ownership rights over land and over other living creatures? Is dominion some sort of sovereignty? Or is it rather some sort of charge, a responsibility, or as this chapter's title suggests, a stewardship?

In truth, the Hebrew text does not here provide a word precisely equivalent to the English word "dominion." Indeed, the Hebrew does not employ a noun at all, but rather two forms of a particular verb: *v'yirdu* and *urdu*. In the first chapter, we discussed the root system of Hebrew verbs and provided some examples. So, in this case, what is meant by the root *resh-dalet-he*? It does mean to rule over and likely is related to a similar root, *yud-resh-dalet*, which indicates going downwards. The word suggests a sense of directionality, and this directionality places the human beings above the animals and the land, exercising some sort of power or responsibility over them, but not necessarily owning or controlling them. In the earlier verse, God *describes* what human beings will do—they will exercise this power or responsibility over land and animals. In the second case, God issues a *command* directly to the male and female persons he has created—you will exercise this power or responsibility. In brief, God has not granted some *thing*, whether dominion or ownership, to human beings, but rather described and commanded a relationship.

In terms of *things*, God does give food to human beings: "And God said: 'Behold, I have given you every herb yielding seed, which is upon the face of all the earth, and every tree, in which is the fruit of a tree yielding seed—to you it shall be for food.'" (Gen. 1:29) Now, one might think that this giving itself functions as a transfer of ownership, and yet, the very next verse continues God's exclamation: "and to every beast of the earth, and to every fowl of the air, and to every thing that creepeth upon the earth, wherein there is a living soul, every green herb for food.'"

(Gen. 1:30) We do not commonly think of animals as owning anything, whatever some wealthy individuals leave in their wills to their pets, so perhaps here the act of giving food does not transfer ownership. After all, we do all sorts of giving—such as giving to our guests food and a place to sleep, and our guests do not thereby obtain ownership over or property rights in anything of ours.

In short, the first chapter of Genesis does *not* appear to provide the first human beings with any ownership rights. If humans possess such rights, these rights must arrive on the scene at a later point.

At one such possible later point, the Psalms of King David appear equivocal on this matter: "The earth is the LORD's, and all that is in it; the world and all who live in it" (Psalms 24:1) and "The heavens belong to the LORD, but the earth He has given to man." (Psalms 115:16) Does the earth belong to human beings, as per Psalm 115, or to God, as per Psalm 24? Well, perhaps both—but how so? One might say, as with the case of guests in one's home, that giving does not necessarily entail transferring ownership. The great nineteenth-century German Jewish leader, Rabbi Samson Raphael Hirsch (1808–1888), articulated as much in the thirteenth of his *Nineteen Letters*:

> The day upon which the newly-created world first lay spread out in its completeness before man that he might possess it and rule over it, this day [i.e., the Sabbath] was to be to him an eternal testimony of the great truth that all things around him were the property of God, the Creator. He was to realize that it was God Who had conferred upon him the power and the right to rule the world, in order that he should administer his trust as the property of God and in accordance with His supreme will. In order to keep this idea ever fresh and vivid in his mind, he should refrain on this day from exercising his human authority over the things on earth. He should not place his hand upon any object for the purpose of exercising dominion over it; that is, for employing it for any purpose of his own. He must, as it were, return the borrowed world to its Divine Owner in order to realize that it is only lent to him.[16]

Although in R. Hirsch's phrasing humans can possess the earth, they do so as borrowers and trustees. And this is how the earth can belong to God at the very same time God gives it over to human beings.

Another explanation, this one from the Talmud, focuses on the blessings Jews recite prior to eating items of food. Shortly we will discuss the blessing made before eating bread; this and all other food blessings conclude in different manners, but all begin with the same six words: *Baruch Ata Adonoy Eloheinu Melech Ha-'Olam* (Blessed are You, Adonoy/Lord, our God, King of the Universe). Six blessings suffice to cover all foods: one for bread; one for wine; one for grains (at least wheat, barley, and three others associated with the land of Israel); one for items that grow on trees; one for items that grow from the ground or from plants or grasses; and a final blessing, ending with the expression "that everything is created by His word," for *all* other food items, including most drinks and animal products and tofu and candy, to identify just a few of them. According to the rabbis of the Talmud, the recitation of a blessing over food effects a kind of transfer of ownership from God to the individual reciting the blessing and consuming the food or drink. As much is evident in the Babylonian Talmud from the characterization of eating *without* reciting the appropriate blessing: "Rabbi Ḥanina bar Pappa said: Anyone who derives benefit from this world without a blessing, it is as if he stole from God and the community of Israel." R. Levi points to the two verses we quoted above from Psalms 24 and 115: "Rabbi Levi raised a contradiction: It is written: 'The earth and all it contains is the Lord's,' and it is written: 'The heavens are the Lord's and the earth He has given over to mankind.' [This is] not difficult. Here [meaning the former verse] before a blessing, here [meaning the latter verse] after a blessing."[17] This text teaches that the transfer of ownership from God to human beings occurs through the mechanism of the blessing's recitation.

Beyond the more descriptive, poetic biblical passages, such as those from the Psalms of King David, a number of actual Jewish laws also suggest that we do not own, at least not fully, our property. To begin, there is a pair of related obligations called *pe-ah* and *leket*, according to which farmers must leave food for the poor and needy to gather. We learn in chapter 19 of Leviticus:

> And when you reap the harvest of your land, you shall not completely reap the corner [*pe-ah*] of your field; and the gleaning [*leket*] of your harvest, you shall not gather. And you shall not glean your vineyard, and the fallen grapes of your vineyard you shall not gather; for the poor and

the stranger you shall leave them; I am Adonoy, your God. You shall not steal, and you shall not deal falsely, and you shall not lie, a man and his people. (Lev. 19:9–11)

In brief, there is a religious obligation for farmers *not* to harvest and collect *all* of the food they have planted and to which they have tended for months. For the mitzvah of pe-ah, they must leave the corners of their fields for the poor, for any of the poor, and for strangers, to come and take. And for the mitzvah of leket, they must leave on the ground whatever has fallen to the ground, for the poor and for strangers to collect.

Let us be clear: farmers plant grains and vegetables and fruit trees and grapevines on their land, and they spend additional time and labor and resources plowing and irrigating and protecting this produce, and yet, in the end, they cannot claim ownership over everything they labored so dearly to grow. It would be one thing if the Torah urged *voluntary* giving, but this is not the situation here. The Torah is telling the farmer: you do not own all of this. And, a libertarian might wonder, if the farmer does not own *all* of it, can we really say he or she owns *any* of it?

Now, one reason such a law might be appropriate, or even necessary, is to remind us of the point that the farmer does not *alone* create a bountiful crop. The farmer is dependent upon the weather, especially the rain—and particularly so in Israel, where a poor rainy season can prove devastating. In this way, the laws of pe-ah and leket remind farmers and everyone else that they remain dependent upon God for everything they eat and possess. The blessing a Jew recites before eating bread functions in a similar way. It goes as follows: *Baruch Ata Adonoy Eloheinu Melech Ha-'Olam, Ha-Motzi lechem min ha-aretz* (Blessed are You, Adonoy/ Lord, our God, King of the Universe, the One Who brings forth bread from the earth). Truly? God brings forth bread from the earth? Who ever witnessed such a thing? The farmer plants, and with appropriate tending and watering, the plants produce the grain, which someone harvests, which someone then grinds into flour, which someone then bakes into bread. Where is God in all of this? Well, traditional Jewish thinkers tell us that God *is* there, and as a Partner. By blessing God for bringing forth the bread from the earth, Jews remind themselves that they do not produce food alone, but rather in partnership with God, that none of it would be possible without God. This recalls the joke about advances in genetic science and technology, the joke in which God and a scientist agree to a contest for creating a human being. In preparation for creating a person, the scientist bends down and scoops up a handful of dirt, to which God interjects: "Get your own dirt." So too, perhaps, with bread. We think we are creating the bread, but we do not cause the rain to fall, and nor do we create the required raw materials.

Returning to the above selection from Leviticus chapter 19, it is striking that the eleventh verse, the one immediately following the laws of the field corners and the gleanings, communicates the prohibitions of stealing and dealing falsely. Why state such prohibitions at this point in the text? It is as if to say that there is some connection, that to withhold from the poor and strangers the gleanings and the food from the corners of the field is to steal from them and deal with them falsely. Although most commentators separate these, associating stealing and dealing falsely with financial matters alone, at least one commentator does detect a connection. The Moroccan-born Rabbi Chaim ibn Attar (1696–1743), in his work *Or ha-Chaim*, argues that one who owns a field and takes from the corner, instead of leaving what is there, should not imagine that he or she is not stealing, thinking that he is simply taking what belongs to him or her:

> You shall not steal, etc. The mitzvah of stealing leans upon [is juxtaposed to] the mitzvah of the corner of the field. Perhaps that it was intended in the way they said it in Torat Kohanim and this is their language: Ben Bag Bag says Do not steal what is yours from the thief, in order that you not appear to be a thief. And here is the intention of the juxtaposition of *Do not steal* to *pe-ah*, that the warning comes to not steal it in thinking that it is his.[18]

That is, one might think as follows: someone stole an item from me, and because the item belongs to me, I have the right to take it back. Ben Bag Bag, in the *Sifra*, instructs me not to use such reasoning, lest I take it back and thereby appear to be a thief myself. In using this reference, the *Or ha-Chaim* seems to suggest that if in the case of something I clearly own I should not steal it back thinking it is mine, then surely in the case of the corner of the field, I should not think it mine and prevent the poor from taking from that part of my field. Not only might I appear to be a thief, but I would actually be a thief for taking for myself the produce from the corner of the field. The key point, perhaps, is not that I might appear to be a thief, but rather that I should not use the reasoning of thinking it belongs to me to justify my actions.

If this were not enough, two additional laws, those of *Shemittah* and *Yovel*, further circumscribe the notion that farmers own the goods they produce and the land upon which they produce them. According to the laws of Shemittah, farmers in the land of Israel must let their land lie fallow every seventh year.[19] The Torah considers ownerless whatever the land produces during that year. Although the means by which Jewish legal authorities have dealt with the practicalities of Shemittah, especially since Jewish resettlement of Zion in the nineteenth and twentieth centuries, makes for a complicated story, what matters for us is what it suggests about the Torah's notion of property ownership. Just like the Sabbath reminds us on a weekly cycle to recall that we do not control and own everything, or perhaps anything, so too the Shemittah, as the Sabbatical year appears to remind us of our fundamental lack of control and ownership.[20] Rabbi Solomon ben Isaac (or Shlomo Yitzḥaki) (1040–1105), known as Rashi and considered the greatest of all commentators on the Torah and the Talmud, points out that Shemittah does not prohibit eating or otherwise deriving benefit from the produce of the field: "rather, that you shall not behave as if you are their owner." *Ba'al habayit*, the term used here for owner, literally means the master of the house, but has connotations, certainly in this context and even in modern Hebrew, of ownership.[21]

If the Shemittah year is a Sabbatical year, then the Yovel is a Sabbatical on top of a cycle of Shemittah years. The Yovel, or Jubilee, is meant to take place every *fiftieth* year, and at this time, all land returns to the original owners. After seven cycles of seven years, the Yovel arrives: "And you will sanctify the year of the fiftieth year, and you will proclaim freedom in the land for all of its inhabitants; a Jubilee it will be for you, and you will return a man to his portion, and a man to his family you will return." (Lev. 25:10) Despite the fact that sowing and reaping are prohibited in this year as with the year before, the forty-ninth year, the inhabitants of the land will eat from the increased production of the fields. (Lev. 25:11–12) The other conditions of the Jubilee year are striking. People are returned to their families, presumably from any sort of servitude. People also return to their portions, meaning the ancestral lands of their families or at least tribes, with all land sold during the previous half-century now reverting to the original owners. (Lev. 25:13–14) And perhaps most intriguing, ten days into this fiftieth year, on the day Jews observe Yom Kippur, a shofar blast is sounded throughout the land, and *dror*, freedom, is declared. (Lev. 25:9–10)

Freedom in what sense? Clearly freedom for any Jews living in servitude, perhaps as a consequence of having been forced by the courts into such a situation over financial problems. Yet what about landed property returning to its original owners? In what way is this a kind of freedom? Freedom for the now displaced "new" owners, who purchased such land fairly? The commentator Rashi cites Rabbi Yehuda from the Mishnah and suggests that dror comes from the Hebrew word root meaning to reside, such as at an inn. In modern Hebrew, a *diyyar* is an apartment, something one usually rents. Dror therefore might best be understood as a freedom of residence, the ability to travel and live where one wishes. The later commentator Sforno points to the prophet Jeremiah, who echoed the biblical use of proclaiming dror, applying it to freedom from famine, pestilence, and war.[22] In any case, the Torah in Leviticus connects the proclamation of freedom with this return of people to their original land and homes.

Perhaps, in some sense, this reinstitutionalization of the old order of things figures as a correction to a possibly extreme concentration of wealth? Perhaps the original, broader allocation of land was more proportionate and allowed for greater freedom for many more people? What is also clear, however, is that far from the notion that individuals cannot own property, we do appear to have here, in practice, widescale ownership of property—because even if land is being returned to its original owners, it would seem we have a recognition of the ownership of private property.

Jewish Ideas Favoring Property Ownership

Israel's first Ashkenazi chief rabbi, Isaac Herzog (1888–1959), author of a two-volume work on the laws of property and the laws of obligation, suggested that for a very long time, ownership simply did not figure as an explicit concept in discussions of Jewish law:

"What is ownership?" is a question which is nowhere directly and abstractly put in any of the writings which are included under the description of sources of Jewish law, early or late, and one will therefore search in vain in the mass of Jewish legal writings of recognized authority for a definition of ownership. Jewish jurisprudence was too pragmatic and concrete in tendency to occupy itself with the definition of legal terms without immediate reference to a practical point.[23]

Jewish law overwhelmingly functions as case law, with little theoretical systematization. "In the *Mishnah* and the *Gemara* [i.e., Talmud] there is nothing even approaching a systematic presentation of the laws of property, the subject matter being scattered throughout the fourth part, or order, of the *Talmud, Seder Nezikin*, and in other *sedarim*, or orders."[24] Regardless of any lack of conscious systemization, and despite the biblical laws and ideals described in the previous section, the fact of the matter is that there exists an extensive body of Jewish law concerning the practicalities of property ownership and business dealings.

For four and a half centuries, the *Shulchan Arukh* has served as the main, normative codification of Jewish law for traditional Jews. Written in 1563 by Rabbi Yosef Karo (1488–1575), this work was, in turn, based upon the structure of the *Arba'ah Turim* of Rabbi Jacob ben Asher: one section concerns laws of prayer, Sabbath, and holidays; another section includes laws of kosher food, family purity, and mourning; a third section contains laws of marriage and divorce; and the fourth part is called *Choshen Mishpat*, literally the "Breastplate of Judgment" (referring to part of the dress worn by the head priest in the Tabernacle and Temple), and deals with financial matters, including laws of courts and witnesses, laws of damages, and the resolution of monetary and property disputes. *Choshen Mishpat* devotes well over a hundred sections to property law alone. Now, if Jews could not own property in any substantial sense, what need would there be for such an elaborate, detailed set of rules and regulations?

From the Mishnah to the Talmud to the *Arba'ah Turim* to the *Shulcan Arukh* to today, Jewish law has dealt with all sorts of property matters, and largely through case law. One classic talmudic discussion concerns what to do when two individuals claim ownership of the same item. Another considers what to do when a purchaser claims to have paid for something, but the seller claims not to have been paid. In our days, there are thousands of articles and audio lectures available on matters of Jewish business law and business ethics. One of the colleges of Yeshiva University is its Sy Syms School of Business. As the scholar Madeline Kochen summarizes,

> All in all, the usual characteristics of property ownership are part of a larger body of Jewish civil (and, to some extent, criminal) law that, notwithstanding certain doctrinal differences, does not look all that different from its counterparts in many, if not most, other legal systems. In biblical and rabbinic law, people can own property, property can have monetary value, and property can properly be bought, sold, bartered, or given away. The institution of property ownership is presumed in the biblical prohibition against theft and in the obligation to return lost property.[25]

Many Jewish legal concepts simply presuppose a notion of property ownership.

For instance, there is the idea of *ye-ush*, of giving up hope in recovering a lost object. Whether speaking subjectively or objectively (in the sense of what would a reasonable person think or do), giving up hope in recovering an object entails relinquishing ownership of it, and making the object available for another to possess. This is the concept of *hefker*, a state of ownerlessness. Indeed, pe-ah (the corners of the field) and leket (the gleanings) discussed above—the very examples we used to question Jewish property ownership—are themselves dependent upon the idea of the food items becoming hefker, ownerless. In the Shemittah year, *all* of the produce of the land becomes hefker, making the food available for anyone to come and take. One can therefore reasonably infer that in non-Shemittah years the farmer does own her or his produce, save for that left for pe-ah and leket.

One of the central obligations of the Sukkot holiday, the festival of booths, is the waving of the four species: the *etrog* (a kind of citrus fruit) and the *lulav* bundle, consisting of palm fronds, willows, and myrtle. On each day of the holiday (save for the Sabbath) Jews pick up these four items, hold them together, recite a blessing, and wave or shake them in six different directions. The choreography and meaning of this mitzvah do not concern us here; what does matter is the fact that in order for the mitzvah to be performed properly and successfully, the individual waving the four species must own them. Even if two or more individuals use the same set, they must transfer ownership from one to another. Not with a contract, but rather the physical giving and taking of the items signals the transfer. Critical here is the fact that minors, those under the age of Bar Mitzvah or Bat Mitzvah, cannot transfer ownership. If, at least on the first day of the holiday, a parent hands the set over to his or her minor child before performing the mitzvah, the parent will be unable to perform the mitzvah with that same set, because the child cannot, in a Jewish legal sense, give them back. So, adults will perform the mitzvah first or purchase for minors an "educational" set, still kosher, but not necessarily of the highest quality or beauty and therefore costing considerably less. In brief, we see here the importance of ownership in the observance and performance of a major Jewish ritual.

As for the holiday of Passover, among the fundamental obligations for a Jew is to not eat, benefit from, or *own* any *chametz* for the duration of the festival. Chametz includes any bread or other product made from wheat, oats, barley, spelt, or rye—grains which may have come into contact with water for more than approximately eighteen minutes. Of course, Passover's bread of affliction/freedom, the *matzah*, itself is made out of wheat, or one of the other grains, but from the moment the flour is mixed with water, the matzah must be cooked within the eighteen minutes. So, it is not wheat and grains *per se* which cannot be owned, but any such grains or foods produced from these grains in any way possibly allowing for leavening or rising. Before the onset of the festival, a Jew must cease to own any chametz, and to ensure this, a number of techniques are employed: consuming, burning, selling, and pronouncing ownerless any chametz one might not have disposed of in any of the other ways. Whereas for Sukkot, one must own the four species, for Passover, one must not own chametz. As Kochen notes, "There are also concrete situations in which a biblical prohibition applies only to that which one owns, thus requiring a determination of ownership for very practical purposes. For example, serious prohibitions regarding leavened bread on Passover are understood by the rabbis to turn on the question of ownership."[26] For these two holidays, why go to such extreme ends if we do not or cannot own property in any meaningful sense?

Earlier we considered how the institution of Shemittah suggested that ultimately God owns everything. Yet leaving the land fallow did not figure as the only regulation of the year. The Shemittah year also brought about the cancellation of debts: "At the end of every seven years thou shalt make a release [Shemittah]. And this is the manner of the release: every creditor that lends anything to his neighbor shall release it; he shall not exact it of his neighbor, or of his brother; because he has proclaimed a release to the Lord." (Deut. 15:1–2) As we see, the very word *Shemittah* means *release*. This is not quite the same thing as letting one's land rest for the year, but both do function as a relinquishing of ownership, whether of one's land or of the monies owed to an individual.

Now, as one might worry or suspect, despite the divine nature of the decree, many people might hesitate at loaning out money for which they have no guarantee of return. Especially as the seventh year approached, one can easily imagine the reluctance to loan money, even to those in serious need of such funds. The renowned rabbinic sage Hillel, who lived towards the end of the period of the Second Temple, understood as much—and he designed a solution to the problem, a means of ensuring that individuals would not cease loaning out money.[27] His solution, called the *prozbul*, used biblical sources to avoid the cancellation of the debts. Some view this as subverting the ideal, others as fulfilling it, or at least fulfilling another ideal, and using legitimate Torah sources to do so.

How does the prozbul work? The release of debts applies only to those between individuals, because the Torah states that "that which is thine with thy brother thy hand shall release." (Deut. 15:3) Between you and your brother. Between two individual persons. The prozbul arranges for the transfer of the debt from the lender to the *beit din*, the rabbinic court, or more literally the house of the law. The debt is now legally owed to the *beit din*. As the rabbinic court is not an individual, but rather an institution, the release of debts of the Shemittah year does not apply.

What empowers the court to undertake such a measure? How does the court acquire the claim to collect the debt? One view, that of the sage Rava, locates the court's authority in the principle of *hefker beit din hefker*, that what the rabbinic court declares ownerless (*hefker*) is or becomes ownerless (*hefker*). This sounds much like the modern concept of eminent domain, by means of which a government can seize property for an at least professed public benefit. R. Shaul Yisraeli, whom we met in the previous chapter in our discussion of Shylock's pound of flesh and self-ownership and who wrote extensively on Judaism and the modern state, characterized the court's power as a responsibility: "Thus, *beit din* is not a blind watchman of the law. It must determine when upholding the normal rights of ownership is actually a perversion of justice, that which is known as *midat S'dom* (the attribute of Sodom) or an impediment to public welfare."[28] From libertarian perspectives, this power of the rabbinic court must appear alarming. Clearly, in the secular world, the employment of eminent domain sometimes appears to benefit specific commercial interests rather than the general public interest. It is difficult to imagine libertarians endorsing any use of eminent domain, and the 2018 *Libertarian Party Platform* explicitly rejects its use.

In the case of the prozbul, what precisely does the rabbinic court make ownerless? Although the talmudic text is not explicit on this point, we can make sense of the situation as follows. Originally, the lender loans money to the borrower, let us suppose a loan of 500 shekels. The lender originally owned the money, and the borrower took possession of it under the condition of repaying the money. The borrower can use the money, but does not truly own it, because the same amount needs to be paid back. The Shemittah year comes along and cancels this debt, meaning that the 500 shekels held by the borrower now becomes the property of the borrower and no longer remains the property of the lender. The rabbinic court enters the picture and declares ownerless 500 shekels belonging to the individual formerly known as the borrower. This need not be the same 500 shekels of the original loan. The court basically confiscates the money by making it ownerless. The court then takes these 500 shekels and makes them the property of the individual formerly known as the lender. The former lender now has a claim on 500 shekels in the possession of the former borrower, because according to the actions of the court, these 500 shekels now belong to the former lender and not to the former borrower. In effect, the Shemittah year forgave the original loan, but the court created something to replace it, a new loan of sorts. Although according to some authorities the prozbul is effected just prior to Rosh HaShanah of the Shemittah year, most authorities hold that it is effected at the very end of the Shemittah year, just before Rosh HaShanah of the following year. It is not clear what difference this might make in conceptualizing what has taken place. Either way, because lenders can expect to receive back the amount loaned out, they will not fear loaning funds as the Shemittah year approaches, therefore accomplishing Hillel's aim of maintaining access to funds for those who need them.

Does this really make any sense? The principle of *hefker beit din hefker* empowers the rabbinic court to make property ownerless, but this figured as the first step only. How does Rava imagine that the court exercises the power to award the now ownerless funds to a new owner? Should the money not be available for anyone to claim? How could making something ownerless make it possible for the lender to receive back the money loaned out? The answer can be located in the scriptural sources of the principle.

Where in the Hebrew scriptures do we find *hefker beit din hefker*? That is, how does the Talmud demonstrate that when the court identifies something as ownerless that it becomes ownerless? The Talmud cites not one, but two verses to make the case. For the first part, there is the book of Ezra: "and that whoever would not come within three days, according to the counsel of the princes and the elders, all his substance [*r'khusho*] should be forfeited, and himself separated from the congregation of the exiles." (Ezra 10:8) Here, the rabbinic court is akin to the princes and elders, and clearly such leaders have the power to take *away* property from those who do not follow their instructions. For the second part, there is a verse from the book of Joshua: "These are the territories which El'azar the priest, and Yehoshua the son of Nun, and the heads of the fathers of the tribes of the children of Yisra'el divided for an inheritance by lot in Shilo before the LORD, at the door of the Tent of Meeting. So they made an end of dividing the country." (Joshua 19:51) Here the rabbinic court is akin to the fathers of the tribes, with the authority to *distribute* property. Now we can understand the need to rely upon two verses and not one. One to substantiate the court's authority to declare property ownerless and another verse to authorize the court to award ownership of the ownerless property, to distribute it.

Speaking of the land of Israel, and an aside from all these legal matters, let us return to Genesis. After the passing of his wife Sarah, Abraham sought out a burial place from the children of Ḥet. There ensues a negotiation over price for Abraham's purchase of the cave and field of Makhpelah from 'Efron of the children of Ḥet.[29] Despite disputes over how to understand the encounter—was Abraham only acting politely in purchasing land already promised to him by God?—the fact of the matter is that we have an entire episode devoted to negotiation and purchase and predicated upon a notion of property ownership. The Bible is sparing in its words and provides few details of the lives of Israel's patriarchs and matriarchs, so this event must bear significance.

Finally, a last thought: in the second chapter of *Pirkei Avot*, Rabbi Yose instructs us to "Let the property of your fellow be as precious to you as your own."[30] The word translated here as property is *mammon*, a term referring to monetary matters in general. Commenting on this teaching, Rabbi Dr. Marc Angel explains that "Respecting the property of others is an expression of love, i.e., sympathetic human interrelationship. Although concern for property seems mundane, it is in fact quite significant. A person's property reflects one's labors, tastes, and worldview." Perhaps this resonates with the Lockean idea of having property *in* something, including in ourselves. R. Angel suggests, in a way likely amenable to a libertarian or at least Lockean orientation, that the things we own function as extensions of ourselves. Whether someone identifies as Jewish or libertarian or as both, a person can value property, and can understand its importance to our identities and lives, and yet not necessarily promote the worship of money and its acquisition.

Jewish Attitudes Towards Labor and the Material World

Beyond the vast nature of Jewish property law, it bears emphasizing that Jewish thought in general simply does *not* frown upon material goods, upon their production or acquisition. Although there is the biblical figure of the Nazirite, who takes a vow to abstain from wine and haircutting, there is little in traditional Judaism to match or value the asceticism and self-flagellation of monastic religious traditions—and although the reason is uncertain, the Nazirite must bring a sin offering. In the words of Rabbi Dr. Jonathan Sacks, former Chief Rabbi of the United Hebrew Congregations of Great Britain and the Commonwealth, "In contradistinction to many other religious systems, Judaism refused to romanticise poverty or anaesthetise its pain. . . . The rabbis refused to see poverty as a blessed state, an affliction to be born[e] with acceptance and grace."[31] Elsewhere, R. Sacks states that "Poverty, for the rabbis, was a curse, with no saving graces. Poverty does not ennoble; it demeans."[32] According to the rabbis in the *Midrash Rabbah Shemot*, a medieval commentary on the book of Exodus, "In the world there is nothing more difficult than poverty, that it is more difficult than all of the tribulations that are in the world." (*Midrash Rabbah Shemot* 31:12) Though recognizing the perennial existence of poverty, Judaism in no way values or sanctifies it. To the contrary, in the words of R. Sacks, "No less important than the values placed on work is Judaism's positive attitude to the creation of wealth."[33]

Indeed, Jewish sources place great value in productive labor and commerce and the generation of wealth: in learning a trade, earning a living, and providing for a family. In *Pirkei Avot* 2:2, Rabban Gamliel states the following: "It is good to combine Torah study with a worldly occupation, for the effort involved in both makes one forget sin. Torah study without an occupation will in the end fail and lead to sin."[34] It can be difficult to square this with the world of the early twenty-first century, where tens of thousands of Ḥaredi Jewish men spend all or most of their adult lives engaged in full-time Torah study and live in poverty, dependent upon Israeli or American governmental support, as well as upon private charity. Rabbi Dr. Natan Slifkin (known as the "Zoo Rabbi" for his books on animals and his Biblical Museum of Natural History, in part a zoo, in Israel) has been a clear and strong voice in challenging the reasoning used to justify this system and its normalization of such nearly universal, full-time learning for men. In challenging this orientation, he points to such sources as the one above, as well as to talmudic discussions of the matter, and to medieval and modern authorities, as well.[35]

Two key passages in the Talmud address the issue of the value of work. On B. Berakhot 35b we read of a dispute between Rabbis Yishmael and Shimon bar Yochai over a phrase from the Shema prayer: *And you shall gather your grain,* [*your wine, and your oil*] (Deut. 11:14). Rabbi Yishmael wishes to understand this in the context of another verse: *This Torah shall not depart from your mouth* (Joshua 1:8). If one understands the latter verse literally, then how can one work to earn a living? Should one not engage in Torah study all of the time? R. Yishmael concludes, however, that one ought to combine the two, learning Torah *and* working. R. Shimon bar Yochai counters that there will always be farming work to do, and therefore Torah study will become neglected. His interpretation sees these two ways of life not as complementary, but rather as alternatives to each other: if the Jews do the will of God, then others will take care of mundane matters for them, but if they do not do the will of God, then they themselves will need to gather their own grain, and moreover, perform work for others.

How does the Talmud resolve this dispute? A later sage, Abaye, reported that many individuals had followed the approach of R. Yishmael, to combine labor and Torah, and found success in their study of the Torah, whereas many who took the path praised by R. Shimon bar Yochai did not achieve such success.[36] Clearly, the Talmud did not give a ringing endorsement to the studying Torah only position.

The second passage, on TB Kiddushin 29a, concerns the obligation of a father to circumcise his son. In this context, the Talmud identifies four or five additional obligations placed upon the father: to redeem a firstborn son; to teach his son Torah; to ensure that his son gets married; to teach him a trade; and possibly to teach him how to swim. The comparison is striking. After all, circumcision is the means by which male Jewish infants enter into the Jewish covenant with God, and it is part of how a male convert completes the conversion process. At least until quite recently, almost all Jewish boys were circumcised, even among families with little connection to Jewish religious life. The word *brit*, or *bris*, used for the circumcision ceremony, means *covenant*. The ritual is foundational, and efforts to ban it, whether by the Greeks at the time of the Maccabees or by some nations and cities in twenty-first century Europe and America, are reasonably regarded by many Jews as severe threats, as efforts to undermine or destroy Judaism. Understandably, Torah study and marriage also figure as crucial dimensions of Jewish religious life and its successful transmission across the generations. The possible obligation of teaching a son how to swim is really about saving or preserving life. It is in the company of such deep-seated obligations that we ought to contextualize and consider the obligation *to teach a trade* and understand its great value and importance.

The Talmud goes even further, sharing R. Yehuda's view equating the *failure* to teach a trade with the teaching of *banditry*! Not literally, of course, but effectively so: without a trade and a source of livelihood, a person might turn to theft in order to secure life's material necessities. The fact that later scholars argued whether or not teaching how to make a living in *business* counted as teaching a *trade* (and did not argue about teaching a trade altogether) also signifies for us the importance of having a means to earn a livelihood more generally.[37]

Many centuries later, in his landmark *Mishneh Torah*, Maimonides offered a stinging criticism of those who would demean the value of work: "One, however, who makes up his mind to study Torah and not to work but to live on charity, profanes the name of God, brings the Torah into contempt, extinguishes the light of religion, brings evil upon himself, and deprives himself of life hereafter."[38] Can one imagine any stronger an affirmation of work and rejection of voluntary dependence upon the work and monies of others to sustain one's life?[39]

R. Slifkin points to some more recent examples, of rabbinic figures held in high regard by the very communities that have rejected work in favor of universal, full-time Torah study for men. R. Moses Sofer (1762–1839), known as the Ḥatam Sofer, a Hungarian rabbi widely considered to be a founding father of today's Ḥaredi world, wrote specifically of the land of Israel in claiming it a mitzvah for men to leave the yeshiva and full-time learning to take up professions, in order to fulfill the Torah obligation of settling the land.[40]

Now, to be fair, there have been two broad arguments made to justify universal full-time male Torah learning, to normalize and sanctify it. The first is that even given what the sources have said, we find ourselves in a time of emergency. More precisely, after the devastation of the Shoah, the Holocaust, and the murder of two-thirds of European Jewry and one-third of the world's Jews in the middle of the twentieth century, there was a need to rebuild the scholarly infrastructure of the lost European centers of learning. And yet, even granting that this was the case some decades ago, it is not at all evident that we remain in such an emergency situation. There has never been more Torah learning by more individuals in the world than takes place now, in the first decades of the twenty-first century. One could make a plausible argument that Jews have more than replaced the esteemed European centers of learning and ended any need for emergency measures.

The second justification is that there are minority opinions upon which to rely, even within the writings of Maimonides. However, as R. Slifkin points out, whatever exceptions Maimonides allowed for individuals to live by means of community support, such exceptions remained limited to those who *teach* Torah, who are contributing and giving back to the community, and *not* for those who learn it full-time. And even those who follow these minority opinions would seem to have little basis to dismiss or demean the positive valuation of work. The writer David Conway, arguing for the harmony between Judaism and libertarianism or classical liberalism, criticizes Israel's Ḥaredi community for failing to understand this: "It is Israel's Haredim above all who need to be made to realise that the kind of society that most accords with the injunctions of their religion would demand of all but a few persons economic self-reliance in adulthood, rather than publicly funded, permanent full-time study." In this regard and in using their leverage to secure state funding for their way of life, he judges them "guilty of departing from the religious teaching and tradition of Jewish orthodoxy."[41] Nevertheless, those individuals and communities embracing the model of lifelong, full-time Torah study by men follow the lead of their esteemed rabbinic leaders, in whose wisdom and authority they maintain complete trust.

Beyond the high value placed upon working and earning a living, one might extend or explain a Jewish valuing of property and ownership by considering Jewish attitudes towards materialism more generally.[42] As many have noted, Judaism is a this-worldly religion. The *Tanakh*—the five books of Moses, the books of the Prophets, and the other writings—does not devote great attention to what comes after this world. Without diminishing God and the nonmaterial world, Jewish thinkers have not generally viewed our world as an illusory and false one, in contrast to the way the world is depicted according to some religious orientations. Indeed, many would say that we are here in this world with purpose, to do something, and to partner with God in some fashion in the doing of it. As R. Sacks has proclaimed, "In Judaism, faith is not acceptance but protest, against the world that is, in the name of the world that is not yet but ought to be."[43] Despite much misunderstanding and perhaps misuse of the expression *tikkun 'olam*, the repair of the world, the term nonetheless conveys an important truth, that our presence in the world has meaning and value, and that our essential task is not to escape the world, but to fix it in some sense.[44]

Jewish mysticism, embodied in the *kabbalah*, describes intricate weavings connecting the material and nonmaterial worlds, and calls upon us to elevate the material to the spiritual. In this worldview, human beings function as something of a bridge between the material and nonmaterial realms. And in this regard, whereas from a halakhic/legal perspective, reciting a blessing before eating food serves as a means of transferring ownership from God to the human being, a Kabbalistic perspective might understand the blessing and then the eating as taking something secular and mundane, an item of food, and bringing some sort of holiness to it, raising it above its material origins:

> When a human being eats food and uses its calories as fuel for performing *mitzvot*, good deeds, and studying Torah, the food itself not only "participates" in those acts, but is credited for enabling them. By assimilating into a human body that moves, speaks and serves G-d [sic], a lower life form gets elevated to the highest possible degree.[45]

For all of their great differences and sometimes difficult history, the rationalist and mystical approaches to Judaism do share an embrace of our material—though not materialistic—lives.

Ownership versus Possession

Perhaps the resolution to the apparently contradictory notions for and against the ownership of private property in Jewish thought can be found in a distinction noted earlier, one suggested by R. Samson Raphael Hirsch, when he wrote of "The day upon which the newly created world first lay spread out in its completeness before man that he might *possess* it and rule over it, [that] this day [i.e., the Sabbath] was to be to him an eternal testimony of the great truth that all things around him were the *property of God*, the Creator."[46] In one sentence, R. Hirsch contrasts two things one might have never considered setting in opposition to one another: property and possession. Everything is the property of God, yet humans can come to possess things. It would seem reasonable, then, to read R. Hirsch as saying that, as humans, we can possess property but not truly own it.

Such an opposition between possession and ownership might at first strike us as odd, at least when we think of possession in terms of pos-sessions, of *my possessions*. A person owns something or does not own it. I go into a store and exchange cash for goods and take them home. I own these goods, and I no longer own the money I used to purchase them. Possession and ownership would appear to be identical in such a case. Clearly, this works fine for small purchases, but what about for rather large ones? I buy a car and take out a loan, for most of the purchase price, or I purchase a house and take out a mortgage. I have made a down payment of 10 percent or 20 percent, and I owe the remainder, the vast majority, to the bank. And yet, I still own the car or the house. I can paint the house, I can tear down walls, I can even sell the house to someone else. I am a homeowner! And yet, how is it that I have come to own something for which I have paid only a small part of the cost? I owe the bank for 80 percent or 90 percent of the cost, and yet I am the owner and not the bank?! Somehow, then, I have purchased a powerful right *in* the property, a right that not even the holder of the mortgage can violate at will. The bank's officials cannot unilaterally and arbitrarily take the house from me, take possession, even though in an important sense, the bank *does* own the house. Only in the case where I fail to uphold the mortgage contract (by not paying the bank as per the agreement) can the bank foreclose on the mortgage. I possess the house and have rights in it, even though I have not fully paid for it. So, do I own it? Or do I not own it, but instead possess it and have certain, if expansive, rights in it?

We ought to keep in mind this framework, these limitations on ownership, as we seek to understand how Jewish theological and legal notions appear to recognize and adjudicate human ownership of property while seemingly claiming we cannot own property, that all property belongs to God. R. Sacks echoes R. Hirsch in making the possession-ownership distinction: "In Judaism, there is a difference between ownership and possession. What we have, we do not own; rather, we hold it as God's trustees. . . . One of the conditions of that trust is that we share what we possess with those in need."[47] As R. Sacks states succinctly, "Ultimately, everything belongs to God. What we have we hold in trust."[48] And Rabbi Saul Berman explains that

> The laws of the sabbatical year teach that not only are the powers of the individual subsumed under the general rights of the community, but also that individuals do not have the right of exclusive dominance over their own property. . . . The Hebrew language itself conveys the same powerful message through the absence of a single word through which the concept of absolute ownership can be conveyed. All Hebrew words which are commonly used to express ownership in reality only express the notion

of possession.... [We] cannot speak of human "ownership," because our theology does not believe that there is rightfully any such notion. God is the "owner" of all, and we humans have simply possession rights in various degrees of complexity.⁴⁹

Writing of ancient Israel, Joshua Berman offers a related distinction between ownership of the land and ownership of the rights of production:

> To understand what it means in this context to say that the people had ownership of the land, however, we must first shed our modern understanding of "ownership" of land. For the most part, we relate to ownership of land in absolute terms. The owner of a tract of land, be it an individual or a corporation, has all the rights to that land—its development, its sale, and its produce. But in the ancient world, it was more common for land tenure to be conceived in terms of the parceling out of various rights. One person, say, an official, or a king, could own the land, while the rights to a portion of its yield could belong to someone else. Peasants had rights of usufruct, or "use-ownership" of the land they lived on, while title to the land belonged to the state."

In this sense, our modern notions of ownership might not fully apply to the biblical context. "The ultimate owner of the land is God, and He grants rights to it to His people, Israel, as an everlasting holding, or in the legal terminology of the ancient Near East, as a land grant. In the ancient Near East, a land grant represented a promise by a donor, often a king, to a recipient, in presupposition of the loyalty of the latter, or in recompense for services rendered."⁵⁰ Perhaps we can see, in our brief discussion of the concepts of home ownership and mortgage arrangements, the beginning of an answer, of a resolution to the paradox—that we can, in effect, or in all practical, meaningful ways, own something while not owning it fully in some other, also meaningful sense.

To bring this further, we can point to, in Jewish law, the concept of *shuttafut*, or partnership.⁵¹ Rabbi Herzog describes the different ways one might understand the notion.⁵² It could be that each joint partner owns a distinct, though possibly indeterminate, portion of the whole, such as a piece of property or a business. Or, it could be that all joint partners share in owning everything. With a flock of sheep, for example, does each joint partner own a specific number of sheep, even if we do not know which ones? Or, does each joint partner own part of each and every sheep? Or, does each partner own part, a percentage perhaps, of each entire sheep, rather than owning some but not all parts of each sheep? How one interprets this has legal consequence; as some commands in Jewish law are written in the second-person singular, their application could depend upon whether there is a single owner or multiple owners. If the latter, if there are multiple ownership partners, then a law creating an obligation but specifying an individual owner might not apply. For instance, does the mitzvah of pe-ah, of leaving the corner of a field for the poor, apply only where there is a single owner or not? If there are ownership partners, the singular command might nonetheless apply if each partner owns a distinct portion of the property. In most or all cases like this, the rabbis of the Talmud identify other verbs written in the second-person plural, therefore establishing obligations upon ownership partners—but at least conceptually, such partnership bears implications for how we understand ownership.[53]

Madeleine Kochen, in her profound and excellent book *Organ Donation and the Divine Lien in Talmudic Law*, articulates all of this and more in fascinating ways. She writes of "the complicated legal interplay between the seemingly all-encompassing institution of divine ownership and the institution of human property ownership, with which it somehow overlaps and, indeed, often runs in parallel."[54] Perhaps it sounds paradoxical, but in Jewish thought it appears possible that God can own everything, and yet human beings can own some of these same things, and at the very same time. (Then again, one of the great theological puzzles confronting Jews and many others is how it is possible for there to be *any* relationship between an infinite God and a finite world.) In good part, Kochen aims to explain how the worlds of divine and human property ownership can coexist. She can therefore reconcile both the normality of Jewish property law and the conviction that God owns everything. And she does not relegate the latter to a theoretical realm without worldly impact. Rather, she brings these two together:

> Beyond the specific property rules described above is a deeply rooted assumption that is ubiquitous in Jewish literature and at the theoretical core of the institution of property law within the Jewish tradition, positing that God is, in some sense, the owner of everything. The notion is referenced

repeatedly in rabbinic texts with more than just homiletic or theological effect. In many contexts it is understood precisely as a declaration of the status of property as being within the divine legal realm.⁵⁵

She weaves the ordinary with the divine by showing how property moves in and out of this divine legal realm.

Let us return to the example of the recitation of blessings before the consumption of foodstuffs. We learned earlier of how the rabbis of the Talmud posited that eating without reciting a blessing ought to be considered theft and how the recitation of the blessing transfers ownership from God to the human consumer. Kochen seeks to understand *how* this takes place. "It is as if ownership of the item shifts from God to the person once the benediction has been recited. Why should that be the case?"⁵⁶ So she seeks to articulate the mechanism producing this transaction. She first notes for us that the blessing recited before eating an apple "is not an expression of gratitude. It is a simple assertion of the fact that God created, and thus owns, the apple."⁵⁷ What does this assertion accomplish? "One acquires ownership by verbally professing God's ownership (i.e., by professing one's lack of ownership)."⁵⁸ Another paradox: it is the very acknowledgment of lack of ownership which effects the change in ownership and makes human ownership possible. In addition, as Kochen suggests, it does not matter if one has purchased the apple or planted the apple tree: "no matter how strong one's claim to ownership of the apple, the act of eating will be considered tantamount to theft (from God) until the appropriate benediction, as a final ritual of return has been made."⁵⁹ In her book, Kochen examines many other cases of property transfer into and out of the divine realm, including tithes, Shemmitah, pe-ah, leket, animal sacrifices, and gifts to the priestly class.⁶⁰

Kochen resolves the paradox of simultaneous human and divine ownership through a consideration of physical location. Jewish law generally requires the physical movement of an object to effect a change in ownership. This differs in a critical way from the transfer of ownership in a system such as that of American law. Rabbi J. David Bleich offers the illustration of a delivery from one city to another.⁶¹ What happens when some natural disaster or accident causes the destruction of the shipment? Let us imagine, for example, that a truck crashes, spilling hundreds of gallons of maple syrup across three lanes of an interstate highway. Who owns the maple syrup on the road? The seller or the buyer? Insurance policies aside, who suffers the monetary loss? In American law, it all depends upon the contractual provisions, including time of sale and payment. In American commercial law, "A meeting of minds is not merely a necessary condition of vesting of title but constitutes the essence of this conveyance." That is, the agreement itself provides sufficient condition for the transaction and transfer of ownership. In Jewish law, by contrast, the buyer does not take possession or ownership until he or she receives the shipment. "Jewish law provides that no transfer or acquisition of property (save by inheritance) takes place other than by means of kinyan, i.e., an overt act that gives effect to the transfer."[62] Jewish law does, of course, also require a "meeting of minds," but as a necessary and not a sufficient condition. In Jewish law, in contrast to American law, the seller of the maple syrup would appear to own the spilled goods.[63] Verbal agreement on a sale does not, in general, result in a transfer of ownership.

At least not between human beings.

Indeed, it is possible for a human, through a verbal declaration, to transfer property to God. How can this be? Kochen explains: "Since the world and all that is in it belongs to God, there is no need to *physically move* the item as if to enact a shift from one domain to another."[64] Anything we might possess always remains within the physical realm belonging to God (and yet, despite the fact that all material items remain within God's domain, Kochen points out that one can only consecrate to God that which one owns). "The notion that property can be moved easily (orally) into the divine realm because it is *already* in the divine realm is one of the surface paradoxes that renders the division between divine and human property ownership somewhat fuzzy."[65] Kochen calls this fuzzy, but her explanation makes the paradox comprehensible. As she writes, "the statement that everything 'belongs' to God can itself be understood, in part, as an expression of the idea that there is no physical domain that is not within God's domain."[66]

The notion of the *divine lien*, featured in the title of Kochen's book, makes some sense out of all of this, further helping to resolve the paradox. Earlier we used the example of mortgaged property. I take out a mortgage with a bank. I own the property but with the mortgage I grant the bank a lien on the property. If I fail to pay my debt, the bank can execute the lien and take possession of or sell the property. The difference between the bank and God, in this regard, is that when I pay off my debt in full to the bank, it no longer retains a lien against the property, whereas God never truly relinquishes the lien. This means that human ownership of property can never be absolute:

> Gifts to the poor are not the only ostensibly non-'sacred' gifts that pass through the divine realm. There is a category of transfers that can be shown clearly to represent the exercise of the divine lien, despite making property available to an even wider group of ordinary people, and that is: land freed up by the laws of *shemitah* and *yovel*. These regularly occurring curtailments of owners' property rights might not seem as 'sacred' (in the popular sense of separate) as gifts for the priests or even for the poor, given that anyone (even a rich person) is permitted to take from any one's land and produce during *shemitah* and *yovel*. Nevertheless, these institutions (together) represent the most powerful and obvious legal and theoretical expression of the underlying claims of divine ownership and concomitant limitations on human property ownership.[67]

In the end, the rabbis of the Talmud understand human ownership as genuine, but necessarily limited, with "all human parties, at all times, less than absolute owners." And in a manner perhaps akin to how a bank maintains a lien on a mortgaged property, "The rabbis thus understood that, in some sense, a divine claim or lien continues to exist in all property."[68] This might prove the best way for us to understand human property ownership in Jewish law and thought: that human beings possess property and thereby own property for most practical purposes in our day-to-day material world, but that such ownership is always mortgaged to God, and paying off the debt completely is simply not possible.

Is the very practical, this-worldly ownership of property in Jewish thought enough to assert a compatibility between Judaism and libertarianism? Can Jewish notions of limited human ownership be squared with libertarian assertions of absolute ownership? Could a religiously observant Jew campaign for political office and endorse the sorts of claims about private property made in the *Libertarian Party Platform*? That property rights are fundamental rights, not to be infringed upon by the government or by individuals? It is not evident that a belief in the divine lien or divine ownership of all property would necessarily preclude such claims and their defense. The situation might prove different in a Jewish commonwealth where the laws of Shemittah and Yovel were observed and enforced, but in the context of a secular polity and contract law, Jewish and libertarian perspectives just might not conflict in the way one might have expected. After all, Jews and Jewish communities seem to manage fairly well and stably with this shared ownership model. And as we suggested earlier with the case of trespassing to save one's life, it is not clear that libertarians, or at least not all of them, actually hold to an absolute notion of property ownership.

Until now, in considering the right to own property, we have focused on its possession, on the possibility of ownership. Yet just as critical is the right to *use* one's property, to dispose of it as one wishes. To have land and not be able to produce from it or sell it, to have money and not be free to spend it—this is not to exercise fully the prerogatives of ownership. Next, therefore, we will turn to the use of property, to the spending of money, whether through private charity or through the collection of taxes and government spending.

Chapter 4

Ownership versus Stewardship: Taxation, Tzedakah, and Charity

> All persons are entitled to keep the fruits of their labor. We call for the repeal of the income tax, the abolishment of the Internal Revenue Service and all federal programs and services not required under the U.S. Constitution. We oppose any legal requirements forcing employers to serve as tax collectors. We support any initiative to reduce or abolish any tax, and oppose any increase on any taxes for any reason. To the extent possible, we advocate that all public services be funded in a voluntary manner.
> – Section 2.4 "Government Finance and Spending,"
> *Libertarian Party Platform* (2018)

When one thinks of libertarian objections to government, taxation often comes to mind first. A powerful libertarian perspective takes most taxation to be government theft of private property. The core issue, however, might not truly be the taxation, but rather the spending. That is, who has the right to spend money and for what purposes? In particular, what is the difference between voluntary charity on the one hand, and on the other hand, government taxation and distribution or redistribution of funds, even if for praiseworthy purposes?

Now, even if we can reconcile, between Judaism and libertarianism, the issues of self-ownership and the ownership of property, will we be able to reconcile attitudes towards taxation and charity? After all, libertarians oppose most, if not all, taxation—and where they support taxation, this taxation must be minimal and limited to funding very specific government functions such as defense and protection against other aggression and fraud. Libertarians, at least for the most part, oppose governments disbursing tax funds to do what can be done through private, charitable giving. In Jewish thought, by contrast, charitable giving is not a purely voluntary matter. Indeed, Judaism *prescribes* certain types of obligatory giving, such as tzedakah and tithes—though it is worth noting that in some cases the obligation functions not so much in formal, legal terms as in moral or theological terms and in communal terms, with more informal, practical means of enforcement.

So, how could one system tolerating only voluntary charity and another system requiring charitable giving possibly prove compatible? How could a religiously committed Jew, one who sees giving as an obligation, champion a libertarian perspective opposed to any such obligation?

Is Taxation Theft?

Most of us experience taxation—in its many forms: income, sales, excise, real estate, and more—as perfectly normal. This is simply something that governments do, taxing citizens to pay for the operations of government. We elect legislators to allocate the collected funds, and government officials then distribute them. Yet ought we to consider this normal? Or, as many libertarians would argue, is taxation basically *theft*, the appropriation of private property by means of force or the threat of force? Is taxation a just and fair exercise of government? Is it a necessary evil? Is it an immoral and unjustified practice? Or, perhaps, to some extent, all of these?

The basic libertarian anti-taxation argument runs like this: when governments tax their citizens, they take from individuals the monies (that is, the private property) these individuals possess, whether this possession came about through earnings or investment or inheritance; individuals who refuse to pay their taxes are subject to fines and/or imprisonment, meaning tax funds will be collected willingly or unwillingly. Insofar as they are collected unwillingly, these are acts of aggression and the improper confiscation of individuals' private property. As the *Libertarian Party Platform* concisely expresses it, "All persons are entitled to keep the fruits of their labor."

The simple but quite serious point here is that the *very same* activities a government engages in to collect and enforce the collection of taxes would be considered immoral and criminal should one person do likewise to another. As Murray Rothbard writes, "In contrast to all other thinkers, left, right, or in-between, the libertarian refuses to give the State the moral sanction to commit actions that almost everyone agrees would be immoral, illegal, and criminal if committed by any person or group in society."[1] When an individual takes money from another without the latter as a willing partner, we call this theft. If this is wrong for an individual to do, on what grounds should it not be equally wrong for a government and its officials to do the same? Or, as Tom Palmer once framed the matter in a *New York Times* op-ed piece,

> Suppose someone were to stop you at gunpoint and demand that you hand over half of your hard-earned income. Wouldn't you consider him a thief and consider yourself justified in resisting the robbery?
>
> Now suppose that the thief is carrying a paper certifying him as an agent of the state. In addition, he claims that the robbery is being carried out for your own good. Is his act any different now?[2]

Even though we have so far described the targets of taxation as unwilling, Rothbard asserts that the fact that most people accept taxation, that they are or have become willing victims, does not make it theft any the less.[3]

If taxation as theft is not enough, some libertarians argue that it is a form of enslavement as well. In what senses? First, when I put labor and time into earning monies I am forced to turn over to the government in the form of taxes, this labor and time effectively belong to someone else. Income tax, Rothbard explains, entails that "all of us work a large part of the year—several months—for *nothing*. . . . [Th]e income tax means that we sweat and earn income, only to see the government extract a large chunk of it by coercion for its own purposes. What is this but forced labor at no pay?" On top of this, employers find themselves legally obligated to withhold taxes from their employees and transfer the withheld funds to the government—and sometimes without any compensation for undertaking this administrative task. As the platform states, "We oppose any legal requirements forcing employers to serve as tax collectors." Finally, workers must devote uncompensated time to filing taxes, or pay someone else to do so. Some would argue that the time and labor devoted to such activities could also be viewed as a sort of slavery.[4]

Isabel Paterson (1886-1961), in *The God of the Machine*, underlines the point that it becomes difficult to limit taxation once one party secures the authorization to take money from others. Speaking in particular about government welfare, she writes, "And that is what the proposal to care for the needy by the political means comes to. It gives the power to the politicians to tax without limit; and there is absolutely no way to ensure that the money shall go where it was intended to go."[5]

Robert Nozick (1938-2002), in *Anarchy, State, and Utopia*, discuss taxation, wages, and the seizure of profits and argues that

> Seizing the results from someone's labor is equivalent to seizing hours from him and directing him to carry on various activities. If people force you to do certain work, or unrewarded work, for a certain period of time, they decide what you are to do and what purposes your work is to serve apart from your decisions. This process whereby they take this decision from you makes them a *part-owner* of you; it gives them a property right in you. Just as having such partial control and power of decision, by right, over an animal or inanimate object would be to have a property right in it.[6]

Nozick implies that taxation contradicts self-ownership, and he uses Locke's language of having property in something or someone.

John Locke took the threat of taxation without representation so gravely that he depicted it as undermining the very purpose of government. In so doing, he suggested a striking distinction, between *absolute* power and *arbitrary* power. At first one might assume that absolute power is greater than and worse than arbitrary power. In Locke's presentation, however, absolute power, circumscribed by reason and by specified ends, has limits, whereas arbitrary power has none. Locke offers the example of military power. On the one hand, military officers wield absolute power over their subordinates: "[T]he Preservation of the Army, and in it of the whole Commonwealth, requires an *absolute Obedience* to the Command of every Superior Officer, and it is justly Death to disobey or dispute the most dangerous or unreasonable of them." And yet, despite this fact and this power that an officer can command a soldier to risk forfeiting his or her life, the officer nevertheless cannot "command that Soldier to give him one penny of his Money." And a general, who can sentence a soldier to death for desertion or disobeying orders, cannot "dispose of one Farthing of that Soldiers Estate, or seize one jot of his Goods."[7] We see here that the *absolute* power of military command does not encompass the *arbitrary* power of taxation. If this is the case in a military context, one would think it the case all the more so that government authorities would not be entitled to such arbitrary power over citizens.

Locke's fascinating characterization does, though, point to one counter to the libertarian definition of taxation as theft: that taxation *with* consent might reasonably be understood as proper and acceptable. Governments, through their legislative powers, "must *not raise Taxes on the Property of the People, without the Consent of the People*, given by themselves, or their Deputies."[8] Locke, here and elsewhere, envisions some sort of active, perhaps renewable and renewed consent, but many nonlibertarians might point to a more passive sort of consent, that as citizens, under a social contract with the State, we have *implicitly* granted the government the right to tax us. Of course, as per the American Revolution, this remains valid only so long as there is representation—and thus no taxation without representation. No doubt, some libertarians would rebut this position by claiming that so long as we do not consent as individuals, each one of us, the taxation remains theft—that no majority of other persons could proffer my consent and bind me.

To review, let us return to that section of the *Libertarian Party Platform* featured as the epigraph for this chapter, where we find the following statement on "Government Finance and Spending":

> All persons are entitled to keep the fruits of their labor. We call for the repeal of the income tax, the abolishment of the Internal Revenue Service and all federal programs and services not required under the U.S. Constitution. We oppose any legal requirements forcing employers to serve as tax collectors. We support any initiative to reduce or abolish any tax, and oppose any increase on any taxes for any reason.[9]

It is worth noting a few things. The brief, introductory line, without saying so explicitly, perhaps suggests the equation of taxation with theft. After all, if we can infer that taxation is the opposite of individuals retaining the fruits of their labor, then taxation must be the improper confiscation of some of these fruits. In addition, however, there is no call to eliminate, as a matter of ideological principle, *all* taxation. There is clearly an effort to minimize taxation and even strip away some of the mechanisms of the tax system, and support for ending any particular taxes, but not a single, unambiguous statement as to the illegitimacy of taxation altogether. Whether this is due to a recognition of the impracticality of shifting to a pure libertarian commonwealth or the reality that some libertarians support some minimal taxation, or both, remains unclear.

And what about nonanarchist libertarians, those who recognize a need for very limited government? How do they propose to fund government operations, such as the military defense of the population? If without taxation, how? And if with taxation, upon what philosophical or moral grounds? For, if it is truly theft, can anything justify it? The Cato Institute's David Boaz begins by pointing out that we are so far from ending taxation that one could make a lot of progress minimizing taxation without having to worry about eliminating it. He also suggests that in such a situation, without the coercion of taxation, individuals and organizations might, voluntarily, be willing to provide funds for basic governmental functions of protection.[10]

John Hospers, in his 1971 manifesto *Libertarianism: A Political Philosophy for Tomorrow*, describes a few possibilities. Like Boaz, he believes that enough people would be willing to pay for the value provided by the police, courts, and the military—enough so that a small number or percentage of "freeloaders" would not threaten the system. Alternatively, even such services as courts and the police could operate on a contracted fee basis, where individuals would have the option of paying for police protection and the use of courts to oversee such matters as business disputes. Most people will want such services and will agree to pay for them.[11] Finally Hospers cites another writer, David Walter, who asks why we would think individuals would forego such services as garbage removal and public transportation should government not provide them? Walter suggests that people would not be so foolish as to wallow in garbage if the government did not arrange for garbage collection, and he presents this clever analogy: "Do men go barefoot because the shoe industry is still a private operation?"[12] It may or may not be the case that government does provide certain services more effectively and more efficiently than would be provided otherwise, but Hospers and others do encourage us to consider what government *must* do, if anything, and to question what we take to be the natural role of government in our lives. If taxation is indeed theft, then Hospers and Boaz and the like have at least provided suggestions for imagining functional, minimal government without taxation.

Taxation in Jewish Thought and Practice

What do Judaism and Jewish history have to say about taxation? Is it acceptable for a governing body to fund its operations by confiscating monies from the population under its rule? Is taxation understood, in any regard, as theft? Well, until 1948, there was a rather long stretch of centuries during which this remained a purely theoretical question on the level of a Jewish state or polity. And even since 1948, there has not been all that much consideration of how a state run under Jewish law might operate in regard to such matters as taxation.

It is possible, perhaps even likely, that a Jewish state would ground its authority to tax in the biblical powers assigned to kings. In the eighth chapter of the first book of Samuel, the people demand that the prophet appoint a king over them. In warning the people of what such a king will do, Samuel at least appears to enumerate the king's powers. And these powers include the confiscation of property (as well as conscription of various sorts):

> (14) And your fields and your vineyards and your olive groves, the good ones, he will take, and he will give them to his servants.
> (15) And your seeds and your vineyards, he will take a tenth, and he will give them to his officers and to his servants.
> (17) Your flocks, he will take a tenth, and you, you will be servants to him.

It is not entirely clear whether Samuel's words figure as a *de*scription or a *pre*scription, whether he is merely characterizing how kings do act in reality or explaining what powers rightly belong to kings. R. Klapper points out that Samuel presents only the powers of the king to take, leaving out the limitations set in Deuteronomy: "While these rules do not explicitly contradict the limitations found in Devarim [i.e., Deuteronomy], they may be read as emphasizing the inability of formally defined rules to restrain an ambitious king."[13] This sounds more like a warning than a mere description. Regardless, for Jewish kings and for non-Jewish kings alike, and likely for ruling authorities of all sorts, including democratically elected governments, these verses provide a basis for the power to tax, to take property from subjects, even without explicit consent.

It is worth noting that although Samuel's monarch possesses the power to tax, he or she does not maintain *arbitrary*, unlimited power, in the Lockean sense or otherwise. That belongs only to God, not a human king. Moshe Halbertal and Stephen Holmes, in their book *The Beginning of Politics: Power in the Biblical Book of Samuel*, present provocative distinctions among models of kingship. Whereas God can be understood as King, and whereas some cultures, such as that of ancient Egypt, have viewed the king as god, Samuel's king is clearly *not* a god. According to Halbertal and Holmes, this model of the king as *not-god* created or made room for a new realm, that of human politics. We will return to this idea in the next chapter, on government.[14]

Exactly how Samuel's words might apply to the modern state of Israel remains a question. As the scholar Meir Tamari explains, Maimonides distinguishes between the foundation of power and legitimacy in two cases, for monarchs in the line of King David and for other rulers. For the Davidic dynasty, the source of power could be located in the laws of kings, as per Samuel. For other rulers, presumably including the rulers of the modern, secular Israeli government, such power would be grounded in *dina d'malkhuta dina*, the law of the kingdom is the law, a concept we have mentioned earlier and will also discuss in greater depth in the next chapter. Because of this, as Tamari summarizes, "Modern Israel presents an important halakhic problem in regard to taxation." Here we have a Jewish state, in the land of Israel, governing the land of Israel, and yet it might not have the Jewish legal status and biblical authority of King David and his line.[15]

Besides the book of Samuel, there are a few other biblical sources suggesting taxation was a legitimate principle or even actual practice in ancient Israel. Manuel L. Jose and Charles K. Moore identify the following five types:

- A *capitation tax*, with a silver half-shekel payment per male individuals ages 20 and up, took place during the forty years wandering in the desert (Ex. 30:12–14, 25–26), and in Neḥemiah 10:33 we learn of an annual tax of one-third of a shekel per person to maintain the Temple (the text here does not specify gender or age restrictions, though this does not mean there were none).
- Although not a tax in ancient Israel, Joseph did impose upon the Egyptians an *income tax* of one-fifth of their produce, and the desert sojourn brought the institution of tithing, a tenth of livestock to be consecrated to God (Lev. 27:32). There also emerged the requirement of bringing first fruits, grains, wine, oil, and wool to the priests (Deut. 18:3–5).
- In 2 Kings, there is a *property tax* paid by King Jehoiakim to the Pharaoh (23:35). According to Jose and Moore, the tax here is upon the value of the land and not the value or even increase in value of what the land produces.
- These authors suggest the existence of a *special assessment tax*, something levied for particular projects rather than on a regular cycle. They point to 2 Chronicles and a directive from King Solomon to obtain funds for the repair of the Temple (24:5). As the verse does seem to refer to this in the framework of an annual tax, it is not clear that this verse provides the evidence the authors suggest.
- Whereas these first four taxes are types of direct taxes, there were also *indirect taxes*, such as customs duties or sales taxes. The two scholars point to the books of Ezra, Chronicles, and Kings for examples of tributes and forced labor.[16]

To what extent any or all of these figured prominently and regularly in ancient Israel remains uncertain. And then there is the question of whether or not we are applying or misapplying a concept of taxation applicable to modern, bureaucratic, nation states onto something rather different. Jose and Moore argue, at least, that we cannot separate the religious or theological from the political, and that we ought to understand these measures as forms of taxation: "In the theocracy of ancient Israel, tithing in a religious context was the same as taxation in a governmental context. It is impossible to distinguish between religious and governmental taxation since religion and government were one and the same in ancient Israel."[17]

Robert A. Oden, Jr., in his examination of "Taxation in Biblical Israel," offers a straightforward definition, borrowed from the late Menachem Elon (1923–2013), a scholar and a justice on the Israeli Supreme Court, that "tax is a compulsory payment, in currency or in specie, exacted by a public authority, for the purpose of satisfying the latter's own needs or those of the public, or part of the public."[18] Oden continues and identifies a number of taxes, the same or similar to those presented by Jose and Moore:

- A *per capita* tax in Nehemiah.
- Under King Solomon, in 1 Kings, taxation through twelve districts, each responsible for supplying the monarch one month of each year (4:7–19).
- Emergency levies in 2 Kings (15:19–20).
- The first fruits in Deuteronomy.
- Forced labor, and also the Sabbatical and Jubilee year gleaning rights, though not everyone would classify these as kinds of taxes.[19]

Oden takes up a number of challenges to the notion of biblical taxation, including the idea that all supposedly biblical taxation is voluntary and so not truly taxation, in the sense of coerced payments: "[T]he phrasing of the taxation laws in the Hebrew Bible often gives some appearance of voluntariness. However, this voluntariness is only nominal, since payments of various kinds were a prerequisite for those who wished to remain full members of the ancient Israelite community."[20] Oden also questions the degree to which biblical taxes entered into actual practice, agreeing with the historian Salo Baron "that most biblical laws have an 'extremely idealistic and doctrinaire slant' and that they were 'enacted by classes which had the right to do so, but had no power to carry them out.'"[21]

Given the lack of clarity or at least certainty in regard to taxation in biblical and ancient Israel, one might best understand the matter by turning to how Jewish communities have operated historically, to consider what authorization Jewish law and tradition have provided to communal authorities and which obligations they have imposed upon community members. According to Meir Tamari,

> Irrespective of the legal source of fiscal policy, communal taxation was an early characteristic of Jewish social life and deeply entrenched in religious law. The widespread instances of Jewish autonomy in almost all periods of history brought with them a common pattern of communal taxation. It is not surprising, therefore, to find a wealth of rabbinic literature on the subject as well as communal ordinances from every country and period of Jewish history.[22]

It is clear that, for various purposes, the leaders of Jewish communities have claimed—and, in principle, may claim—monies from members of the community. The scholar Joseph Isaac Lifshitz notes that the entire enterprise of Jewish communal taxation to provide for the poor emerged, at least in part, as a consequence of the transition from agricultural to urban living:

> The changing of the commandment to give charity from one that has a connection to agricultural life, to one connected to urban living, is what seems to have added a public aspect to such actions. This was the background to the appearance of the institution of charity collectors (*gabba'ei tzedaka*) and the right of the community to force individuals to give charity in the Mishnah and the Talmud.

Lifshitz suggests that perhaps the biblical obligations of pe-ah and leket and the like sufficed in the agricultural context, a more formal framework becoming necessary only when sufficient numbers of individuals concentrated in towns and cities.[23]

Rabbi Dr. Aaron Levine, an expert on matters of economics and ethics and Jewish law, writes that "Judaism's charity obligation consists of both a public and a private component." He describes levies to raise money for the poor in the times of the Talmud, but points out that the public collections were not enough on their own. R. Levine uses the public-private distinction to discuss coercion, attributing an idea to Rabbi Chaim Soloveitchik (1853–1918), who lived in the nineteenth and early twentieth centuries. "The purpose of the coercive levy, he posits, is not to ensure that the individual members of the community qua individuals discharge their charity obligation, but rather to allow the public sector to carry out its own distinctive social welfare responsibility." That is to say, the public collection for the poor was an entirely separate matter from the obligation of individuals to provide tzedakah and assist those in poverty. R. Levine also notes that "from the standpoint of Judaism's social welfare program, income transfers are not the ideal approach."[24]

The scholar Elisheva Carlebach paints a quite nuanced portrait of Jewish communal organizations over many centuries prior to the modern era. While making the important caveat that there was considerable variation across lands and centuries, Carlebach describes the authority exercised by communal leaders to tax their fellow community members as core to communal authority:

> These organizations evolved at different paces, with governance styles and patterns that varied according to time and place. Some aspects of self-governance were common to most communities: the responsibility of Jews to select representatives, to legislate, to adjudicate disputes, to apportion taxes, to punish civil infractions, and to organize their own social welfare, educational, and religious life. The emergence of communal organizations was far more contingent, their relationship to one another more decentralized, and their structures far more diverse than had previously been believed. At the same time, their presence and utility remain indisputable.[25]

A large portion of communal taxation was required to satisfy demands from the non-Jewish rulers and their agents. Jewish communal leaders sought to distribute the burden appropriately in order to raise the necessary funds.

These same authorities also, in effect, taxed the community members to fund services provided for and by the community:

> In addition to the taxes paid as a condition for Jewish collective existence, communities raised taxes to cover a wide array of their own expenses. Depending on the size of the community, its religious functionaries, such as rabbis, teachers, and undertakers, its butchers and bakers, the upkeep of communal buildings, the welfare of members, and charity for local and distant causes all added to the sums that had to be raised from community members.[26]

Carlebach also considers the theological-religious basis upon which Jewish communal authorities could exercise the power of taxation:

> The mechanism by which the community had the right to appropriate the property of individuals in the form of taxes had been one of the thorniest halakhic issues regarding the functioning of communities. There is scant provision in Jewish law for this type of tax collection... The first rabbinic monograph devoted solely to the questions raised by Jewish communal taxation of individuals appeared in 1600.[27]

Carlebach's conclusion appears to be that the authority of Jewish taxation was grounded primarily in the facts and happenstances of its development and not upon any consciously and proactively articulated set of principles:

> Ibn Ezra summarized the dilemma of halakhists who ruled on disputes related to taxes imposed by the communities: there was no body of sources to rely on, only scattered references and diffuse correspondence. The entire structure of medieval communal taxation, like communal governance itself, rested legislatively upon the innovations required by new political realities. They were, therefore, to be classified as minhag ("custom"), rather than din ("law").[28]

Regardless of any possible theological underpinnings, actual Jewish communities had, for centuries, found themselves ensconced in a practical reality of taxation and authority to tax.

Can we reconcile the libertarian hostility to taxation with biblical and talmudic sources and the extended historical record of Jewish communal taxation? To start, neither the biblical and talmudic precedents nor the historical facts of taxation impose clear requirements upon the secular state in the modern world. As Adam Chodorow shows, the biblical examples of the Temple tax, the agricultural tithe, and tithing of income, as well as talmudic accounts of communal distribution of funds, all "bear the marks of the religious purpose they served or the historical circumstances from which they sprang." Given the anchoring of such practices in specific historical contexts, Chodorow expresses doubt over their use in our days: "Thus, while it may be tempting to look to the examples of taxation in the Bible and Talmud for evidence of what Judeo-Christian values require in a modern, secular tax system, such examples provide little or no guidance when they are placed in context."[29] As for the more nebulous difference in philosophies or sensibilities, although the attitudes might conflict—as in other cases we have considered—it is not at all clear that actual practice must. First of all, neither Jewish theology nor religious law necessarily *requires* that the legal or customary practices of the autonomous Jewish community be transferred to the secular state. And, secondly, libertarian political philosophy does not necessarily *require* that subcommunities within a secular state accept upon themselves libertarian approaches to taxation. Before arriving at a conclusion, however, we must consider further the question of whether charity is truly voluntary in a Jewish theological context.

Tzedakah Versus Charity in Jewish Thought

In the English-speaking world of the late twentieth and the early twenty-first centuries, the Hebrew word *tzedakah* has often been translated as charity, but are tzedakah and charity really the same things? Is tzedakah a mitzvah, an obligation? If so, what sort of mitzvah? And if tzedakah is truly an obligation, and yet we think of charity as voluntary, how could they be the same? Can what we think of as voluntary be involuntary? As many others have remarked before, the truth is that charity probably does not make for the best translation for tzedakah. Returning once again to the Hebrew linguistic root system, tzedakah comes from the root *tsadi-dalet-kuf*, and this root connotes a sense of justice. The import here is that whereas charity is a voluntary offering, the notion of justice suggests that this act of giving for the welfare of others serves to correct something unjust.

Now, this is not at all to imply that the giver of tzedakah has done some injustice for which she or he must atone and make right. Nor does it mean that the individual suffering poverty, the recipient of the funds, has been treated unjustly, by the giver or by someone else. Rather, I would suggest that some people have in mind some more nebulous cosmic imbalance, perhaps in contrast to some ideal, or at least more just, distribution of goods.

And, indeed, we find in Jewish thought an idea that when we give tzedakah we are not really giving what we own to someone else, not giving over to another person our own possessions or wealth and thereby making a voluntary sacrifice, but rather that we are acting as conduits on God's behalf to transfer money to someone in need. The recipient might be gaining something, or at least taking possession of something rightfully his or hers, but the donor is not losing anything in this sense.

Rabbi Jacob ben Asher (c.1269–c.1343), known as the Ba'al HaTurim or the Tur (based upon the name of his famous book on Jewish law the *Arba-'ah Turim*, or *The Four Rows*), underscores this point in his articulation of the laws of tzedakah: "And the idea should not arise in one's heart to say, How can I lessen my own money to give it to the poor?, because he should know that it is not his money, but rather a deposit with which to do the will of the Depositor. And it is His will that it should be distributed from it to the poor." As the Tur explains, the money was given (by God) to the giver of tzedakah for the express purpose of giving it as tzedakah. The Tur follows this up with a theological guarantee, in the Name of God, that one will not become poor as a result of giving tzedakah, accompanying this assurance with the additional indication that one will actually become wealthier.[30] Note, however, that neither the promise of additional riches nor the guarantee against poverty function as any sort of *right*, on the part of recipients, to specific reimbursement or to a claim upon communal funds. R. Yosef Karo, writing more than two centuries later in his landmark work the *Shulchan Arukh*, confirmed that "No person is ever made poor from [giving] *tzedakah*, and no evil thing and no harm is caused on account of it, as it is written, 'And the work of righteousness [*tzedakah*] will be peace' [Is. 32:17]."[31] Often, tzedakah gets translated as "righteousness," which has a different sense than does "justice," yet certainly justice and righteousness overlap. Rabbi Daniel Sperber, in emphasizing the greater importance of providing monies to the needy above donating money to build synagogues or even the Temple itself in Jerusalem, quotes Maimonides in understanding tzedakah as righteousness:

> One is obligated to take care in the [practice of the] mitzvah of *tzedakah* more than all other positive commandments. For [it] is the characteristic of the righteous of the seed of Abraham our forefather, as it is said, "For I know him, that he will command his children and his household after him, that they shall keep the way of the Lord, to do *tzedakah* and judgment..." (Genesis 18:19). And the throne of Israel will not be established and the

religion of truth will not stand fast but through *tzedakah* [a reference to Proverbs 16:12], as it is said, "In righteousness (*bi-tzedakah*) shalt thou be established" (Isaiah 54:14). And Israel will not be redeemed but through *tzedakah*, as it is said, "Zion shall be redeemed with judgment, and her converts with righteousness (*bi-tzedakah*)," (Is. 1:27).[32]

What becomes clear is that tzedakah cannot be translated simply as charity, that it has no single-word equivalent in English, but rather includes other connotations, such as those of justice and righteousness. In terms of its claimed efficacy, tzedakah is said not only to bring peace (as reported in the *Shulchan Arukh*, citing Isaiah) but is described in the liturgy as one of three means of overturning or at least mitigating a bad verdict during the days of judgment from Rosh HaShanah to Yom Kippur: "And repentance and prayer and tzedakah remove the evil decree."

Interestingly, one can understand the ownership of funds for the poor from another perspective. According to the scholar Noam Zion, referencing a medieval text, "Failure to pay taxes collected for the poor was regarded as theft of the poor because it was their entitlement and the taxpayer's obligation."[33] We discussed taxation as theft from the taxpayer, but here we see a reversal of sorts, with the taxpayer as the thief, keeping from the poor funds rightly belonging to the latter. Of course, we are not here talking about the taxpayer in the modern nation state, rather this is a community member assessed an obligation, but the sense is plain: to refuse to part with these funds is to steal them from their rightful owners.

This notion that the giver of tzedakah does not own the funds to be given fits well with our earlier discussion of property ownership and matters such as leaving for the poor the corners of one's fields. As Madeline Kochen explains, "property is set aside by the (initial) owner on behalf of the poor. While it might appear as a gift of property from the owner, it is not; the owner does not own property acquired by the poor, nor does he have the right to select the identities of the recipients." The landowner sets aside property or produce, but cannot even choose the recipient, something that might seem odd in the context of voluntary charity.[34] In this sense, acts of tzedakah do not function as acts of charity. Or, to flip this around, one might say that it is not simply that tzedakah is not charity, but also that charity is not tzedakah. Charity is voluntary and is an act of kindness, of mercy, even sometimes pity. Tzedakah may be fixing something unjust in the distribution of wealth, and it may appear merciful or kind, but it remains an obligation, with no pity involved.

Perhaps because money used for tzedakah does not truly belong to the donor, there is a strong prohibition against turning away from giving tzedakah. That is, not only is there a positive mitzvah to give, but there is also a negative mitzvah to not *not* give, to hold back from giving. Here is how R. Karo, in the *Shulchan Arukh*, phrases it:

> It is a positive *mitzvah* obligation to give *tzedakah* according to one's ability, and many times we were commanded in it with a positive commandment. And there is a negative commandment to [not] raise one's eyes away from it, as it says: Do not harden your heart and do not shut your hand [Deut. 17:7]. And all who raise their eyes away from it are called wicked, and it is as if they worship idols. And there is very much [a need] to be careful in this, because it is possible that blood will be spilled, that the requesting poor person will die if one does not give to him immediately, as in the story of Nachum, a man of Gam Zu.[35]

The law here emphasizes that not giving tzedakah could lead to the death (perhaps from hunger?) of a person in need, making the refusal to give a sort of murder, or at least manslaughter. It might not seem quite as clear, however, on what grounds the refusal to give tzedakah is likened to idol worship.

It is possible that one could derive this connection—between idol worship and refusing to be charitable—from what the refusal to give tzedakah implies about a person's understanding of money. If I believe the money belongs to me, then my refusal to part with it might be unkind or even immoral, but is it really similar to worshipping statues or false gods? From the perspective that humans do not own, or at least do not fully own, the money they possess, we can understand how a refusal to acknowledge God's ultimate ownership of the money could be considered a rejection of God. Such a rejection could be taken as a kind of idolatry, namely *placing some other value above God*. And in our days, we find ourselves all too familiar with the worship of money and wealth, among other things clearly lacking in divinity.

In addition, there exists a notion in the Jewish tradition that God requires tzedakah not only, and perhaps not even primarily, to address inequality and to help the poor, but rather that God created inequality in wealth in order to provide the opportunity to give tzedakah. In Deuteronomy 15:7 we are told "If there will be among you [*vicha*] a poor person from any one of your brothers, within any one of your gates, within your land that HaShem your God gives to you, you shall not harden your heart, and neither shall you shut your hand from your brother, the poor one." Why *vicha*, among you? Why not simply "If there will be a poor person, you shall not harden your heart, and neither shall you shut your hand"? One commentator cited earlier, *Or ha-Chaim*, seeks to explain this seemingly extraneous word. As Rabbi Avrohom Chaim Feuer explains the view of the *Or ha-Chaim*, "We must remember that the reason they suffer poverty is for our sake! Since the Almighty wished to provide you with the opportunity to gain the merit of charity, He purposely made some people poor and strategically placed them בְּךָ, *in your midst*, so that you could easily perform this mitzvah." Moreover, where the poor person lives among the non-poor it becomes more difficult for the latter to look down on the former or see them as strangers.[36]

The poor also serve as a reminder to those not currently poor that one day they, or their descendants, might become poor or that once upon a time they too, or their ancestors, used to be poor. The Rama, Rabbi Moshe Isserles (1530-1572), in his Ashkenazi supplement to R. Karo's *Shulchan Arukh*, makes such a point:

> And a person should take it to heart that each hour he should request from the Holy One, Blessed be He, his livelihood, and like he requests that the Holy One, Blessed be He, will listen to his pleas, so he should listen to the pleas of the poor. Also, he should take this to heart, that it is the returning wheel of the world [i.e., that things go around and come back around in the world], and it is the end of man that it will come [to] him or his son or his grandson according to this character trait, and all the mercy he [bestows] upon others, [God] is merciful upon him.[37]

Furthermore, we learn from the Bible itself that poverty will never disappear entirely: "For the poor will never cease from the land; therefore I command you, saying, 'Surely you will open your hand to your brothers, to your poor, and to your needy in your land.'" (Deut. 15:11) Despite the possibility that this entire framework might strike us as problematic—why should some suffer in order for the rest of us to have the opportunity to help them, for if there were no such suffering, then we would have no need to practice such kindness and to help alleviate it?—it might simply be that God created a world where free will, where human choices and actions (on behalf of oneself and on behalf of others), will most likely, if not inevitably, result in poverty for some. In such a world as this, such a world as ours, we would be wise to keep this in mind, that given the presence of the poor among us, those who are not poor should provide assistance. And that we should know that the world God created also functions in such a way that poverty will fall upon all of us, if not personally, then upon members of our families, or upon our descendants. And perhaps all of this figures as integral to the world we have, to a world God wanted—that we ought to act as partners with God in improving the world, and that the continued existence of poverty ought to provide us with a motivation to build societies and a world where poverty will disappear from the land.

In the end, the notion of tzedakah does not translate simply as charity, but rather is caught up in a much more complicated web of relationships among people and within societies. As Noam Zion points out, the definition of tzedakah has varied over time. Indeed, although we have been discussing tzedakah and giving money to the poor, the two have little association in biblical texts. For example, the biblical obligations of pe-ah and leket and Shemittah, discussed in an earlier chapter, do not at all reference tzedakah. The first time we find any association of tzedakah and giving to the poor does not occur until the fourth chapter of the book of Daniel, and in that context helping the poor figures as a means of gaining merit to offset sins and not as a means of increasing justice in the world.[38] In the later world of the rabbinic texts tzedakah can refer both to obligatory communal giving and to voluntary giving, and even to *ḥesed*, or kindness, in contrast to legal justice. All of this suggests there is something novel in the modern linking of tzedakah as aiding the poor and tzedakah as justice. Although those who today connect the two might be inaccurate in attributing a textual or linguistic linkage to ancient times, this does not mean they are necessarily mistaken, that the Jewish tradition does not contain a powerful emphasis on justice, if not quite matching our concept of social justice today. No doubt, and unsurprisingly, meanings have expanded or shifted. In any event, tzedakah clearly differs from charity in its obligatory nature, in the fact that it is not, or not exclusively or entirely, voluntary. And what about within the world of libertarianism? How do libertarians view charity? Could libertarians entertain any sort of notion of involuntary charitable giving?

Libertarianism, Charity, the Welfare State, and the Critique of Government Spending

Ayn Rand famously praised selfishness and ridiculed altruism:

> If it is true that what I mean by "selfishness" is not what is meant conventionally, then this is one of the worst indictments of altruism: it means that altruism *permits no concept* of a self-respecting, self-supporting man—a man who supports his life by his own effort and neither sacrifices himself nor others. It means that altruism permits no view of men except as sacrificial animals and profiteers-on-sacrifice, as victims and parasites—that it permits no concept of a benevolent co-existence among men—that it permits no concept of *justice*.[39]

She even titled one of her books, an essay collection, *The Virtue of Selfishness*. To Rand, the widespread acclaim accorded altruism perverts true morality. Rand's notion of ethics "holds man's life as the *standard* of value—and *his own life* as the ethical *purpose* of every individual man." Life is an end in itself, so for any individual person his or her life would be an end in himself or herself. Morality means—to Rand, it *requires*—striving to fulfill such an end. "To live for his own sake means that *the achievement of his own happiness is man's highest moral purpose*."[40] By Rand's framing, therefore, to sacrifice oneself for another in any regard would be immoral, and a kind of human sacrifice, akin to human sacrifice in some ancient cultures. Rand is not arguing that when one does something seemingly altruistic, the individual gets some personal benefit out of it, if only feeling good about oneself, thereby making the act selfish. Rather, she is arguing that it is immoral to *not* act in one's own interests, immoral to sacrifice oneself, whatever other benefits doing so might trigger.

Some might mistake Rand's position for that of most libertarians. They would err in making such a judgment. Libertarian attitudes towards charity have little to do with Rand's egoism or with her contempt for altruism. Libertarians fully engage in charitable endeavors. Where they differ from modern liberals is in defining the proper vehicle for such charity. For libertarians, governments should stay out of the business of distributing charitable funds (or of providing tax deductions for charitable giving).[41] That is, governments should not acquire funds through taxation and then redistribute these funds for charitable ends. If libertarians would generally reject Rand's disdain of charitable and altruistic endeavors, they might agree to some extent with Rand's view of the poor and their benefactors in her ideal society, in the words of one of her disciples: "If *you* want to help them, you will not be stopped."[42] In brief, libertarians do not reject the *ends* of charity or the *motivations* of charity, but rather government allocation as a *means* of providing such charity. In a sense then, one might say that libertarians tend to view charity in a rather Christian manner, as "voluntary benevolence" or "self-less love," as Noam Zion has suggested to me. The chapter after the next one will elaborate upon this with a discussion of non-governmental, voluntary communities, some of which pursue charitable aims.

Rand's rhetoric aside, what problem do libertarians have with governments helping people, among them the poor and homeless? After all, most governments provide some sort of assistance to those in need, and liberals and conservatives alike agree on this role of government, even though they disagree on the parameters of such assistance—that is, as to the amount of money or as to the definition of worthy recipients. Indeed, for many conservatives, corporations and already wealthy individuals tend to figure as deserving of government largesse, as evidenced by corporate welfare and tax laws and tax cuts favorable to the rich. Libertarians, when they reject welfare, at least remain consistent in dismissing *both* social and corporate welfare.

Libertarian critiques of welfare spending do not really differ much from general libertarian critiques of government spending—that is, why should government officials know better than you and me how best to spend the money you and I have earned? As Isabel Paterson asks, "But if taxes are to be imposed for relief, who is the judge of what is possible or beneficial? It must be either the producers, the needy, or some third group."[43] What motivates government officials to function as better stewards of my money (or of God's money?!) than you or me? Where the challenge to this libertarian critique of welfare spending differs from the challenge to the similar libertarian critique of government spending in general is in the stakes. It is, perhaps, one thing to argue over the wisdom of government spending in commercial, business matters, or over which tax credits local, state, and federal governments offer for what sorts of projects. Yet even for those who understand in principle the libertarian critique of government spending, one question still nags when it comes to charitable or welfare spending: If a government *stops* providing such assistance, would people not just die? Would private charity really pick up the slack? Does government not need to function as a harbor of last resort?

The United States government, for instance, requires by law that any hospitals receiving federal funding provide treatment for all individuals, regardless of their ability to pay, and regardless of their citizenship status. In order to help pay for this "uncompensated care," the government provides extra funds to hospitals delivering such services. This is an example of what is meant by the "safety net." Imagine a situation in which the federal government did not help cover uncompensated care. Hospital administrators, in their allocation of more limited resources, might need to turn people away. And we are not talking about individuals showing up at the emergency room with routine and non-emergent conditions, such as strep throat. We are talking about true emergencies. Maybe some of us have read or watched too much dystopian science fiction, but is it all that difficult to imagine emergency room intake requiring proof of ability to pay before okaying the provision of treatment? Would people not die prematurely and unnecessarily by bleeding out or developing infections in untreated wounds?

Even outside of the hospital setting, with general medical care, what is to guarantee that individuals with minor ailments, curable with antibiotics, for example, would not die needlessly due to lack of ability to pay? One might suggest that private charity would step in to fill any gaps in the safety net caused by the absence of government funding. Yet, would they really do so? Would a safety net woven together by private charity alone do the job to prevent such death and much more non-fatal suffering? And even if we hope or think that it would do so, what if it failed to do so? As imperfect as the status quo might be, do we really want to engage in such a risky experiment?

It would seem to many people that private charity is simply not up to the challenge. Yet what if this *seems* the case only because government stepped into this area once dominated by private charity? Perhaps charitable giving and such things as mutual aid societies have declined as a result of government occupying this space in the socio-economic sphere? As Tom Palmer writes,

> In the case of welfare institutions, prior to their displacement by the welfare state, there was a remarkable proliferation of voluntary institutions to help people to deal with the problems of life, from the need for medical care during times of misfortune to a friendly hand up when life had gotten one down. Historians have documented the remarkable story of the "friendly societies" that provided such "mutual aid" before the welfare state crushed them. Such societies provided social solidarity, insurance against misfortune, moral support, and much more, all on a voluntary basis.[44]

If government stepped back out, libertarians might reason, the religious and cultural mutual aid societies and other charitable efforts would very well fill the hole—and much more efficiently so.

It is possible also that this account romanticizes an imagined (and perhaps never actualized) comprehensiveness to private charity, yet it no doubt remains true that various nineteenth and twentieth-century developments, such as industrialization and the growth of the state, have severely fractured traditional communities and communal organizations and organization. Such clearly describes well the fate of traditional Jewish communities in Europe. As Noam Zion summarizes, "What is important to note regarding the Jewish municipal *kuppa* is that it is granted legal power by the Jewish community to tax and distribute aid to the poor. Often this coercive authority was confirmed by the non-Jewish monarch in a charter." A *kuppa* is specifically a collection box, but here refers more broadly to the activities of local Jewish authorities to collect and distribute funds for the needy. As Zion notes, the power and legitimate authority of the communal leaders could be located in both the local Jewish community and in the non-Jewish authorities. Over the last two and a half centuries, this world largely came to an end, as Zion explains in his massive, three-volume and nearly 2,500-page-long opus on the history of tzedakah and social justice: "After the Emancipation, when Jews won citizenship in the 19th [century], their communities lost their judicial, legislative and civil-economic governmental functions, and therefore the tzedakah traditions to be studied in this book lost their legal force after almost 1800 years and maintain only their rhetorical moral power."[45] This loss of authority included the loss of coercive authority: "After the emancipation of the Jews in the 19th C., there was a radical transformation of the municipal Jewish government which lost their authority to legally coerce its 'members' to do anything including contribute to the tzedakah funds."[46] In brief, the modern world has broken down traditional, communal structures. Is the libertarian notion of a state wholly removed from the activities and responsibilities of taxing and using the wealth of its citizens to provide social welfare an impractical and impracticable dream, or is it not only possible but more just and more likely to succeed than the efforts of the modern welfare state? And, in any case, does "Judaism" endorse or dismiss the welfare state? Does it do neither? Or both?

Government Spending and the Welfare State in Jewish Thought

Returning once more to the possible biblical roots of Jewish taxation, Meir Tamari adds one more dimension to our understanding. As an economist and scholar of Jewish business ethics, Tamari sees in the biblical collection of half-shekel coins not simply an indirect means of taking a census but also the at least symbolic effect of bringing rich and poor together as equals in one society. In Tamari's characterization, although personal and voluntary charitable giving exists within Judaism and Jewish communities, a notion of collective responsibility led to the formalization and institutionalization of communal welfare efforts. Even without any sort of state of their own for close to two thousand years, Jewish communal leaders have taxed their communities in state-like ways:

> Perhaps the most Jewish of the underpinnings of taxation is the now universally accepted concept of society's responsibility for the needs of its members. One must bear in mind that the welfare state, with its publicly financed education, health care, and subsidies to the poor, is only a recent phenomenon amongst other nations. On the other hand, the Jewish provision of such services through the public purse, as opposed to relying on personal charity, dates back to antiquity. It must be stressed that the financing of these services bore all the hallmarks of government activity; that they were, in fact, undertaken by autonomous communities is

irrelevant. For the individual Jew, these communities had all the authority and power to tax and punish evasion that the state has today.[47]

Is Tamari on point in characterizing Jewish autonomous communities as, effectively, welfare states? Or, does this description go too far? And even if he is on point, does this necessarily mean the nongovernmental dimensions of autonomous communities are "irrelevant"?

Some scholars have distinguished between the welfare *state* and the welfare *society*. Alex Robertson explained this succinctly in 1988: "[A] welfare state is a 'legal state', in which entitlement to a range of goods is guaranteed by statutory rights. It is thus an essentially administrative entity. A welfare society, on the other hand, I take to be a social system in which welfare assumptions are an organic part of everyday life."[48] John J. Rodger elaborated upon this distinction in his 2000 book *From a Welfare State to a Welfare Society*, though pointedly contrasting two views of the matter. A modernist view sees the development in tandem of welfare state and societies, whereas an anti-modernist approach sees the two as at odds, with the welfare state emerging only out of the collapse of the welfare society and its presumably more intimate and bygone communal and familial life.[49] Given the distinction, one might suggest that Tamari's Jewish communities, though exercising administrative functions in the provision of welfare, look more like welfare societies recognized by the bonds of family and community.

Noam Zion would appear to disagree, or at least he describes a more nuanced arrangement. On the one hand, "Biblical welfare is still conducted by law, not merely by voluntary charity and neighborly help. In that sense the Biblical system of maintenance for the poor is closer to a welfare state with its legally mandated welfare, than a welfare society of voluntary gifts."[50] On the other hand, as Zion notes, this legal framework for welfare does not include the modern welfare state's administrative mechanisms for collection and enforcement, or for distribution for that matter. The autonomous Jewish communities—though not guided in their welfare efforts by a comprehensive legal code, nor providing a modern state system such as social security where all pay in and from which all receive benefits—nonetheless exercised authority over collection and distribution of funds for the poor. Whatever the relationship to the welfare state, both biblical and rabbinic frameworks include what we would understand as a welfare society:

> What is exemplary in the Jewish "welfare society" are private gifts of tzedakah to beggars, associations providing voluntary private aid, like free loans (Deuteronomy 15) or *g'machs*, sharing funds, services and goods, and the sharing of mutual brotherly help. Even the Rabbinic municipal welfare state is fully integrated within an extensive welfare society based on voluntary private *gemilut hasadim*, acts of lovingkindness, providing nonmonetary services for the ill, aged and needy as well as those marking happy life cycle rites.[51]

Perhaps, then, Jewish communities have often functioned as hybrids of the two models? Or, perhaps neither biblical nor later Jewish models quite fit the academic dichotomy between welfare society and state?

The Judaic studies scholar Michael Satlow offers some intriguing reflections upon how Jewish communities have addressed poverty over the centuries. He notes that whereas the modern state rationalizes, objectifies, and standardizes poor relief, likely making it fairer in its distribution, it also dehumanizes the recipients, as their needs and even they themselves become quantified. Satlow detects in Jewish history, by contrast, a shift *away* from this latter approach:

> While all early rabbinic texts are not in complete agreement about this, there is a gradual move over time from an objective definition of poverty to a subjective one. Medieval and recent rabbinic texts declare that when determining whether someone should be considered poor for the purpose of receiving communal support, the person's entire context should play a role.

Against the objectivizing inclination, "Jewish texts (or at least some of them) resist this move in ways that do not map easily onto our modern political approaches" taking "the full humanity of the poor into account, something that is very difficult if not impossible for large, state-scale programs to do." Satlow proposes another interesting idea, an idea one might say would address the question of whether or not a libertarian state would or could play absolutely no role in the provision of welfare. The modern welfare state also "reinforces a system designed to relegate responsibility for our poor to the 'government,' away from us. It turns poor relief in[to] a 'commons problem' that allows it to slip between the cracks as few want ownership of it." That is, intentionally or not, Satlow suggests, in line with a libertarian critique, that the welfare state—far from providing a comprehensive solution to the problem of poverty, a comprehensive solution unavailable without the power and reach of the state—decreases a sense of communal responsibility, creating holes in any government safety net. For libertarians who argue that we cannot assume private groups and individuals would not meet the needs of those in need, this idea perhaps only bolsters their case.[52]

Tamari does raise one other challenge to the thought that Jewish and libertarian approaches to charity and welfare could be compatible: "In Judaism, however, taxation was introduced as a manifestation of the concept of the rights of the community and of less fortunate individuals *in* the property of all the other individuals."[53] Take note of Tamari's phrasing, reminiscent of what we learned, in the previous chapter, from John Locke: "the rights . . . *in* the property" of others. To be clear, Tamari is declaring that *the poor in the Jewish community possess a right to the property of those who are not poor*, and that taxation of community members figures as a legitimate means of exercising this right. This solidly places Jewish care for the poor within the framework in which we do not entirely own the wealth we possess. If correct, such a formalized quasi-government assertion that people can hold property rights *in* what is ostensibly owned by other people would be abhorrent to libertarians.

Yet not all would necessarily concur with this depiction and this chasm between Judaism and libertarianism. Disagreeing with Jon Levenson, author of the essay "Poverty and the State in Biblical Thought," Noam Zion recalls that

> Jon Levenson argues that the Bible does *not* promote a "welfare *state*," but rather reflects fear of *any* centralized state and its unjust taxation system . . . [S]ocial justice is not the task of the urban elite led by the king, but by agricultural brothers. The people's desire for a monarch is portrayed by Samuel (I Samuel 8, 12) as a mistaken request of the people that will lead to the requisition of the lands and the drafting of the children of free holders. The taxes will not be used to support the poor but to finance war and ostentation that exacerbate poverty and exploitation.[54]

Any requirements of aiding the poor, by such means as the Jubilee year or the leaving of the corners of fields, figured as part of a nonstate society. Zion himself disagrees with Levenson's conclusion, writing that "It is the abuse of the state when too much power is centralized, not the idea of a state that arouses the prophetic critique."[55] And yet, in our discussion of rooting the right of state taxation in the first book of Samuel, we considered primarily the right to tax rather than the uses made of such power. In this regard, Levenson is not wrong to see that such taxation was not invoked or applied for the welfare of the people, let alone the poor and others in need.

Zion himself presents another provocative and significant idea in helping us understand the collection of funds for tzedakah and their expenditure. Lest we think the fact of such collection and distribution and the coercive authority of communal leaders in this regard is proof of Jewish support of the modern welfare state, this fact does not in itself provide justification for such a state's often much broader aims. "The Rabbis also collected tzedakah, if necessary, by legal coercion to guarantee the basic needs for all the poor, but they never envisioned condemning or confiscating the surpluses of the wealthy for the sake of establishing an equality of ownership of property among all citizens as a goal in itself."[56] Joseph Isaac Lifshitz notes that, according to the Talmud, such coercion applied to the wealthy alone and not to others, even when others were obligated to give charity. Furthermore, according to Lifshitz, some later authorities interpreted coercion to mean persuasion.[57] Either way, we do not have here a *universal* taxation, backed up by the authority of the state. In the rabbinic framework for tzedakah, the purpose remains limited rather than expansive. One does not see here clear evidence or justification for the modern welfare state.

In evaluating the notion of the welfare state in Jewish ideas and values and history, one critical distinction remains, the distinction between *legality* and *morality*. Sometimes we confuse the two, thinking that if something is morally good, we ought to codify and promote it through legal means—and that we ought to legalize against that which is morally bad. Yet is this the case? Ought it to be the case? Noam Zion writes descriptively that "The moral obligation incumbent on the individual is institutionalized collectively in the tzedakah system of every Jewish municipality, at least for subsistence support of basic needs."[58] Note the language of *moral* obligation. Much of what we have discussed about tzedakah has taken place in a moral context—and much charitable giving, Jewish or otherwise, takes place outside of a legal framework. Just because something is morally good—indeed, just because something is morally obligatory—does not necessarily mean we need governmental laws to enforce it. Communal norms and social pressures often prove quite effective at this. Although Judaism entails moral obligations, they remain fundamentally religious obligations, not automatically placed under the jurisdiction of the state. Even more so, there is no reason to think Jewish laws or values require that secular governments institutionalize such moral values in the specific form of the modern welfare state. It might be that Jewish theology and history would be quite compatible with a modern welfare state, yet for all the importance of justice and tzedakah as a form of justice in the Jewish tradition, this does not clearly equate with the modern welfare state. The general libertarian view on such matters is that laws should prevent only unwarranted aggression against someone, against his or her liberty. Otherwise, governments should stay out of legislating morality, whether in terms of speech or private sexual behavior or drug use. Or charitable giving. From this perspective, it is not the job of the law and not the responsibility of the state to prevent citizens from doing what is foolish or morally wrong or even unkind. For libertarians generally, such things ought not to be either proscribed or prescribed.

Finally, Lifshitz offers us one additional way to think about or to rethink the relationship between tzedakah and property ownership. "In Judaism, sovereign control over one's property is not conditional on giving charity. The opposite is true: The ability to give charity is conditional upon private wealth." In this sense, he echoes the distinction between legal and moral obligations and motivations: "Charity is a deed that flows from the strength of character rather than from the weakness of one's claim to property." The moral obligation upon the wealthy fails to create a legal right for those in need. In this way, he challenges the entire notion that the laws of tzedakah and the laws of providing for the poor serve as *limitations* on property ownership. "All the limitations placed by Jewish religious law on property rights are of a moral nature—they have no legal or monetary standing, and there is nothing in them that changes the legal definition of property rights." Instead of imagining that our charitable giving justifies our property ownership or that our ownership of private property is conditional upon acting charitably, Lifshitz conceives of a just society not as one that redistributes wealth from rich to poor, but rather as one that protects private property rights so that individuals can better carry out their moral obligations to help others.[59]

Despite the idea that donors of monies to those in need do not truly own the funds they disburse, and despite Tamari's explicit linking of Jewish notions of property rights with communal care for those in need, it remains unproven that all Jewish approaches to welfare must contradict all libertarian ones. In good part, this is due to the fact that Jewish communal efforts do not fit neatly into the model of the welfare state. As will become more clear in the chapter after next, it might very well prove to be the case that Jewish ideals, even when mandated, could take place within voluntary communities, that the example of required giving and lack of ownership do not necessarily entail the creation or endorsement of the welfare state or any state mechanism for providing care for those individuals in need.

Voluntary Taxation?

Earlier, we pointed to libertarian writers who suggested that in a fully libertarian polity citizens would voluntarily fund the government, and that the existence of a few noncontributors would not endanger a system of minimal government funding. In its platform, the Libertarian Party of the United States invokes such a system: "To the extent possible, we advocate that all public services be funded in a voluntary manner."[60] Could this actually work? And what might Jewish attitudes be like towards such an approach to raising funds?

The perhaps surprising answer to the first question is yes, it could work. How do we know? Can we find even one example of such a system? We can find one, and, interestingly, we can find it in recent Jewish history. We need look only to the decade or so prior to the declaration of Israel's statehood. The scholar Assaf Likhovski has described the situation:

> While compliance with British taxation was low, the Jewish community of Palestine established a system of autonomous voluntary taxes designed to finance Jewish military expenditures in face of the growing and often violent Arab opposition to Jewish presence in Palestine. At first, these

taxes were paid on a local basis, but in 1938, during the Arab rebellion of 1936–1939, a national organization was established, and progressive income and property taxes, as well as indirect taxes (collectively known as *Kofer ha-Yishuv*), were levied on the Jewish community. The revenue collected was used to finance the major Jewish militia, the *Haganah*, and also to support illegal Jewish immigration to Palestine from holocaust and post-holocaust Europe.

What distinguished this from regular charitable giving was clearly its organization on a national scale with levied, though presumably recommended, tax payment amounts. But how did it work? Outside of the existential threat, what motivated people to comply and pay the taxes levied upon them? "Special movies, slide shows, public conferences, lectures, exhibitions, direct letters, pamphlets, newspaper ads and articles all exhorted the Jews of Palestine to pay. Social ostracism of those who did not comply was utilized. Evaders were also prevented from using the services of Jewish community institutions (which provided health, housing and employment benefits)."[61]

A variety of educational and social means appears to have provided sufficient motivation. In the late 1950s, after the creation of the state and a decline in levels of taxpayer compliance, officials initiated a number of approaches to increasing compliance. These included rationalizing or making more scientific and efficient the entire process of assessment and collection. There was also an attempt to "train" people to act as good citizens:

> Another important method for creating compliance was tax education and propaganda, which was used to convince Israelis that when they paid taxes, they were paying themselves. Newspaper ads, explanatory pamphlets, public meetings with taxpayers, and organized tours of tax offices were employed. School materials were created seeking to familiarize secondary school students with the notion of taxation and instill compliance.[62]

In this we see a conscious, organized effort to create a "tax culture."

More interesting than the question of why people dodge taxes might be, in Likhovski's phrasing, the "major puzzle [in] the social-science literature" of why so many people in the West remain compliant and pay their taxes, especially with lax enforcement and low penalties? Perhaps the answer can be found in the Israeli case: the development of what scholars call a tax culture. Likhovski seeks to distinguish his analytic approach by focusing on historical factors rather than the more abstract dimensions of human psychology. For him, it was not simply something about human nature that explains tax compliance in the Israeli situation—or presumably in other situations—but instead particular historical and societal factors. And, for our understanding, we might suggest that if a tax culture can develop in certain circumstances, maybe a concerted effort to promote a tax culture could work, even on a national scale, even in a place such as the United States—where, after all, one might have expected much less compliance given a general laxity in enforcement and punishment.

Utilizing the concept of a tax culture, we might reasonably suggest that most Jewish communities, including the autonomous communities of Europe up until the Enlightenment, possessed such a culture. As Meir Tamari writes, "The religious and moral teachings of Judaism, however, created an ideological climate in which the individual's obligations to the communal well-being were constantly reiterated, so that they became an integral part of him."[63] This, after all is what we mean by enculturation, when a behavior comes to feel natural, even intuitive. Jewish communities have long functioned in this manner, with the sorts of inclinations and expectations that characterize a system of voluntary taxation, along with appropriate collection and distribution mechanisms.

Putting aside for the moment the important and daunting feature of national coordination, one might argue that many or most forms of charitable giving are akin to voluntary taxation, especially within the context of institutions or social groups or cohesive communities. To mention one example, an increasing number of synagogues appear to be abandoning fixed dues in favor of recommended and voluntary contributions. The writer James L. Payne insists that taxation is not the only way and not even the traditional way to raise money for public uses: "There is another way to raise public funds. It has been around for thousands of years, and until the twentieth-century love affair with government, it was the principal way money was raised for social purposes. It's called voluntarism." Payne then addresses the motivations, the reasons why most individuals in a society would take part in such a system:

Instead of using force, one collects money on a voluntary basis by offering donors a positive satisfaction in return for their contributions. In many cases, the satisfaction is that of fulfilling a high religious ideal or social duty. But voluntary giving can operate with mundane, personal motives as well. Vanity, for example, is a common impulse behind charitable giving. In ancient Greece, the desire to stand out and be well-thought-of undergirded an extensive philanthropic system called "liturgy." Wealthy, prominent citizens made public gifts of buildings, military equipment, bridges, plays, and festivals.[64]

There are many reasons to give money for public goods, and together they just might motivate enough people, with so-called "freeloaders" not amounting to a significant problem. Individuals would likely feel more positively about giving voluntarily and more in control when they do not experience their wealth as being taken coercively. And as Payne also notes, such an approach would likely lead to vast savings in money and time, as compliance with taxpaying absorbs countless hours of effort for individuals and businesses. Even if the voluntarily donated funds went to the government instead of private charities, the bureaucracy required to handle this would be streamlined compared to the current needs, in the United States for example, to assess, collect, police, investigate, and prosecute.

One might also consider another way that the entire system of tithing and returning land to the original owners and leaving produce for others to take might have been voluntary in an important sense, or at least not coercive. In the context of the ancient Near East, Joshua Berman characterizes the entire system of land and property we have discussed as part of a large system of mutual aid or social insurance, preventing "the permanent development of an indigent underclass," and thereby generating a kind of egalitarianism and warding off extreme disparities in wealth. In such a world economics cannot be separated from social and religious life and the norms of daily life, of membership in a community of mutual responsibility. "Acts we moderns perceive as altruism may well reflect a socially mandated norm and the economic wisdom of informal insurance." In a world of tribal bonds, having built-in means of resetting economic status provides economic and social insurance, ensuring that people do not become dependent without hope of living freely.[65]

Here, then, with this paradoxical notion of voluntary taxation, perhaps we can find a meeting point of libertarian and Jewish thought—and practice. That the historical example of Jewish communities taxing their members might provide grounding not for the modern welfare state of coercive taxation, but rather for the voluntary tax culture many libertarians envision. That Jewish ideas of tzedakah, if not opposed in principle to the modern welfare state, do not necessarily entail its support, let alone require its establishment. Despite our initial thought that libertarian and Jewish ideas of taxation and the provision of charity or welfare necessarily conflicted with each other, we must conclude otherwise: that they do not necessarily conflict, and that instead they might prove quite compatible.

Chapter 5

Government Tyranny versus Government Protection

> The protection of individual rights is the only proper purpose of government. Government is constitutionally limited so as to prevent the infringement of individual rights by the government itself.
> – Section 3.0 "Securing Liberty," *Libertarian Party Platform* (2018)

Taking together libertarian views on freedom, ownership, and taxation, we can see clearly the libertarian rejection of all or most government. From most libertarian perspectives, governments can do little, if anything, better than private citizens and organizations can. Libertarians tend to see even limited government as, at best, a necessary evil. By means of laws and by means of police and military force, libertarian government has a single purpose: to protect people from unwanted aggression, whether physical aggression or financial aggression (in the sense of confiscating property, violating contracts, and engaging in fraud, not in the sense of merely savvy business practices). Anything government does beyond this will likely be coercive and unnecessarily restrictive of human freedom.

This view of the vices of government and the relative virtues of limited government ought not to be confused with a conservative or right-wing position—for libertarians oppose not only redistribution of wealth for public benefits programs, but also for the purpose of corporate welfare, as well as for farm subsidies, and they reject trade protectionism and tariffs. In the nonfiscal realm, libertarians oppose government involvement in matters of morality, including what goes on in bedrooms and the privacy of homes. By contrast, social conservatives endorse governmental activity in the realm of personal behavior, and many or most traditional conservatives have little trouble supporting government aid to the wealthy and to corporations and business interests while at the same time decrying government spending on welfare and other such aid. Libertarians deserve credit for their consistency in opposing most or all government intrusions, whether in financial or social and cultural matters.

Have Jews traditionally shared this minimalist or anarchist view of government? Ought they to do so? In the United States, at least, a majority of Jews have long supported the Democratic Party and the general contours of the welfare state. No doubt, many Jews would base such support upon values of justice and kindness they find in Jewish traditions and texts. In light of this, can religiously observant Jews even contemplate supporting, let alone campaigning on, a libertarian vision of limited to no government? In answering this question, we first ought to consider the Jewish historical and textual evidence concerning the practice, experience, and evaluation of governments. Have Jews viewed governments positively or negatively? And, over the centuries, have they experienced governments positively or negatively?

Government Protection of the Jews

Jews have long known that rulers and governments can prove necessary and beneficial in a dangerous world. In *Pirkei Avot*, Rabbi Ḥanina (of the first century of the Common Era) warned that one should "Pray for the welfare of the government, for were it not for fear of it, people would swallow one another alive."[1] This is far from an enthusiastic endorsement of government, yet it nevertheless does recognize government's value and the preference for it over the likely alternative. As R. Marc Angel explains in his commentary on this teaching, "As an often endangered minority group, Jews have well understood that their security depended on the ability of governments to maintain stability, law, and order."[2] Jews have been helped by governments protecting minorities from those who would discriminate against them, or harm them physically, injuring or killing them. A nation of laws and good government—or in the case of nondemocratic government, a benevolent ruler—can protect Jews and others against the whims of antisemites and racists.

Despite the not unreasonable sense among many Israeli Jews and Jews worldwide that the regime in Iran in the first quarter of the twenty-first century has posed an existential threat to the state of Israel, it is nevertheless the case that historically Iran has proven rather hospitable to a large Jewish community. Although most Persian Jews and their immediate descendants now live in Israel and the United States, Iran's Jewish community still counts somewhere close to 10,000 individuals today, two decades into the twenty-first century. Jews have lived in Iran and Persia for millennia, since biblical times, the age of the prophets. The story of Purim takes place in Persia, and although the Jews faced the possibility of a genocide at the instigation of Haman, the evil councilor to the king, the situation became upended with the Jews receiving the monarch's protection. It is also related in the books of Ezra and Neḥemiah that the Persian king Cyrus the Great encouraged and aided financially the return of Jews to Jerusalem to rebuild the destroyed Temple. Of course, the intervening centuries have witnessed both periods of persecution and periods of protection, but Iranian Jews have tended to fare better than their sisters and brothers in the Arab states of the Middle East.[3] For some, the Purim story figures as a kind of archetype, of benevolent protection following a time of persecution.

Jews have resided in North Africa for thousands of years and in European lands for not quite as long a time, and Jewish populations in both areas have received protection from rulers at various levels at various times, allowing for flourishing between periods of persecution, including discrimination, deportation, and massacres. Without providing the varied details of the many different Jewish communities, one can still conclude that Jews have benefitted from and recognized the value of protection provided by rulers and their governments, and far too often they have experienced the absence of such protection.

The history of the Jews under the Nazis offers a case in point. Whether eagerly or under duress, the leaders of many European nations aided the Nazis in their efforts to annihilate the Jews. Yet one example stands out in contrast to this cooperation. Although it is likely only apocryphal that Denmark's King Christian X actually wore in public a Star of David on his clothes to show solidarity with Danish Jews, he at least voiced such a sentiment and did support financially the movement of Jews from Denmark to Sweden. Over 90 percent of Denmark's Jews were saved in this manner, and over 99 percent of Danish Jews survived the Nazis.

Of course, no survey, no matter how brief, of government protection of Jews would be complete without acknowledgement of the *goldene medina*, as many Jews once referred to the United States (and, apparently, to South Africa as well), this golden country promising opportunity and prosperity. For sure, Jews in the United States have never entirely escaped prejudice and violent antisemitic attacks, yet overall the country has provided a remarkably stable and extended period of tolerance and support. As George Washington wrote in his famous letter to the Jewish congregation in Newport, Rhode Island,

> It is now no more that toleration is spoken of as if it were the indulgence of one class of people that another enjoyed the exercise of their inherent natural rights, for, happily, the Government of the United States, which gives to bigotry no sanction, to persecution no assistance, requires only that they who live under its protection should demean themselves as good citizens in giving it on all occasions their effectual support....
>
> May the children of the stock of Abraham who dwell in this land continue to merit and enjoy the good will of the other inhabitants—while every one shall sit in safety under his own vine and fig tree and there shall be none to make him afraid.[4]

In the United States, Jews have experienced the freedom to practice unhindered their religion or to not practice it at all, as has rather frequently proven the case. Jews have participated in virtually all spheres and all levels of public and private life. If this is due in good part to the cultivation of a culture of tolerance, it is also due in no small part to the protection provided by national, state, and local governments and authorities. If there are still horrific attacks against Jews, including the October 2018 massacre of eleven Jews in a Pittsburgh synagogue, it has been the case that the United States government prosecutes the terrorist rather than persecuting his surviving victims.

Government Persecution and Neglect of the Jews

Above, we looked to R. Angel's explanation of the teaching from *Pirkei Avot* for the notion that Jews recognize the value of governments ensuring law and order. He does, however, qualify the imperative to pray for the welfare of the government. Such instruction applies only to *just* governments. After all, law and order do not, on principle alone, provide any guarantee of safety or protection. Indeed, the rise to power of Adolf Hitler and the Nazis took place within the legal framework of the Weimar Republic. Through elections and parliamentary coalitions, they attained power by legal means. And once in power, the Nazis persecuted the Jews and others within the law: "Laws were passed depriving Jews of all rights. It was legal to round up, imprison, and murder Jews. All those who participated in these heinous actions were following the law of the land!"[5] R. Ḥanina's aphorism cited above rightly notes the dangers of anarchy, of the absence of government and order, yet this does not exclude the possibility or reality of governments themselves proving dangerous, whether for Jews, other minorities, or entire populations under their rule. And, of course, R. Ḥanina shared his teaching long before our age and the spread of democratic governments. Monarchs too can provide order and security. And they can orchestrate or encourage or ignore disorder and chaos as well.

Where does one even begin? The persecutors of Jews paraded through biblical and ancient Jewish history: Egyptians; Ammonites; Amalekites; Babylonians; Greeks; Romans. Christian and Muslim rulers of the last two millennia have sometimes tolerated, often oppressed Jewish populations under their rule. On ostensibly religious missions from Europe to the Holy Land, the Crusaders murdered Jews on the way. For centuries, Jews and entire Jewish communities faced expulsion from their homes and lands, including from England for more than 350 years, from the end of the thirteenth century to the middle of the seventeenth. Centuries of a Jewish presence in Iberia came to a brutal end with the Inquisition.

In Eastern Europe in the late nineteenth and early twentieth centuries, in such places as Russia and Romania, antisemitism became encoded in laws and regulations and economic restrictions as official state policy.[6] Under Tsar Nicholas II, the Russian government provided financial support to anti-Jewish publications and sought to arrange pogroms and blood libels. This activist policy followed a period more aptly described as neglectful, beginning with mob-led pogroms in the 1880s. As the noted historian H. H. Ben-Sasson explains in his monumental volume *A History of the Jewish People*, "Those Jews who placed their trust in the protection of the authorities were helpless. . . . The authorities displayed total incompetence as well as an unwillingness to defend the Jews and, in several cases, as in Kiev, army units stood idly by while the rioters wrought havoc all around them."[7] In these cases and others, governments either encouraged or failed to prevent murderous attacks on Jews and Jewish communities.

Indeed, the flip side of government protection is not only or always government persecution. There is also the neglect, disinterest, and absence of government protection. Most notoriously, perhaps, this took place in the middle of the seventeenth century with the Khmelnitski massacres. In 1648 and 1649, Bogdan Khmelnitski led Cossacks against the Polish nobility and rioted against and murdered Jews in the process.[8] Historians have varied on their estimates of the number of Jews murdered during this period, but even the more recent and lower figures reach as high as ten or twenty thousand. The authorities did not or were not able to prevent this terrorism, destruction, and murder. Not too much later, the Ottoman Empire demonstrated its own ineffectiveness in protecting Jews: "In the second half of the seventeenth century there was a change for the worse in the status of the Jews. They continued to hold important positions in economic life, but the weakening of the rule of the sultans meant that the latter could not guarantee efficient protection."[9]

There have also been less violent threats to Jewish persons, though still targeted threats to Jewish ways of life. Turning to more recent years, one can see such danger for Jews, within a governmental legal framework, in Western democracies. Of course, there is no comparison to the legalized crimes of the Nazis or tsarist-sanctioned pogroms, but a different legalized sort of threat to Jewish communities can be found, for example, in efforts to ban circumcision and kosher slaughter. Despite the fact that no kosher slaughter had taken place in the country for at least a decade, in 2014 the government in Denmark felt compelled to ban the kosher slaughter of animals for food. More recently, two out of three Belgian regions have banned Jewish and Muslim ritual slaughter, with this ban coming into effect in Antwerp and the Flemish region on January 1, 2019. The professed issue is this: Claiming that stunning prior to slaughter makes animal slaughter more humane, some European authorities have focused on this technique, something prohibited according to the Jewish ritual practice. As of March 2018, the following nations mandated stunning: Denmark, Belgium, Iceland, Norway, Sweden, Slovenia, the two Belgian provinces, Switzerland, and Lichtenstein, with the last two allowing exceptions for poultry. Although one might at first wish to give advocates the benefit of the doubt, the fact of the matter is that such laws ignore the massive brutality perpetrated upon food animals during the entire period from birth up until slaughter. It is difficult to understand the enthusiasm for such a focus on Jewish and Muslim practices at the moment immediately prior to slaughter, while ignoring widespread animal cruelty perpetrated on animals day after day.[10]

In the end, we are left with a question: Ought we to understand the frequent failure of rulers and governments of various sorts to protect Jews as evidence of the value of stable government *or* as evidence that ruling powers have mostly proven bad for Jews? Should the history of the Crusades and the Khmelnitski massacres provoke Jews to embrace government in general as an ideal, or to embrace minimalist government as an ideal? The answer is not obvious. The history of government over Jews has swung across time and space like a pendulum, between the benefits of government protection on the one end and the persecution by and failure of government on the other side. So far, we have been discussing government protection and persecution in terms of basic physical security and survival, in matters of life and death, yet what about Jews and government and economic freedom and security?

Capitalism, the Free Market, and the Jews

In the words of the scholar Jerry Z. Muller, the Jews "have been particularly good at" capitalism. They have been so good at it that some wonder how it is possible so many Jews have supported and served in leadership roles in communist and socialist movements and even in less radical, liberal ones. More generally, the famed economist Milton Friedman (1912-2006) pondered how it could be that after World War II so many intellectuals in the West could favor collectivist ideologies and large governments. In his noted 1972 paper "Capitalism and the Jews," Friedman famously characterized this as a paradox, presenting the case of the Jews as a striking example:

> Two propositions can be readily demonstrated: first, the Jews owe an enormous debt to free enterprise and competitive capitalism; second, for at least the past century the Jews have been consistently opposed to capitalism and have done much on an ideological level to undermine it. How can these propositions be reconciled?

As a Jew supportive of capitalism, Friedman viewed himself as a member of *two* minority groups:

> I was led to examine this paradox partly for obvious personal reasons. Some of us are accustomed to being members of an intellectual minority, to being accused by fellow intellectuals of being reactionaries or apologists or just plain nuts. But those of us who are also Jewish are even more embattled, being regarded not only as intellectual deviants but also as traitors to a supposed cultural and national tradition.[11]

The word "traitors" is perhaps too emphatic a word here, but no doubt, among Jews who anchor in "Jewish values" their support for such things as large government and a strong welfare state, there have been and are many Jews who thereby do view Friedman and the like as advocating positions contrary to Jewish values and tradition. To such individuals, a religiously committed Jew promoting capitalism and severely limited government might appear puzzling, if not an oxymoron.

How do Friedman and others characterize the situation? They flip the identification of the traitors: to Friedman and like-minded critics, many or most Jews from the nineteenth through the twenty-first centuries have acted, in effect, as the equivalent of class traitors. That is, in much the same way that some liberals or leftists would criticize working-class citizens as voting against their own economic or class interests by supporting and voting for pro-business politicians seeking to lower taxes on the most wealthy individuals and creating a regressive tax burden hurting these very same working-class citizens, so have Friedman and others claimed that Jews have supported and voted for governments and policies harmful to their own best economic interests, which ought to be aligned with free market capitalism, by means of which so many

Jews have prospered. According to Friedman, "Except for the sporadic protection of individual monarchs to whom they were useful, Jews have seldom benefited from governmental intervention on their behalf."[12] Why would they seek to inflict harm upon themselves? Why not, on the contrary, aim to expand such beneficial methods in order to increase prosperity for more and more individuals?

Writing of the Jewish intellectuals entranced by socialism and Marxism and such ideologies in the 1930s, Irving Kristol expressed the following thought many decades later, at the close of the twentieth century: "In Israel as well as in America, Jews to this day continue to combine an almost pathologically intense concern for politics with a seemingly equally intense inclination towards political foolishness, often crossing over into the realm of the politically suicidal. How is one to understand this very odd Jewish condition—the political stupidity of Jews?" In Kristol's understanding, the problem arises out of the fact that Jews went stateless for so many centuries. The consequence of this was a lack of experience in the realms of foreign policy and political relations and a corresponding and naïve embrace of utopian universalism. "But ultimately it is just one more variant of the universal humanism which was the unofficial religion of the Enlightenment—to which Jews, lacking a realistic political tradition, were especially susceptible, and still are. In the United States, as well as in certain circles in Israel, such a universal humanism has acquired the status of a quintessentially Jewish belief." That is, such universalism has become almost a religion for many Jews, and, in the view of Kristol, a religion not particularly amenable to an age of nation states and their political relations.[13]

In seeking to remove "the exploration of Jews and capitalism" from the hands of the "apologists, ideologues, and anti-Semites," Jerry Muller offers a more nuanced account of the history of Jews and capitalism, looking to "patterns in modern history that tend to be neglected by social scientists" to explain that Jews have done fairly well under capitalism, and that Jews have opposed capitalism, but for various reasons—"the stuff of economic history as well as of social history, of political history as well as cultural history, of the history of business, but also of the family and the nation-state"—and *not* from anything inherent in Jewish tradition.[14] In other words, neither Milton Friedman and his allies nor their critics are justified in describing the other as traitorous to some true Jewish ideal.

In the words of the philosopher Marilyn Friedman (presumably, no relation), "Jewish teachings show no necessary incompatibility with the basic tenets of either socialism or welfare-state capitalism. My conclusion is that we should not take the compatibility of Jewish religious belief with free-enterprise philosophy as evidence that free-enterprise philosophy is *uniquely* suited to the world-view of a person of Jewish origin."[15] To adapt this slightly to our concerns, even if Jewish thought is compatible with libertarian thought, this does not mean the former is necessarily incompatible with all other political philosophies. R. Jonathan Sacks would appear to concur: "It would be quite wrong to identify a great religious tradition with any particular set of economic institutions."[16]

Perhaps the question in the early twenty-first century ought to be this one: Which accusations of aberrant, traitorous commitments are most in need of *correcting*? Although clearly committed Jewish libertarians and other capitalist or politically conservative Jews ought to understand that there exist plenty of good reasons—historical, sociological, and philosophical—why other Jews might adopt anti-capitalist or pro-capitalist liberal, progressive, or more radical orientations, why they might endorse a strong welfare state, it is likely the case that the inverse situation requires greater balancing. That many more Jews of the latter perspective mistakenly view the Western liberal welfare state as the *only* type of government consistent with what they take to be Jewish values, whether such individuals remain religiously observant to some degree or not at all. No doubt, however, both myths demand demystifying—and perhaps some of this work has been carried out in these pages.

Dina d'Malkhuta Dina, or the Law of the Land is the Law

Of the later rabbinic authorities, those teaching and writing after the talmudic era, none has ever managed to find a biblical source for what has become a strikingly important point of Jewish law: *dina d'malkhuta dina*, the law of the land is the law. That, in some important sense, Jews must obey the laws of the place in which they live, even in some cases where such laws might contradict Jewish religious law. Actually, a literal translation of the term would be the law of the *kingdom* is the law. And according to Rabbi Aaron Rakefet-Rothkoff, the term "is more meaningfully paraphrased as 'the law of the non-Jewish government is the law.'"[17]

Whether or not it nevertheless applies to the modern state of Israel is another matter.[18]

The principle was first proclaimed by Mar Shmuel (180–257), who lived in Babylon during the third century of the Common Era. As R. Isaac Herzog summarizes, "It cannot be traced to an earlier source, nor is there any indication of the ultimate source or authority for this far-reaching maxim . . . nor is the question as to source, or authority, anywhere raised in the *Talmud*."[19] The Talmud cites the precept in Mar Shmuel's name in four different locations.[20] In one case, it concerns divorce, sales, and gifts; in two cases it concerns (not) deceiving tax collectors; in the final case it concerns the purchase of property. The first case, the original teaching from the Mishnah, declares that documents produced by non-Jewish courts are valid, even if the documents bear the signatures of non-Jews; there does appear to be disagreement as to whether this applies to all documents or excludes bills of divorce and documents freeing slaves. One suggestion is that the signatures themselves are from laypersons and not officers of the court. Another suggestion is that in the case of a sale, the court document merely registers a transaction that has taken place rather than effecting the transaction itself. A problem remains with gifts, as clearly the documents themselves effect the transfer of the gifts. For this Mar Shmuel is invoked, that court documents for such gifts remain valid, because of *dina d'malkhuta dina*, and the Talmud does not appear to challenge this claim.

The next two cases are no doubt interesting in our days, as to the horror of many, there have been cases of Jews, who claim to be religiously devout and look the part, being convicted and imprisoned for tax fraud or other sorts of fraudulent actions against the government. In these cases, Mar Shmuel is again called upon to establish that Jews *cannot* deceive tax or customs collectors, because the law of the kingdom is the law. The Talmud offers one important modification: that Shmuel's principle applies only to duly authorized tax collectors who collect specified amounts but does not apply to self-appointed tax collectors or collectors who set amounts arbitrarily. Therefore, where the tax collectors are legitimate representatives of a legitimate government, Jews must obey the law of the land and pay their taxes. Certainly, the United States and probably most nations today figure as such legitimate cases, leaving no grounds for tax evasion.

The final case figures as perhaps the most intriguing of the group. As we discussed in the earlier chapter on property ownership, the issue here is that according to Jewish law, ownership generally requires the physical taking of possession of the property, whereas in many legal systems, a signed contract causes the transfer of ownership. What happens, then, when such a contract is approved by a non-Jewish court, and yet prior to the Jewish purchaser taking physical possession of the property, another Jew does so, by working a parcel of land, for instance? Does this other individual become the owner, or does the purchaser become the owner? If the law of the land requires a contract, how can the nonpurchaser individual own it? And yet if Jewish law requires physical acquisition, how can the purchaser own it? Does *dina d'malkhuta dina* mean that the contract remains valid even though it does not follow Jewish laws for the transfer of ownership? The examples provided in the talmudic discussion do not offer complete clarity in the matter.

In any case, these four cases provide the context and known beginnings of this concept, a concept critical for how religiously observant Jews ought to behave when Jewish law and secular law clash. If the principle is simple and seemingly sensible and practical, it is nonetheless stunning. True, it makes sense that Jews ought to obey the laws of the secular states in which they reside. The alternative would prove chaotic and impractical, as organized polities cannot function with selective observance of the law, whether by subgroups of the larger population or by individuals. Jews would likely earn and deserve reputations as bad and disloyal citizens, causing ḥillul Ha-Shem, the desecration of God's name (as they do in our days when caught and tried and convicted for such crimes as tax evasion and tax fraud).[21] And yet, what if such laws explicitly contradict Jewish laws, whether set down in the Bible or elaborated later by the rabbis? How can one suggest that the rules of secular sovereigns could ever supplant those ordained by God? On what grounds? And to what degree?

Rabbis and others have long debated the extent of the application of the rule that the law of the land is the law. Despite the differences of opinion in this regard, all agree that the rule does *not* apply universally, particularly not applying to ritual matters. That is, the rule does not require that Jews obey a law prohibiting circumcision, or a law requiring Jews to consume nonkosher food. Rather, the opposite: Jews would be obligated to disobey such laws. As R. Rakefet-Rothkoff summarizes,

> The Talmud and all related literature clearly states that this maxim is confined to aspects of *dinei mammonot*, i.e., to the monetary, civil, and real-estate laws of the Jewish legal system. Only those statutes may be waived when contravened by the prevailing non-Jewish secular legal system. However, issues of *issura*, i.e., rituals such as *kashrut* or Sabbath observance, are not subject to convention, or waiver.[22]

Basically, then, the principle remains limited to financial matters, and to the fair administration of relevant laws and regulations, as "the laws must be just, equitable, and applicable, to all citizens and residents of the state."[23]

Where later authorities do seek to understand the justification for the principle, some look to something akin to social contract theory, others to the legitimacy of monarchs. Our question is whether or not the principle makes any difference in understanding if religiously observant Jews could accept living in a libertarian polity? In terms of financial matters, obeying the monetary laws of the state—for libertarians, the minimal laws of the state—the principle should *not* provide any obstacle, as it would not within many other systems, whether democratic or not. And in terms of matters of *issura*, the permitted and forbidden of ritual law, a libertarian-leaning government would likely offer less interference than most other types of government. We can find no reason why *dina d'malkhuta dina* ought to exclude such an arrangement, and therefore no reason why a religiously observant Jew could not, at least in this one, particular regard, run for office promoting in good faith a libertarian approach to government.

The Politics of the Hebrew Scriptures

A number of modern-day thinkers have shared their understandings and their theories of politics embedded in or embodied by the holy Jewish texts, the five books of Moses, and the prophetic and other books. Spoiler: they are not all in agreement. The question for us remains one for the potential Jewish libertarian candidate for office: What vision or visions, if any, do the Hebrew scriptures provide of ideal or legitimate government organization? Do they prescribe any such ideal model of government? Do they proscribe or rule out any such models?

Michael Walzer serves as the undisputed dean of the field, with decades of writings on justice and politics, both general and Jewish. He has served as one of the editors of the massive set of three volumes (with a planned fourth one) examining the "Jewish Political Tradition," and among the books he has authored is *In God's Shadow: Politics in the Hebrew Bible*. Although Walzer sees in ancient Israel some democratic features, or perhaps inclinations—a kind of consent embedded in the notion of covenant and a kind of equality in the covenant's inclusion of all members of the community, and even strangers living in the midst of the community—he does not see any sort of explicitly democratic politics. That is, despite such democratic leanings and despite moral and religious teachings, the Hebrew scriptures do not specify a particular form of government: "Which of the regimes described in the histories is the authentic biblical regime—the kingship of God? the kingship of (Davidic) kings? the priestly kingdom? the mixed government of kings, judges, priests, and prophets suggested by Deuteronomy 16-18?" The only political teaching Walzer can identify is one that deems *unimportant* the relationship between rulers and those they rule. The only truly important relationship is between God and Israel, and this is simply not a political relationship. He writes: "This indifference might simply leave politics free, open to prudential and pragmatic determinism. Indeed, pious men and women have a biblical license to consider institutional alternatives without reference to religious doctrine." Although the ancient texts detail "what political leaders, whoever they are, ought to do," they do not appear interested in *how* leadership and government are organized.[24] One suspects, therefore, that the esteemed Michael Walzer would offer no objection to, or find no theological contradiction in, religiously observant Jews running for political office as libertarians.

In their book *The Beginning of Politics: Power in the Biblical Book of Samuel*, Moshe Halbertal and Stephen Holmes take Walzer's ideas in something of a novel direction. If they agree that the Hebrew scriptures do not specify a single type of government, they also do not think the texts remained wholly uninterested in politics. Rather, they see in the book of Samuel the creation of politics as an entirely new, previously unknown realm. Halbertal and Holmes argue that we find here a rejection of two theses: the more ancient notion that an earthly king was a god, and the more recent notion, evident in the book of Judges, that God is King. The book of Samuel eclipses the latter orientation by removing God's sovereignty over political matters and placing such matters instead into the hands of a king who is *not* God. Politics is thus a realm of human sovereignty, and if the text does not delineate the proper or ideal form of political rule and organization, it certainly takes an interest in politics, giving birth to it.[25]

In the first volume of *The Jewish Political Tradition*, edited by Michael Walzer, Noam J. Zohar, and Menachem Lorberbaum, the last of these three likewise writes of a split between the divine realm and the human realm, with religious law belonging to the former and secular politics belonging to the latter. "Politics is recognized as a nontheocratic, this-worldly activity geared to the better ordering of human society . . . and human beings are recognized as competent political agents." Although the division between the two realms opens up a space for human action and leadership and also protects against tyrannical leaders seeking to root their authority in divine law, this separation of religious and secular also requires a sacrifice: "the ideal of an all-encompassing divine law."[26] That is, perhaps something is lost in giving up on the possibility of a fully divinely ordered world. And perhaps out of this loss has sprouted the notion of infusing with religious and spiritual meaning all parts of our lives, including the seemingly "secular" pursuits such as work?

R. Aryeh Klapper delves deeply into these matters, considering the biblical and prophetic texts as well as later rabbinic commentary on these. Unsurprisingly, a variety of views emerge over the centuries. Looking at the second chapter of Mishnah Sanhedrin, he takes the rabbis to understand the rules laid out in Deuteronomy as producing ineffective government. Given the much less desirable alternative of anarchy, the rabbis react by "deemphasiz[ing the] restrictions" on the monarch and thereby "develop a concept of royal dignity nowhere mentioned in that text." Without rejecting any of the "cautions and concerns" evident in Deuteronomy, the rabbis manage to elevate the position of the king, presumably to encourage more effective governance. Centuries later, a group of commentators known as the Tosafists respond to the Talmud's examination of Mishnah Sanhedrin and of the rules set out in Samuel by aiming to restrain unlimited power. In considering, from the second book of Kings, the case of King Ahab seeking to purchase and possibly confiscate the vineyard of Nabot, R. Klapper understands the Tosafists to be reasoning that the monarch had the right to take land for state purposes but not for his personal use (perhaps reminiscent of Locke's previously noted distinction between absolute and arbitrary power). They further propose that a monarch can confiscate purchased fields though not hereditary ones. R. Klapper comments, "This passage seems interested in providing a society of free landowners, and may very well be a reaction to the manner in which Joseph increased the power of the Egyptian monarchy. Read this way, it provides at least an ideological rejection of absolutism." R. Klapper reviews commentary from Maimonides and concludes with a consideration of Rabbi Zvi Hirsch Chajes (1805–1855), writing in the nineteenth century, who suggests a kind of social contract between the people and the monarch, a contract that is not absolute and is revocable.[27]

Presenting a contrary view to those of Walzer, Halbertal, Holmes, Lorberbaum, and R. Klapper is the scholar Yoram Hazony, who argues that the Hebrew scriptures actually do present a clear political teaching. Hazony identifies what he calls a "consistent political theory," that of limited government for a single nation. He sees in the holy texts a rejection of both the "imperial state" and "political anarchy." Whether in the form of the oppressive Egyptian regime and God's approval of rebellion against it, or in the form of Israelite monarchs who abuse their positions with their expansive appetites, Hazony finds a biblical critique of broad state power: "Of course, restraining the appetites of the state means restraining the appetites of the rulers, and the narrative emphasizes that this problem is not one that is unique to monarchy. It haunts all political leadership." And in the rejection, in the book of Judges, of a world in which individuals did "that which was right in [their] own eyes," some sort of a state, in this case a monarchy, became necessary. Not necessarily ideal, but certainly necessary. For Hazony, there is a scripturally approved form of government: "The Hebrew Bible thus endorses the integrity of a single, limited state as preferable both to anarchical order and to the imperial state. This limited, national state, in which the king will be chosen from among the people and will be one of them in spirit, is in fact the biblical ideal." Though an ideal, it remains one "suspended at the midpoint between two competing evils." Although Hazony's emphasis on nationalism may set it apart, overall this sounds very much like a notion amenable to a libertarian spirit.[28]

We find in Rabbi Dr. Philip Z. Maymin one writer insisting that the Hebrew scriptures promote not merely a political teaching, but a specifically libertarian one. In order to make such a case, Maymin needs to overcome the obstacles of some clearly nonlibertarian biblical rules and accounts, such as the stoning to death of a Sabbath violator. Maymin's strategy, not entirely unlike what we have described elsewhere in this section, is to distinguish between divine and human jurisdiction over various matters. Maymin then argues that in all cases where *human* jurisdiction holds sway, we find a libertarian orientation: "An examination of the types of commandments based on whether they are interpersonal commandments or holy commandments shows that the interpersonal ones seem to be primarily libertarian while the holy ones are not necessarily so." Aside from religious matters and divine punishment, the Torah tells a story of free will and liberation from slavery. Maymin insists that

> in contrast to the possible anarchy that could result from a total lack of structure, significant laws are established that seem on the whole to support and enforce individual ownership rights, including a commandment to establish and maintain a legal court system.
>
> These concepts of liberty, self-government, autonomy, property, sovereignty, and an independent judiciary are the hallmarks of libertarianism.

In this way, in seeing these ideas in the text and in bracketing off "holy" matters, Maymin argues that the Torah figures as the "quintessential libertarian text."[29]

In his important and riveting book *Created Equal: How the Bible Broke with Ancient Political Thought*, the Bible scholar Joshua Berman places the biblical covenant between God and the people of Israel in the context of other treaties in the ancient Near East and presents an account quite unlike the others we have described.[30] While not speaking specifically about libertarianism, Berman's analysis of the God-Israel covenant reveals dimensions that somehow seem, at one and the same time, both antithetical to and harmonious with modern libertarianism. He describes a framework of laws and values aimed to produce a certain kind of egalitarianism, to promote solidarity not only on a tribal level, but a national one as well, to prevent extremes of wealth and poverty through a sort of mutual aid and insurance. His account does not readily provide an answer to the question of whether the Torah promotes a libertarian polity. Trying to answer such a question while reading Berman's account can be confusing, like looking at one of those drawings, such as that of the young woman and the old woman, that can be seen in two ways—yet not at the same time; one must flip back and forth.

In some ways, the society he describes looks entirely foreign to a libertarian sensibility, with a system designed intentionally to create a more or less egalitarian society, with controls—such as the cancellation of debts and the freeing of indentured servants and obligatory gifts to the poor—helping to bring this about. And yet, the entire enterprise also forces a diminishment of centralized political power, with any mortal king wielding rather restricted powers, and this certainly resonates positively with a libertarian orientation. "It is a system that rejects both statism and feudalism. . . . Absent a strong, centralized monarchical bureaucracy within the narrated world of the Pentateuch, the sovereignty of God is left unmitigated, unrefracted. All land, all persons are under His direct sovereignty."[31] Even the very measures meant to produce egalitarianism do so not through a state-like structure but rather through something that functions much more like a mutual aid society, a kind of social insurance not at all antithetical to libertarianism. And although one might have thought the absence of a strong earthly monarchy would partially eclipse divine authority, Berman tells us that the opposite is the case, that the perceived power and honor of gods and earthly kings bolstered and reinforced each other, making the weak monarchy of biblical thought all the more odd.[32] In this regard, perhaps the most striking insight Berman advances is that whereas in general the treaties of the time and region were between a king and a subservient vassal king, the biblical covenant appears to govern the relationship between God and all Israelite men, the "common man," as if each and every one existed as a vassal king. Not even Moses, the greatest prophet in Judaism, served as a king on behalf of the Jewish people.[33] In the end, reading Berman's account, probably one would not describe the Torah as the "quintessential libertarian text," though neither would one describe it as the opposite. It enters the scene from an entirely different angle.

Jews, Libertarianism, and Government

Can one identify *any* necessary relationship between Jews and government? Anything certain from Jewish texts and Jewish history concerning what role government ought to play in our lives?

As we have seen, Jewish history reveals a rather mixed story—sometimes positive, sometimes negative—of the relationship between Jews and the governments under which they have lived. Jews have experienced, in varied times and places, both government protection and government persecution. *Dina d'malkhuta dina* has played some role in maintaining flexible relations with and attitudes to various sorts of rulers and governments. One might even suggest that the principle allows Jews to accept a libertarian polity, but also many other just arrangements. And what about the Hebrew scriptures? Do they demand or even recommend any particular form of government? Do they at least rule out unjust governments, ones engaged in coercion of the people under their rule, for example? Or, do these ancient writings do something rather unexpected and make room for a secular politics of various sorts?

As with our other examinations, our discussion here neither demonstrates nor dismisses conclusively a fundamental connection between Jewish and libertarian ideas. Nothing we have learned in this chapter would necessarily disqualify a religiously committed Jew from running for office as a libertarian candidate. In the next chapter, the last chapter, we will go beyond government to consider ideas of community and individualism. Will we, perhaps, encounter an essential conflict there?

Chapter 6

Individualism versus Community

> Libertarians support free markets. We defend the right of individuals to form corporations, cooperatives and other types of entities based on voluntary association.
> We encourage certifications by voluntary associations of professionals.
> Section 2.8 "Marketplace Freedom and Section";
> "2.9 Licensing," *Libertarian Party Platform* (2018)

Our last obstacle, our one remaining challenge, is that of the apparent conflict between Judaism and libertarianism over the valuing or devaluing of individualism and community. At first blush, we might presume that Judaism favors the latter and devalues the former, whereas libertarianism champions the former and holds the latter in contempt. Such a first blush will prove unwarranted.

Libertarianism and Individualism

If we imagine that libertarianism is all about *me*, the individual, the self-made man or woman, we might turn first to Ayn Rand, who based her entire worldview on almost a worship of the self. As we noted earlier, she even titled one of her books *The Virtue of Selfishness*. Rand argued that not only is egoism rational, but that it is the *only* rational way to approach the world, that self-sacrifice is fundamentally irrational, and also—or perhaps thereby—immoral. She writes:

The moral purpose of a man's life is the achievement of his own happiness. This does not mean that he is indifferent to all men, that human life is of no value to him and that he has no reason to help others in an emergency. But it *does* mean that he does not subordinate his life to the welfare of others, that he does not sacrifice himself to their needs, that the relief of their suffering is not his primary concern, that any help he gives is an *exception*, not a rule, an act of generosity, not of moral duty, that it is *marginal* and *incidental*—as disasters are marginal and incidental in the course of human existence—and that values, not disasters, are the goal, the first concern and the motive power of his life.[1]

Yet, most human beings do live their lives, at least in part (and not only out of religious commitment), for the sake of other human beings—most notably, their own children.

Rand's view echoes the American myth of the rugged individual against the world, the idea that each person creates himself or herself through willful acts, without the need of other people or societal infrastructure. Such is evident in Rand's novels, in such characters as *The Fountainhead*'s Howard Roark and Dagny Taggart and in John Galt of *Atlas Shrugged*. Galt even proffers an oath, engraved in granite: "I swear, by my life and my love of it, that I will never live for the sake of another man, nor ask another man to live for mine."[2] As Galt's oath implies, Rand finds detestable such an attitude and behavior, living for the sake of others.

Now, most libertarians do *not* identify as Randians or as Objectivists, the appellation for those subscribing to Rand's overall philosophical worldview, which she dubbed Objectivism (and, for that matter, Rand herself did not identify as a libertarian).[3] And very few libertarians would consider immoral the making of sacrifices for others. As David Boaz quips, "When I hear communitarians like [Amitai] Etzioni describe the libertarian view of individualism, I wonder if they've ever read any libertarian writing other than a Classic Comics edition of Ayn Rand."[4] Nevertheless, one recognizes that self-ownership, the dignity of the individual, and individualism figure as central libertarian values. Writing elsewhere, Boaz presents individualism as the first of nine key concepts of libertarianism:

Libertarians see the individual as the basic unit of social analysis. Only individuals make choices and are responsible for their actions. Libertarian thought emphasizes the dignity of each individual, which entails both rights and responsibility. The progressive extension of dignity to more people—to women, to people of different religions and different races—is one of the great libertarian triumphs of the Western world.[5]

For the development of the modern notion of individualism, Boaz points to the likes of John Locke and John Stuart Mill, Thomas Paine and Thomas Jefferson, and also to abolitionists and early feminists, such as Frederick Douglass and Mary Wollstonecraft, respectively, and the sisters Sarah and Angelina Grimké in merging the two movements.[6] Boaz sees abolitionism, women's rights, and gay and lesbian rights as fully within the libertarian tradition.

For libertarians, "the dignity of the individual" are not empty words or merely a nice-sounding slogan. There is content to the notion. Libertarians ground their outlook in respect for individuals—in their ability to make choices, in their responsibility to make decisions. The rejection of all or much of government is not merely over the issues of aggression, taxation, and coercion, but out of a conviction that government activity often denies individuals their ability to make decisions for themselves and thus robs them of their dignity.[7]

John Stuart Mill (1806–1873) expressed eloquently what many libertarians and others value about individualism:

> A person whose desires and impulses are his own—are the expression of his own nature, as it has been developed and modified by his own culture—is said to have character. One whose desires and impulses are not his own, has no character, no more than a steam-engine has a character. . . . It is not by wearing down into uniformity all that is individual in themselves, but by cultivating it and calling it forth, within the limits imposed by the rights and interests of others, that human beings become a noble and beautiful object of contemplation.[8]

Mill makes the point that there do exist limits upon the expression of individuality, but these limits are generated only by the individual rights of others.

The 2018 *Libertarian Party Platform* refers to the *individual* or *individuals* forty times, usually in the context of rights and their protection. Following the Preamble, the first section of the platform is devoted to Personal Liberty. Not simply liberty in general, but the freedom of the individual:

> Individuals are inherently free to make choices for themselves and must accept responsibility for the consequences of the choices they make. Our support of an individual's right to make choices in life does not mean that we necessarily approve or disapprove of those choices. No individual, group, or government may rightly initiate force against any other individual, group, or government. Libertarians reject the notion that groups have inherent rights. We support the rights of the smallest minority, the individual.[9]

The individual as a minority of one is deserving of protection against others, whether other individuals, groups, or the government itself.

For libertarians, government exists to protect individuals, their rights and property, and not to promote some individuals or groups or interests over others. Not to protect groups at all, save in the sense that groups are associations of individuals.

Judaism and Community

In seeming contrast to the holding of individualism sacred on the part of libertarians, Jewish thought prizes community as a sacred value. The Jewish people started as a family, expanded into tribes, and became forged into a nation in its decades-long journey from Egyptian slavery to freedom in its Promised Land. In Jewish tradition, the Torah contains 613 commandments, and although one will not likely discover two identical lists of the 613, what all lists share is the fact that no individual Jew can observe all 613. And this is not due to any deficiency of effort or character, nor of any lack of time. Rather, some commandments are limited to the priestly class, the Kohanim, and some can be performed only in the land of Israel. Some can be undertaken only by farmers, others by people engaged in business transactions. In general, minors are not obligated in the performance of the commandments, because only upon reaching the age of Bar Mitzvah or Bat Mitzvah, literally the Son of Commandment and the Daughter of Commandment, does a Jew become so obligated. In short, it takes the entire community to observe and fulfill the entire Torah.

Jewish community does not end, however, with the practical necessity of an entire community to observe the full complement of commandments. For many, the people of Israel form a single entity in a spiritual sense. R. Joseph B. Soloveitchik, the foremost Modern Orthodox thinker and rabbinic leader in the United States in the twentieth century, wrote that "The community is not just an assembly of people who work together for their mutual benefit, but a metaphysical entity, an individuality; I might say, a living whole." In his understanding, God promised and gave the land of Israel *not* to the collection of individual Jews, but rather to *knesset Yisrael*, the Jewish community as "a distinct juridic metaphysical person."[10] Mystics have characterized this unity as akin to a body: "When a single Jew sins, it is not he alone who suffers, but the entire Jewish people." In this sense, the actions of individual Jews affect the spiritual health of the entire people.[11]

There is a further, practical import to this notion of a mystical or metaphysical unity of the people: we are responsible for one another. As is quoted in a number of places in rabbinic literature, *Kol Yisrael areivim ze la-ze* (or, alternatively, *ze ba-ze*), All of Israel are responsible for one another.[12] Here is how the perennially eloquent R. Jonathan Sacks describes this:

> The governing assumption throughout the Hebrew Bible is that when Israel is rewarded, it is rewarded collectively. When it is punished, it is punished collectively. It experiences fate as a people. Judaism is a collective faith whose central experiences are not private but communal. Jews pray together. They mourn together. On the Day of Atonement they confess together. The idea that 'All Israel are responsible for one another' is presupposed by every syllable of Judaism.[13]

The sense of responsibility suggested by the rabbis is one of guarantorship, as if we are all cosigners on each other's loans. Although the rabbis mean to characterize mutual responsibility within the Jewish community, Rabbi Aryeh Kaplan extends this responsibility: "Each Jew's moral responsibility extends beyond the Jewish people to the entire human race, as moral corruption in any place affects the entire world."[14] The notion of serving as cosigners on a contract such as a loan can be applied as well to the relationship between the Jews and God.

As scholars of the ancient Near East have observed, the Torah is a contractual document, in some ways similar to other contractual documents of that ancient period and place. As Michael Satlow explains, "The several covenants in the Torah are largely modeled on contemporary sovereign-vassal treaties of the Ancient Near East: Israel pledges its loyalty to God and God defends Israel."[15] At Mount Sinai, in the view of Jews, the nation sealed a covenant with God. Not that each individual entered into a separate covenant with God, but that the entire community did so—and not merely the community at the foot of the mountain on that particular day. In the words of Moses: "And not with you, you alone, do I make this covenant, and this oath, but with those who are here, who stand with us today before the Lord our God, and with those who are not here with us today." (Deut. 29:13–14) According to tradition, Jews not present, not yet born, would be bound by the covenant agreed to by their ancestors. This is understood in different ways, with some saying that the souls of all Jews, even those to be born centuries later, were present at Mount Sinai.

In one famous midrashic account, God raises Mount Sinai into the air, holds it over the assembled Hebrews, and offers an ultimatum: accept the covenant or this will become your grave.[16] Not only are future members of the community bound to the covenant, but those present appear to have been coerced. Usually, one does not take such a midrash literally, so what lesson might the rabbis have been seeking to teach? Maybe that, if the Sinaitic covenant would bring freedom, as discussed in an earlier chapter, then it would be a kind of suicide to reject it. Or, if the Torah is taken as akin to a tree of life, then to reject it would be to welcome death. Another explanation points to the fact that the midrash characterizes the situation in terms of God holding an inverted barrel over the people—and whereas a dropped mountain would crush anyone underneath, a barrel would enclose them instead. Perhaps as a tomb would enclose, and perhaps death in the sense of cutting off.[17] Regardless, the tradition does provide a corrective of sorts to the problem of involuntary commitment to the covenant: that at the time of the Purim story, the Jews consciously and willingly accepted the covenant. They reaffirmed their commitment as voluntary and uncoerced.

While the matter of if and how one can bind someone to a contract without her or his explicit consent is beyond the scope of our inquiry, two things are clear: that traditional Judaism accepts the binding of future generations to the Sinaitic covenant, and that such a contract would be incomprehensible to libertarians. The freedom to enter (and not enter) into contracts is fundamental to libertarians. To enforce a contract not accepted willingly is viewed as a kind of slavery, with a military draft and conscription and of course actual slavery serving as the prime examples of such involuntary servitude. Now, for most of human history, most individuals found themselves born into a particular community, whether sociologically or politically or both; choice did not figure into this belonging. In such a world, perhaps binding the members of future generations to a covenant did not strike people as discordant as it does for many or most of us today. The fact is that, although the expression "Jews by choice" generally refers to those who convert into the Jewish religion and people, it is largely the case today in our modern world that even Jews by birth are largely Jews by choice. Indeed, most Jews today have thrown off any sense of obligation to the covenant established at Sinai. So, even when religiously observant Jews in our days say their observance is rooted in the obligation set at Sinai, and not out of personal choice, the experiential reality suggests otherwise for most, at least for most of those not living in relatively isolated communities. Today, most Jews who submit themselves to the yoke of Heaven do so willingly. Regardless of the reasons for keeping the covenant, its centrality demonstrates the overriding significance of community in the Jewish tradition, perhaps at the expense of individual choice, or perhaps as a higher value.

Judaism values community in numerous other ways. We have already discussed tzedakah and the power of communal leadership to levy taxes to support communal needs. Communal prayer requires a quorum, and although individuals can pray on their own, communal prayer serves as the ideal. The prayer liturgy itself, even when recited by individuals outside of a quorum, includes many expressions of communal solidarity, with language often crafted in the first-person plural instead of the first-person singular, as *we*, *us*, and *our*, rather than as *I*, *me*, and *my*. The 'amidah, the Standing Prayer—also referred to as the 'avodah, the Service—rests at the center of every prayer service, and in this prayer an individual does not say, for example, "Heal me," but rather "Heal us," and not "I thank You," but "We thank you." When a quorum is present for morning and afternoon services, after the individuals recite quietly the 'amidah prayer, the prayer leader then repeats aloud the entire 'amidah, and the members of the prayer community respond *amen* to the blessings. A quorum allows the recitation of certain other prayers, including the *kaddish* and the mourner's *kaddish*, as well as a formal, public reading from the Torah scroll.[18]

Beyond any theoretical or textual valuing and beyond any legal obligations of community, one ought not to ignore the actual, lived experience of traditional Jewish communities. Of course, for many centuries many Jews found themselves forced to live in isolated communities or neighborhoods, including ghettos. In the modern, in the postmodern world, in a world of automobiles and buses and trains, the traditional Jew cannot travel on the Sabbath. If traditionally observant Jews wish to take part in a prayer community on the Sabbath, they must therefore live near enough each other to be able to walk to synagogue. If they wish to eat in each other's homes on the Sabbath, they must live within walking distance of each other. Living amongst each other facilitates relationships and brings children together for play and learning. For adherents of less traditional orientations, in which no taboos or expectations on the use of cars are to be found, people can and do live far away from each other, in some ways weakening the bonds of community.

Indeed, Rabbi Ismar Schorsch, the chancellor of Conservative Judaism's Jewish Theological Seminary between 1986 and 2006, characterized the 1950 ruling, from the Committee on Jewish Law and Standards of the movement's Rabbinic Assembly, to allow driving to synagogue on the Sabbath as a great mistake, arguing that the movement thereby "gave up on the desirability of living close to the synagogue and creating a Shabbos community."[19] Although many leaders rejected this evaluation and although the decision might have boosted membership for an extended period, Conservative Judaism's membership has declined substantially over the last decade or two, as detailed by Daniel Gordis, himself ordained as a rabbi by Conservative Judaism's Jewish Theological Seminary:

> In 1971, 41 percent of American Jews affiliated with the Conservative movement, then the largest of the movements. By the time of the 1990

National Jewish Population Survey, the number had declined to 38 percent. In 2000, it was 26 percent, and now [in 2014], according to Pew, Conservative Judaism is today the denominational home of only 18 percent of Jews. And they are graying. Among Jews under the age of 30, only 11 percent of respondents defined themselves as Conservative.[20]

Steven M. Cohen paints a similar picture using raw numbers:

> The sheer number of American Jewish adults who identify as Conservative and belong to a synagogue has fallen by about 21 percent – from 723,000 adult Jewish congregational members in 1990 to 570,000 in 2013. And the number of non-synagogue Conservative Jews – those who say, in effect, "I'm Conservative, but I don't belong to a congregation"—fell by an even more precipitous 47 percent, from 739,000 to 392,000.[21]

Now, certainly the permissive decision on driving to synagogue does not alone explain Conservative Judaism's steep decline in membership, but the resulting geographical separation could reasonably explain a weakening of communal bonds.[22]

One cannot deny the importance of community within Jewish history and Jewish religion, yet does this mean that the individual has little or no significance in the tradition? Is the individual always or essentially subservient to the community?

The Final Frontier: A Digression

There is a pair of famous scenes in the second and third films of the original *Star Trek* crew, *Star Trek II: The Wrath of Khan* and *Star Trek III: The Search for Spock*. In the former, as Spock (spoiler alert) sacrifices his life, he declares to Captain Kirk that "Logic clearly dictates that the needs of the many outweigh the needs of the few," to which Kirk responds, "Or the one."

Before moving on to the companion scene in the sequel, two digressions upon the digression:

First of all, one of my high school social studies teachers, Anthony Pennino, was of a libertarian bent, and in his openness to different ideas he had all of us subscribe to both *The Progressive* and *Reason* magazines during that school year. Anyway, he explained to us that Gene

Rodenberry, the creator of *Star Trek*, was similarly inclined towards libertarianism or at least towards ideals of liberty, and if I recall correctly, we could gain extra credit by watching an episode of *Star Trek* and then writing and submitting a report explaining how it demonstrated values of freedom.

Secondly, although I have no idea whether or not they ever voiced libertarian views, both William Shatner (Captain Kirk) and Leonard Nimoy (Mr. Spock) were born Jews.

In any case, to return to the original digression, one can imagine that libertarians and particularly Randian devotees (and perhaps Gene Rodenberry himself) were or would be horrified at Spock's declaration and Kirk's assent. Fortunately for the horrified, *Star Trek III* came along two years later to rectify the error. Kirk tells (another spoiler alert) the recently resurrected Spock that "the needs of the one . . . outweigh the needs of the many."

Judaism and Individualism

For us, the point of this digression is that—despite what one might expect—Judaism does *not* side unequivocally, or even equivocally, with the first vision over the second. Indeed, there are many pieces of evidence suggesting a balance, if not the contrary. To begin, there is the famous notion from the Mishnah and Talmud that to save an individual person is to save a world: "Whoever destroys a soul, it is considered as if he destroyed an entire world. And whoever saves a life, it is considered as if he saved an entire world."[23] Bolstering this idea is a talmudic discussion of the creation of the first human being. Why did God create a single human being, Adam (the name derives from the root word meaning soil), and not multiple human beings? Note that despite the popular notion that Eve was created from a rib of Adam, there is another, perhaps better translation and interpretation that posits a single human, male and female together, with two faces on opposite sides of a single head, and the splitting in half of this being, the taking of a *side* rather than a rib, from this androgynous or hermaphroditic Adam. And this is no modern invention, but is to be found in the Talmud itself.[24] So why one original human and not many? This teaches us at least two things, whether or not we take such an account literally: that all human beings reach back to a single source, and therefore no one can trace his or her lineage to some greater ancestor than others can; and that like the first individual was a world, so too is each of us a world, a world subject to both destruction and saving. The Talmud offers one additional image to establish the distinctiveness of individuals: "A human being imprints/mints many coins from one mold/stamp and all of them are similar to one another, and the King of Kings of Kings, the Holy One, blessed be He, imprints/mints each human being from the mold/stamp of the first human being [i.e., Adam] and no one of them is the same as his fellow."[25] Whereas when human beings make many of a thing, such as coins, they produce identical copies, when God creates human beings, God does so with a single mold, yet each comes out different, with no two looking or thinking exactly alike.[26]

Within Judaism, one also finds the principle of *kavod ha-beriyot*, literally "honor of the creations," though probably better expressed in English as "the dignity of the individual." This idea is a powerful one, elevating the dignity of the individual to such a level that it can override certain biblical laws. For example, it is biblically forbidden for a Jew to wear a garment made of both wool and linen, and yet if, while in a public place, an individual realizes he or she is wearing such a garment, one does not remove it immediately, due to the threat to individual dignity of walking unclothed in public. This might seem obvious, but violating a biblical prohibition is a serious matter. One can—indeed, one must—break the laws of the Sabbath in order to save a human life, yet one might have supposed that removing a garment, even exposing one to partial nudity, might not justify transgressing a biblical command—and yet it does. Elsewhere, we learn that embarrassing someone is akin to murder. As R. Daniel Sperber reminds us, "Whoever humiliates his fellow man in public, the Talmud declares, is as if he has shed blood."[27] One must also remember that the transgression of a biblical law is not so weighty just because of the Bible; rather, we are talking about obligations set by God. God has instructed Jews not to wear *sha'atnez*, the mixture of linen and wool. To go against this is to defy God. Thereby one understands that the principle of individual dignity, concerned with relations among people, can even override the relationship between people and God. We have already seen another area where Judaism promotes individual dignity—in earning a livelihood. Likewise, in the giving of tzedakah (which is not exactly the same thing as charity, as we learned in an earlier chapter), every effort is made to protect the dignity of the recipient, in terms of what is provided and in what manner.[28]

Judaism values the individual to such an extent that Jewish law prohibits a person from killing another person even to save his or her own life! If someone tells me to shoot and kill another person or else be shot and killed myself, I am not allowed to shoot. Even if the threat and consequence would be that both of us would be shot and killed, and not just one of us, I am forbidden to cause the death of this other human being. Even if there is an entire group of Jews threatened with one or all of them being killed should they refuse to identify and turn in one of their own, it is forbidden to cause the end of a life in this way. In addition, there is a concept of *kavod ha-met*, "honor of the deceased," and many rules and rituals around death to preserve an individual's dignity.

R. Sacks roots Judaism's individualism in the theological notion that humans were created in God's image. "Of all the great religions, Judaism has the strongest conception of the freedom and dignity of the individual, beginning with the principle that the human person as such is the one bearer of the image of God."[29] Elsewhere, R. Sacks expands on this idea of individual dignity:

> Jews have always been the irritant of empires because of our insistence on the dignity of the individual and his or her liberty. Anti-Semitism is either the last gasp of a declining culture or the first warning sign of a new totalitarianism. God commanded our ancestors to be different, not because they were better than others—"It is not because of your righteousness that the Lord your God is giving you this good land" (Deut. 9:6)—but because *by being different we teach the world the dignity of difference*. Empires seek to impose unity on a plural world. Jews know that unity exists in heaven; God creates diversity on earth.[30]

Diversity and pluralism are possible only with individualism and the valuing of the dignity of the individual. Given Judaism's conception of God's creation of a single individual in God's own image, in the idea of God minting humans, each one unique, there is no way one can imagine that Judaism undervalues or does not value the individual. Community is important in Judaism, yet Judaism is not only about community.

Finally, we have mentioned previously the late Israeli scientist and public intellectual Yeshayahu Leibowitz. He argued forcefully that even in Israel, religion and religious authority ought to be separated from the state, for both the health of the state and the health of Judaism. Always an iconoclastic thinker, Leibowitz did not find particularly fruitful this entire debate over individualism and the community: "As for the Halakhah, it is impossible to determine definitively whether it centers on the individual Jew or on the Jewish community which observes it. ... It is concerned with man as he stands before God, not with man by himself nor with human society. Both are regarded as natural data, not as values." Leibowitz rejected definitively identifying Judaism with all sorts ideas and values, often midrashic, from stories, and without any legal force and open to contradictory interpretations. Indeed, as the words just quoted indicate, he did not see "individualism" or "community" as values at all. "It is doubtful whether any one of the many views from Jewish literary sources concerning the individual and society represents the definitive outlook of Judaism." Leibowitz's Judaism was that of the halakha, Jewish law. In his understanding, this totalizing system of obligation fully constitutes Judaism. In his view we find religious meaning in and only in standing before God and doing what God obligates us to do. Other actions and activities might be beautiful or moral, but they remain empty of *religious* meaning, according to this perspective.[31]

Clearly, whether one, like Leibowitz, denies that Judaism embodies values at all, or one sees Judaism valuing individual dignity, one cannot consider Judaism to be anti-individual in its prizing of community. And just as we have challenged such a notion, we must dispel the myth that libertarianism, in its veneration of the individual, is anti-community.

Libertarianism and Community

Although Ayn Rand's idolization of egoism and vilification of altruism might figure for some as a defining principle of libertarianism, the reality falls far from this. What libertarians oppose is not altruism per se, but rather altruism as organized and coerced by government. What libertarians oppose is not community per se, but rather community as promoted or as constrained by government. They see government's role as the protection of individual liberties, which certainly includes the rights of free association and assembly. Libertarians thus favor *voluntary* communities. As we saw in the brief *Libertarian Party Platform* excerpt opening this chapter, "We defend the right of individuals to form corporations, cooperatives and other types of entities based on voluntary association." For libertarians, communities—whether political, commercial, or social—must be formed and joined by means of individual choices. There is even a term for this: Voluntaryism.

The British philosopher Auberon Herbert (1838–1906) first employed the word, possibly in the 1890s, in such essays as "The Principles of Voluntaryism and Free Life," one of the pieces collected in the posthumously published volume *The Voluntaryist Creed* (1908).[32] The writer Carl Watner defines the term in the following manner:

> Voluntaryism is the doctrine that relations among people should be by mutual consent, or not at all. It represents a means, an end, and an insight. Voluntaryism does not argue for the specific form that voluntary arrangements will take; only that force be abandoned so that individuals in society may flourish. As it is the means which determine the end, the goal of an all voluntary society must be sought voluntarily.[33]

Herbert not only argued that voluntary associations were morally and pragmatically positive, but he also characterized the consequences when government interferes with them:

> Grasping greedily at the common compulsory fund, out of which every sort of thing is provided, the people lose their faith in free enterprise and their natural inclination to form voluntary societies of their own in order to provide for all the growing wants of life; and instead of setting themselves to build up with their own hands a new civilization—the real work which cries aloud to be done—they waste priceless time and energy in struggling for miserable handfuls out of the devil's quarreling fund—as it has been well called—thus playing the politician's game to his heart's content.[34]

That is, when a government funds what could have been voluntary institutions, people begin fighting over the government spending, in order to procure some of it. Such energy and time could be better employed in creating and maintaining such institutions.

Importantly, the notion of voluntaryism was never an independent principle. Rather, it grew out of or at least found links in other libertarian principles we have discussed in earlier chapters. In particular, voluntaryism is rooted in the concept of self-ownership and in the non-aggression principle. If we understand ourselves as owning our bodies and possessing the right to utilize them as we wish, and if we believe no one has the right to initiate aggression or coercion against us, then the logical consequence must be that all human engagements and associations—political, social, religious, economic—ought to be entered into voluntarily:

> We, who call ourselves voluntaryists, appeal to you to free yourselves from these many systems of state force, which are rendering impossible the true and happy life of the nations of today. This ceaseless effort to compel each other, in turn for each new object that is clamored for by this or that set of politicians, this ceaseless effort to bind chains round the hands of each other, is preventing progress of the real kind, is preventing peace and friendship and brotherhood, and is turning the men of the same nation, who ought to labor happily together for common ends, in their own groups, in their own free unfettered fashion, into enemies, who live conspiring against and dreading, often hating each other.[35]

Notice the language of compulsion and chains. In the eyes of Herbert, state interference in voluntary associations is akin to the chains of slavery, an unwarranted aggression against one's self-ownership and right to remain free from coercion.

Three-quarters of a century after Herbert's death, the term experienced a rebirth as the name of a magazine, *The Voluntaryist*, published beginning in 1982 (and continuing through at least 2017) by a group of libertarians opposed to electoral politics and other political methods of achieving their aims. Of course, they oppose violent means as well, favoring education. Their opposition to electoral politics is grounded in the belief that any participation only helps justify and strengthen the state.[36]

The notion of voluntaryism can help us better understand libertarian views on taxation and charity, discussed in an earlier chapter. It is not that libertarians oppose charitable giving; rather, they oppose governments taking money from some people and giving it as charity to others. Instead, libertarians say to let people organize charitable groups and do as they see fit with their own money.

Of course, voluntaryism is not only or even primarily about charitable organizations. As Tom Palmer writes, "Libertarians follow religious traditions, family traditions, ethnic traditions, and social traditions such as courtesy and even respect for others."[37] People can and do form many sorts of voluntary communities: amateur sports leagues; book clubs; religious fellowships; political parties; cultural organizations; and countless others, even labor unions.[38] Indeed, far from being a society of isolated individuals, a libertarian society might prove a fertile setting for diversity and pluralism.[39]

In line with libertarian opposition to coercion, the point is to allow groups to flourish through voluntary commitment and organization, absent government constraints or forced participation in collective activity.

Palmer argues forcefully that the critique against libertarians as being anti-community, as not even recognizing community as a value, is erroneous, if not cynical. Of course, he writes, libertarians recognize that no one lives as an isolated, self-sufficient individual, free of influence from other people and from his or her surroundings.[40] Murray Rothbard echoes this response:

> Individualists have always been accused by their enemies of being "atomistic"—of postulating that each individual lives in a kind of vacuum, thinking and choosing without relation to anyone else in society. This, however, is an authoritarian straw man; few, if any, individualists have ever been "atomists." On the contrary, it is evident that individuals always learn from each other, cooperate and interact with each other. . . . The libertarian welcomes the process of voluntary exchange and cooperation between freely acting individuals.[41]

From a conceptual, philosophical perspective, Palmer likewise rejects such accusations:

> A theory of obligation focusing on individuals does *not* mean there is no such "thing" as society or that we cannot speak meaningfully of groups. The fact that there are trees does not mean that we cannot speak of forests, after all. Society is not merely a collection of individuals, nor is it some "bigger or better" thing separate from them. Just as a building is not a pile of bricks but the bricks *and* the relationships among them, society is not a person, with his own rights, but many individuals *and* the complex set of relationships among them.[42]

The metaphors make his point. A forest may not be a *thing* in the same way each tree is a thing, but it still exists, whether as the spontaneously ordered grouping of trees or as a human concept for characterizing the relationships among trees. In the second metaphor, communities are like buildings, humans the bricks. Different arrangements of bricks and other materials produce different sorts of buildings, and different arrangements of humans produce different sorts of communities. Libertarians need not and do not see human individuals as trees without forests or bricks without buildings. They do not reject the reality of forests or the construction of buildings. They simply believe that governments ought to stay out of the business of managing forests or constructing buildings, of directing how human bricks or trees ought to be organized.

Rothbard offers a similar critique of reifying "society" or the "nation," as if such entities possess the characteristics of conscious individuals:

> The libertarian, however, is an individualist; he believes that one of the prime errors in social theory is to treat "society" as if it were an actually existing entity. "Society" is sometimes treated as a superior or quasi-divine figure with overriding "rights" of its own; at other times as an existing evil which can be blamed for all the ills of the world. The individualist holds that only individuals exist, think, feel, choose, and act; and that "society" is not a living entity but simply a label for a set of interacting individuals.[43]

Just like trees interact to form a forest and bricks to arise as a building, so too individual persons interact to create a society. Rothbard brings his argument a bit further, pointing out that attributing to society such human attributes as feeling and choosing paves the way for some people to hijack the term, to present themselves and their interests as those of society and to act in its name:

> Treating society as a thing that chooses and acts, then, serves to obscure the real forces at work. If, in a small community, ten people band together to rob and expropriate three others then this is clearly and evidently a case of a group of individuals acting in concert against another group. In this situation, if the ten people presumed to refer to themselves as "society" acting in "its" interest, the rationale would be laughed out of court; even the ten robbers would probably be too shamefaced to use this

sort of argument. But let their size increase, and this kind of obfuscation becomes rife and succeeds in duping the public.[44]

Rothbard wishes us to make the inference: What is the difference between the members of a small gang adopting the mantle of society to plunder others and the elected or unelected officials of a government from using force to tax individuals for the "good" of society?

Just over 300 years ago, one writer presented another metaphor, one making Palmer's initial point and extending it. Bernard Mandeville published his *Fable of The Bees: or, Private Vices, Public Benefits* in the early eighteenth century. This controversial poem, along with later elaborations by Mandeville, presaged the insights of Adam Smith and others. In brief, each bee goes about its own business and pursues its own selfish interests—and yet, the hive prospers. This unfolds naturally. If one sought to improve the society of bees by forcing each member to stop acting in its own interest, the result would prove disastrous. The mere fact of trees standing together connects them into a forest, but the bees' community emerges from the different actions of many, many individual bees.[45]

Economists have termed such natural development Spontaneous Order, and the notion might very well figure as the least well-known important idea in libertarian thought. Spontaneous order has been utilized most of all as an economic concept, to describe the ways individual actors, as producers and consumers, come together without any grand plan to forge an orderly society. Adam Smith famously characterized this as the action of the "invisible hand." Somehow, something of a balance is achieved in markets when individuals are left to themselves to pursue their individual interests. Many libertarians and others would argue that efforts at conscious, large-scale, government planning of an economy necessarily disrupts spontaneous ordering, with unwelcome consequences.

Furthermore, the concept of spontaneous order has been employed beyond the economic sphere to describe, for example, the evolution of laws, through what is known as common law. For libertarians, the notion could be applied to social organization more broadly. Libertarians might characterize as healthy a society allowing for the voluntary and spontaneous organization of individuals into a wide variety of groups, clubs, communities, institutions, and societies. The effort of governments to disrupt such spontaneous order with an imposed order does not improve the lives of those involved. So, far from objecting to or denigrating the notion of community, libertarians celebrate it, and seek a context within which they can thrive, all through the voluntary actions of many individuals.

In his primer on libertarianism (the original edition was called a primer, the more recent edition a manifesto), David Boaz identifies spontaneous order as one of nine "key concepts":

> A great degree of order in society is necessary for individuals to survive and flourish. It's easy to assume that order must be imposed by a central authority, the way we impose order on a stamp collection or a football team. The great insight of libertarian social analysis is that order in society arises spontaneously, out of the actions of thousands or millions of individuals who coordinate their actions with those of others in order to achieve their purposes. Over human history, we have gradually opted for more freedom and yet managed to develop a complex society with intricate organization. The most important institutions in human society—language, law, money, and markets—all developed spontaneously, without central direction.

Boaz notes that the concept applies outside of these institutions:

> Civil society—the complex network of associations and connections among people—is another example of spontaneous order; the associations within civil society are formed for a purpose, but civil society itself is not an organization and does not have a purpose of its own.[46]

And this is a central concern of our discussion here: the importance of voluntary associations, and the great value placed upon them by libertarians. By pointing out that civil society is not an organization, but rather a network of spontaneously emergent and ordered associations, Boaz recalls for us once again the metaphor of forest and trees. In this case, the trees represent voluntary associations instead of individual human beings, and the forest represents civil society as a whole instead of a single association.

Another writer, Jason Brennan, characterizes libertarianism as supporting both *"radical tolerance"* and *"radical voluntarism"*:

> In a free society, some will choose to follow traditional lifestyles. Others will choose new ways of living. Some will choose tight-knit communities. Some will choose communes. Some will choose a life alone.... Libertarians want all human interactions to be based on consent, not force.[47]

This combination—of voluntary communities with tolerance for other voluntary communities—makes the libertarian ideal something very far from a society of selfish individualists.

This emphasis on the voluntary can be found in the 2018 *Libertarian Party Platform*. The document clearly embraces the notion of voluntary communities, invoking the notion of voluntary action a dozen times. Some of these focus on economic activity, but some invocations speak to other sorts of groups, or at least encompass both economic and noneconomic relationships:

> [W]e oppose all interference by government in the areas of voluntary and contractual relations among individuals.
>
> We defend the right of individuals to form corporations, cooperatives and other types of entities based on voluntary association.
>
> We encourage certifications by voluntary associations of professionals.

Other statements in the platform refer to political and charitable organizations:

> As private voluntary groups, political parties should be free to establish their own rules for nomination procedures, primaries and conventions. We call for an end to any tax-financed subsidies to candidates or parties and the repeal of all laws which restrict voluntary financing of election campaigns.
>
> The proper and most effective source of help for the poor is the voluntary efforts of private groups and individuals.

Clearly, the Libertarian Party opposes coercion not only in terms of the preservation of freedom or the collection of taxes, but also in regard to all kinds of human collective organization.

Now, the celebratory characterization of voluntary communities does have one problematic dimension. In discussing libertarian notions of voluntary associations, one cannot avoid an important and, to many, disturbing corollary of prohibiting government interference. If all voluntary relationships are allowed, this leaves permissible discriminatory associations. Most Americans, libertarian or not, do not think sexist and racist groups ought to be outlawed altogether, at least not in terms of individuals who freely associate, so long as they do not plan or commit violence against others. However, as we have reported, libertarians think all human relationships ought to remain voluntary, even economic ones. When libertarians refer to voluntary relationships, they do not mean simply a group of individuals sitting in some social hall or other room and discussing ideas. Rather, they believe that individuals should be free, for example, to enter into commerce without government restriction. In the language of the *Libertarian Party Platform*, "Members of private organizations retain their rights to set whatever standards of association they deem appropriate, and individuals are free to respond with ostracism, boycotts and other free market solutions." From this perspective, if an individual does not wish to sell wedding cakes to gay and lesbian couples, the subject of a recent United States Supreme Court case, the government should not force him or her to do so. Or, if the owner of a diner does not want to serve African Americans or Jews, he or she should be at liberty to do so. Why? Well, one argument is that the free market will curtail or end such businesses, that individuals can and will use nonviolent means such as boycotts to exert pressure on businesses and consumers, making racist and other discriminatory businesses unprofitable. Whether or not such market pressure would truly prove effective remains unclear. Based upon what we know of both human nature and political allegiances, many racist businesses might very well thrive in the United States and elsewhere. Regardless of the reality of the market, there is a more philosophical or maybe a more practical perspective favoring such a libertarian orientation: it is unclear where one should draw a line in permitting and prohibiting various economic relationships. Should one expect elected or appointed officials or even justices to make the best decisions as to where to draw the lines?

Judaism and Spontaneous Order

In his book *Judaism, Law & the Free Market: An Analysis*, Joseph Isaac Lifshitz presents a fascinating, historical argument for what he calls a

"Jewish spontaneous order." He looks at Jewish scripture, at the Torah and the Talmud, and highlights the lack of both "an economic theory" and "any system of organization of the tribes or about how to elect elders." Lifshitz suggests that we consider this omission *intentional*. Despite the opportunities to implement a God-ordained system—opportunities in the form of a number of covenants, including those at Mount Sinai and at the close of the forty-year wandering through and across the desert—we find nothing of the sort in the classic books.

> The description of the creation of the Jewish nation in the Bible is one of a process: beginning with the forefathers, and continuing to its existence as slaves in Egypt, to its redemption, to the receiving of the laws and a covenant with God, wandering in the desert, and finally to its arrival in the Holy Land. It is a description of a slow process—seemingly a development, rather than an organization that simply resulted from one act.

From this foundation, Lifshitz further suggests that "the Torah assumes a spontaneous order," and intentionally does not specify a single political order. He sees this playing out in the talmudic characterization of the people of Israel as a *kahal*, a community; he notes that the Talmud does not point to any decision authorizing the kahal, no social contract or court ruling, but simply assumes its existence. For the many centuries of the Jewish diaspora, historians have detailed groups of Jews as living in the context of a *kehilot*, small, partially self-governing communities of Jews.[48]

Lifshitz brings three other elements to his discussion of spontaneous order and the Jewish people. For one, he introduces the notion of destiny, that a common purpose might serve as a catalyst, if not a necessary condition for spontaneous order: "In this framework, spontaneous orders are generated precisely when people *do* have a common purpose or destiny in particular spiritual and temporal conditions, even though—and this is crucial—the purpose may be indifferent to any particular form of political organization." Following this, the writer hypothesizes that this commitment to spontaneous order in the unfolding of the Jewish people in history implies an endorsement of another type of spontaneous order, that of the free market and a rejection of planned economies. Finally, he links spontaneous order to God: "Appreciation for spontaneity is appreciation for the hand of God that dwells within the public sphere, be it through politics or society more broadly." Similar in some sense to the way that one might acknowledge the inability of human wisdom to understand God, perhaps the Jewish tradition teaches us to maintain modesty in our efforts to understand and impose our control on markets and society.[49] In the end, or rather throughout the past, Jewish communities do appear to have emerged and functioned as spontaneously generated communities, living out this libertarian principle.

Although he does not invoke the concept of spontaneous order, Joshua Berman does paint a portrait of an unplanned (at least from the human perspective) society, and a free one, based in the system of biblical laws: "It envisions an association of free farmers and herdsmen, subsumed within a single social class, where the common ownership of the means of production is vested within extended kinship groups."[50] R. Sacks echoes this, at least in part: "At the heart of the Hebrew Bible is the God who seeks the free worship of free human beings, and two of the most powerful defences of freedom are private property and economic independence."[51] This sort of free, voluntary association fits well within a libertarian framework. Even if it appears coercive from the outside, it does not necessarily feel so from the inside, and importantly for a libertarian sensibility, this biblical model minimizes the state and its authority and reach.

Individuals and Communities

In his best-selling book, *Don't Hurt People and Don't Take Their Stuff: A Libertarian Manifesto*, the writer Matt Kibbe draws together individualism and community in a libertarian worldview, or rather, he points to the way they are intimately linked: "Can governments require that people care, or force people to volunteer? It seems like such a silly question, but some seem to think the answer is 'yes.'" For Kibbe, the answer is the opposite, and here is his explanation: "Some people just don't see the link between individual initiative and the cohesion of a community."[52] He is telling us that requiring individuals to "care" or forcing individuals to "volunteer" does not produce strong, effective communities. What does produce such communities are individuals—expressing their individual desires, talents, and goals—who freely build and participate in them.

As Jason Brennan notes, "Many libertarians in fact think that community spirit is needed to make free society work."[53] As David Boaz encapsulates the point: "There's no conflict between individualism and community. There's a conflict between voluntary association and coerced association."[54] Individualism and community are far from opposed in this libertarian orientation. Rather, they mutually reinforce each other; individuals and communities help each other thrive. And one might say the very same thing about Judaism, where the framework of community and communal norms and the respect for individual, human dignity benefit each other, where a myriad of individuals can perform the very same mitzvot, fulfill the very same commandments, each in his or her own way.

As we have now learned, libertarians do not reject community, and Jewish texts and thinkers neither reject individualism nor have reason to oppose the libertarian principle of voluntary communities. After all, what is a religious community if not a spontaneously ordered and (at least in our modern world) an ultimately voluntary association and an important part of a larger civil society? And, one might add, not only Jewish *religious* communities, but secular ones as well. Although we commonly think of the Israeli kibbutz as a secular and socialist institution, it really presents us with an excellent example of a voluntary community, of people joining together in a common project with mutually agreed upon rules.[55] We began this last chapter of our discussion thinking we needed to confront perhaps the greatest challenge to the compatibility of Jewish and libertarian philosophies. And yet, now, it appears that in the matter of the supposed conflict between the individual and the community, libertarianism and Judaism may prove the most compatible—a point upon which a religiously observant Jew ought to find no difficulty campaigning.

# Conclusion

Standing on One Foot

We began with a question: Can a religiously committed Jew, in good faith, run for political office as a libertarian candidate, promoting the platform of a libertarian party? To answer this question, we set ourselves a task: to examine possible points of conflict between libertarian and Jewish ideas and experience. Would any differences prove fatal to such a candidacy?
Let us review.
Freedom. Unsurprisingly, we saw that liberty figures as an essential libertarian principle. In Jewish ideas and texts, we encountered a kind of coexistence of freedom and servitude. On the one hand, the founding story of the Jewish people is that of the liberation from Egyptian slavery. On the other hand, the submission to and service of God appears foundational in Jewish theology. We considered different understandings of liberty and determined that we could not dismiss some sort of overlap in Jewish and libertarian thought in their valuing of freedom. Or perhaps one might say that the more expansive notions of liberty within Jewish thought could still encompass a narrower libertarian conception. Although a religiously observant Jew might embrace a theological servitude under God, she or he would not necessarily thereby need to dismiss a libertarian political notion of freedom. That is, one can believe oneself

a servant of God—indeed, one can understand and experience this as freely chosen—while still championing practical freedoms in a political context.

Self-Ownership. Another basic libertarian principle, one clearly specified in the *Libertarian Party Platform.* Although for many Jews today it appears self-evident that we do not own ourselves, and self-evident that God does own us, we did learn that there are other, perhaps even more strongly grounded positions, pointing to some sort of *shared* ownership, to a partnership with God. It does seem possible, if not likely, that a Jew who believes in a complete lack of human self-ownership would have some anxiety or difficulty in standing at a podium and announcing her or his commitment to a party platform embracing it unambiguously, that such an individual would prove unable, concerning the principle of self-ownership, to express commitment to it both faithfully and compellingly in responding to a question from a journalist or voter. Well, maybe such an individual would not be able to run in good faith as a libertarian candidate, yet this would not prevent other religiously observant Jews from doing so, those who adhere to a shared ownership model, and who also realize that for most practical and policy purposes this would not prove problematic.

Private Property. A third foundational libertarian notion, and again one where we began with reason to doubt its compatibility with Jewish views. And yet, here too we found complexity in Jewish views, with a fascinating and important distinction between ownership and possession. We also found that the Jewish legal system abounds with rules about ownership and its transfer from one person to another, and even between people and God. In any practical sense, private property finds a place in Jewish thought and Jewish law and Jewish communities historically. We were unable to identify a clear reason why a Jewish candidate could not advocate for a libertarian defense of private property.

Taxation, Charitable Giving, and Welfare. As with other matters, Jewish and libertarian ideas about taxation and charity do not fall into neat boxes, let alone plainly separate ones. Although many libertarians view taxation as theft, many libertarians recognize its need to pay for minimal government functions—or, at least in a practical sense, they recognize taxation will not disappear anytime soon, making a political goal of reducing and minimizing taxation much more realistic than a call for its abolition. And although the Hebrew scriptures offer evidence of taxation in ancient times and although Jewish communities have long exercised a kind of power of taxation over its members, it is not at all evident that Jews living in a secular society would possess any directive or license to impose such practices on others. In a libertarian polity, organized Jewish communities could, in effect, tax their members. In this regard, a Jewish candidate should discover no problem in campaigning in good faith for minimal or even no government taxation in a secular framework.

In regard to charitable giving and welfare, we started out thinking that libertarians—in being opposed to most government activity—would be opposed to charity in the form of welfare, and that Jews—in so prioritizing, even commanding charitable giving—would enthusiastically support charity in the form of welfare. And although libertarians do mostly reject government welfare, whether for the poor or the wealthy, whether for individuals or businesses, they wholeheartedly welcome a culture of private charitable giving. Libertarians do not oppose helping people, they just tend to think private individuals can do this better and more efficiently than can government officials. And although tzedakah and helping others do figure prominently in Jewish thought and history, and although the collection and distribution of funds for those in need can be compelled in some cases, we found no reason to conclude that Jewish notions of tzedakah must be translated into the language of secular governance.

In discussing charity and welfare, I must share that the original, working title for this book was *My Brother's Keeper?* By this title—by referencing the tale of Cain and Abel and Cain's response to God upon being confronted about his missing brother—I aimed to encapsulate this critical point, to flip on its head what we think we know about both Judaism and libertarianism. One might have thought that a libertarian would reject any responsibility to serve as the keeper of his or her brother or sister. To the contrary, many libertarians (though not necessarily all disciples of Ayn Rand) might very well agree that we *are* such keepers, that we possess some sort of moral responsibility for caring for others, our family, our friends, our neighbors, our countrymen and countrywomen, all of humanity even. The key point is that the acknowledgement and acceptance of such responsibility remains a *moral* one and does not require that one support the notion of government carrying it out, as an administrative function, on our behalf.

Somehow, in our world, in the twentieth and twenty-first centuries, we have confused two distinct matters, government activity and responsibility for our fellow human beings. We have jumbled them, coming to believe that those who endorse the latter must endorse the former and those who oppose the former must oppose the latter. One can be an anarchist, and a fair number of libertarians are anarchists, and still embrace such responsibility to one's fellows. As for Jews, many do read the story of Cain and Abel as teaching the lesson that the answer to Cain's question is a loud "Yes, certainly!" Yet, if we do indeed learn this crucial lesson, perhaps it ought to figure as a theological and moral principle and not additionally as a practical, political one. Even if one might wish to employ it in the establishment of some sort of theologically Jewish commonwealth, it is not at all evident that one can leap from the story of Cain and Abel to the modern welfare state, that one can invoke the former to justify the latter. As we will discuss shortly, this does not necessarily mean Jewish thought and Hebrew scripture are opposed to the modern welfare state— that a religiously observant Jew could not run as a candidate for office as the candidate of a liberal or socialist party (that is for another book to explore)—but it would seem to mean that Jewish notions of responsibility for our fellows does not undoubtedly require support for a government that seeks to exercise this responsibility. Values and methods of actualizing values remain two separate things. A religiously committed Jew could, therefore, remain dedicated to tzedakah and serving as one's sibling's keeper and yet still campaign in good faith as a libertarian candidate opposed to government support programs for the poor or for the corporations.

Government. Although libertarians promote either anarchism or, to one degree or another, very limited government, Jewish thought and history entertain mixed views on the value of government, which has served as protector and oppressor in various times and places. Neither in practice nor in theory, theological or otherwise, do we find an unambiguous judgment about the value of government. Certainly, the principle of *dina d'malkhuta dina*, the law of the land is the law, has allowed for considerable flexibility to Jews and Jewish communities in adapting to different sorts of governments. As we have seen, some writers do argue for a kind of affinity for libertarianism in biblical and other Jewish accounts. Yet even without a special affinity, we did not discover anything undermining a

Jewish compatibility with libertarian principles of government organization. One might even suggest that a theologically Jewish commonwealth could take the form of a libertarian polity.

Individualism/Community. Perhaps here we were met by our greatest surprises and reversals. Expecting Judaism to be all about community and libertarianism to be all about the individual and individual liberty, a much more complicated picture emerged. Jewish thought places great value on both the individual—to save one life is to save an entire world— and the community. Although libertarians certainly view government as tasked with protecting individuals, they also see communities as welcome and valuable in a free society—so long as such communities remain voluntary ones. And we found no reason to imagine that religiously observant Jews should not or would not find voluntary communities a worthy and beneficial model. After all, religious communities are self-organizing and voluntary, and their members tend not to want government interference.[1]

On the whole, then, our investigation has, unsurprisingly, revealed numerous cases of tension. And, yet, the tension never grew to overwhelming proportions. Although perhaps we found ourselves unable to bring Jewish and libertarian thought into a complete and smooth harmony, we always seemed to find some room for accommodation, and perhaps a bit more.

Insofar as our investigation took as a rough model the talmudic framework of the give-and-take, the back-and-forth of a sugya, have we resolved the contradiction with which we began? Surely we cannot say that the contradiction has been upheld, that Judaism and libertarianism are fundamentally incongruous and incompatible. But can we assert that it has been definitively refuted? Perhaps we would be justified in concluding that the contradiction was merely apparent but not real? Or, ought we to conclude with teyku, to sit back and let the contradiction stand?

Along the way, we discovered that many of our initial assumptions about libertarian and Jewish thought turned out to be far too simplistic, obscuring the richness of both traditions. Where libertarians might be thought to hold absolutist positions, such as over taxation or abortion, we found exceptions. Where Jews might be thought to hold to a single view, such as over the role of government in charitable endeavors, we found a diversity of opinions.

Chapter after chapter, topic after topic, we found no clinching argument for the incompatibility of libertarianism and Judaism. In each and every case, some counterexample or counterargument provided room for seeing them as compatible, or at least as not incompatible.

One might even detect some notions running through the chapters, or across the arc of the book, notions independent of any one topic or theme. One of these, perhaps the primary one, is the realization that nothing in Jewish scripture or thought or history seeks to compel us to think Jews have ever had much interest or motivation, let alone a sense of obligation of or grounds for, imposing Jewish rules or values upon the rest of the world. (This mirrors the common historical attitude, among Jews, towards conversion: sincere converts are to be welcomed and embraced, but there is no interest and no mitzvah in proselytizing, in seeking out converts—Jewish theology does not require or envision a world inhabited only by Jews and does not prescribe Judaism as the one and only path to God and to a world beyond the one in which we live.) We have mentioned, but not dwelled upon the idea of a theologically Jewish state and government, yet no such entity exists or appears likely to come into existence anytime soon. Not even with the modern state of Israel. True, self-proclaimed religious parties have sought to use government to obtain funding and to exercise control over such matters as marriage and divorce, but these groups have neither expressed much interest nor explored what it might take to run the infrastructure and economy and general court system of a modern state according to Jewish law. In the chapter dedicated to "The State of the Halakhah and the Halakhah of the State," from his book *Halakhah: The Rabbinic Idea of Law*, the scholar Chaim Saiman does explore in a fascinating way whether the system of halakha can even provide a legal and governance structure for the modern, administrative state.[2] In any case, the fact that nothing in Judaism or Jewish history and thought requires imposing a theologically Jewish framework upon secular governments leads to the conclusion that Jews, as citizens or candidates, can freely support or oppose various sorts of secular governments.

If, therefore, Judaism and libertarianism can accommodate each other, if they do not prove incompatible, does this tell us anything about the relationship between Judaism and other political philosophies? Is Judaism compatible with anything? Does the principle of *dina d'malkhuta dina* make Judaism indifferently flexible? Or, could one argue that Jewish thought meshes better with some political frameworks than with others? Is there something special about the connection between Judaism and libertarianism?

Jews and Libertarianism

Or, might we ask, is there something special about the connection between *Jews* and libertarianism? Unsurprisingly, given the prominence of Jews in a broad and diverse array of political movements over the last century and a half in the United States and Europe and South Africa and likely elsewhere, individuals of Jewish heritage have figured importantly in the development of libertarian thought and politics. Yet does this hold any significance for our understanding of libertarianism or Jewishness or their relationship? And if so, how?

One can imagine two ways Jewishness might have played an important role. First of all, in terms of ideas and values. And secondly, in terms of biography. That is, did the experience of any of these figures as Jews under particular governments or in particular societies lead them to cultivate libertarian ideas? For instance, did Alissa Zinovievna Rosenbaum's experience as a Jewish girl and young woman in the last years of Russia's Tsarist regime and the first years of the Soviet Republic give rise to her understanding and prioritization of individualism—and result in or contribute to her transition or transformation into Ayn Rand?

The earliest prominent "Jewish libertarian" was perhaps the British banker, Parliamentarian, and economist David Ricardo (1772–1823), who was drawn to economics after reading Adam Smith and who later authored *On the Principles of Political Economy and Taxation*. From a Sephardic Jewish family with roots in Portugal, Ricardo eloped with a Quaker woman and converted to Unitarianism as a young adult—though apparently he was known to many as Ricardo the Jew.[3] The Dutch economist and writer Arnold Heertje has researched Ricardo's family history, seeking "to trace Ricardo's bent for abstract reasoning to his Portuguese-Jewish ancestors."[4] Heertje provides circumstantial evidence to this effect. Ricardo spent a few of his teenage years with family in the Netherlands, possibly receiving a "rich" informal education within the Jewish community there, in or around the Portuguese Synagogue:

> The Portuguese Synagogue has been a weekly meeting point since 1675. It is a religious place, business is done and intellectual disputes are carried out. Elderly people try to broaden and deepen their insights, youngsters informally receive a broad education that competes with regular schooling. And there is the study of Talmud and Torah. The concentrated attention, the reduction of many-sided phenomena to a few basic principles, the unraveling of description, analysis and normative judgement are building blocks in the sharpening of minds who request structure. In order to judge Ricardo as a deductive economist, one cannot circumvent the study of Talmud according to an age-long tradition. On the one hand, he learned to think within a dogmatic system of strong rules and, on the other hand, at the same time he developed a talent for thinking independently.[5]

Heertje deduces further the following: "In general, one does not encounter Jews among the institutional, descriptive economists, but rather in great numbers among the abstract, deductive thinkers. That seems to be related in one way or another to their often forced movements in space, the permanent crossing of borders and the necessity of linking the past with the future."[6] Did Ricardo's lived experience or did some infusion from his Jewish heritage make him the sort of thinker he became? And even if there was an influence upon how he thought, does this say anything about the libertarian-oriented content of his thought?

The Nobel Prize winning economist Ludwig von Mises (1881–1973), author of *Human Action* and *Socialism: An Economic and Sociological Analysis*, was another prominent Jewish libertarian. He and Friedrich Hayek are considered to have been the leading theorists of the Austrian School of Economics. If von Mises does not sound like a Jewish name, this is because his father's family, engaged in the railroad business, was granted entry into the Austrian nobility. As for whether the Nobelist's Jewish heritage influenced his economic thought at all, it appears he would have firmly rejected any such association:

> Today the Islamic and Jewish religions are dead. They offer their adherents nothing more than a ritual. They know how to prescribe prayers and fasts, certain foods, circumcision and the rest; but that is all. They offer nothing to the mind. Completely despiritualized, all they teach and preach are legal forms and external rule. They lock their follower into a cage of traditional usages, in which he is often hardly able to breathe; but for his inner soul

they have no message. They suppress the soul, instead of elevating and saving it. For many centuries in Islam, for nearly two thousand years in Jewry, there have been no new religious movements. Today the religion of the Jews is just as it was when the Talmud was drawn up.[7]

In at least one regard, the libertarian Mises found himself in agreement with Karl Marx, who also identified no connection between Judaism and capitalism. David Gordon, speaking and writing about possible connections, withholds his judgment on the matter:

> I do not think that Mises's remarks by themselves settle the questions at issue, even if one accepts Mises's highly dubious characterization of Judaism as pure ritual, devoid of appeal to the mind. Mises's comments do not exclude the possibility that legal regulations of the kind Mises describes in such unflattering terms influenced the development of capitalism, either by their content or by the qualities of mind and character that people who adhered to the rituals tended to develop. But these are no more than possibilities: whether these regulations in fact had such effects is another question.[8]

In any event, we find here no clear case of the Jewish background of Mises influencing his economic thought.

Ludwig von Mises' students included Murray Rothbard, widely considered one of the most influential figures in the movement.[9] Rothbard's works include *For a New Liberty: The Libertarian Manifesto* and *Man, Economy, and State*. It is not evident that Rothbard placed much value in his Jewish heritage. His biographer, Justin Raimondo, tells of an autobiographical portrait Rothbard wrote at the age of seventeen:

> In his high school "Autobiography," Rothbard noted that "I was brought up with only rare entrances to temples or synagogues and with no adherence to orthodox customs." The orthodoxy of his mother's parents did not impress him: "my frequent first-hand observations of their adherence to religious traditions does not cause me to change my nonreligious views."

Rothbard also referred to his father as having been raised "in an environment of orthodox and often fanatical Jews who isolated themselves from the Poles around them, and steeped themselves and their children in Hebrew lore."[10]

Another student of Mises and the Austrian School is the London-born American economist Israel Kirzner (b. 1930). Unlike at least Ricardo, Mises, and Rothbard, all of whom were estranged from Judaism, Kirzner is an ordained and practicing Orthodox rabbi. He was a leading student of one of the most prominent twentieth-century American rabbinic figures, Rabbi Yitzchok Hutner, dean of Yeshiva Rabbi Chaim Berlin. Despite this dual prominence, in libertarian and religious Jewish circles, there appears to be no public record of Kirzner connecting the two in his own life and thought.

Other Jews associated with libertarian ideas include the economists Milton Friedman and Rose Friedman (1910–2009), the economist Walter Block (b. 1941), and the philosopher Robert Nozick. According to a 1981 New York Times profile, Nozick "has for years regarded himself as a 'committed part of the Jewish people' and has lived and taught in Israel and written on Jewish affairs."[11]

And to return once more to where it usually begins, Ayn Rand (1905–1982) was born to a Jewish family in Russia. At least one of Rand's biographers, Anne C. Heller, "tried to document how Russian and Jewish culture and history color some of the most interesting features of her character and work."[12] She offers the rather intriguing observation that Ayn Rand's early novel Anthem contained an unpronounceable word "I," perhaps paralleling the Tetragrammaton, the unpronounceable four-letter name of God.[13] Given Rand's worship of the self, there might be something to this. Overall, Heller portrays a girl and then woman who grew up with a religiously observant mother with whom she felt little connection, describing Rand as someone who "rarely spoke about her Jewish ancestry."[14] In an interview, however, the author points to the young Alyssa Rosenbaum's encounters with antisemitism as an important influence:

> For one thing, the anti-Semitism she witnessed in her youth helped to shape her worldview. For example, the Jewish entrepreneurs, industrialists, and capitalists of Nineteenth and early Twentieth Century Europe, including the Russia of her childhood, were punished for their virtues by those less gifted, just as her entrepreneurial heroes would be, and her hatred of altruism and "death-worship" were partly tied to her childhood disgust with the Russian Orthodox idolatry of the cross, of suffering, and of sacrificing the "best" to the worst.[15]

As with Mises and Rothbard, Rand appears to have experienced and expressed little positive about Judaism and Jewish heritage.

Rand and these others are only a few among many. One website identifies more than two dozen "Historic Jewish Libertarians," including some of those named above, and more than ten dozen "Notable Jewish Libertarians." The latter group includes individuals from the academic, business, and entertainment worlds (with Geddy Lee from the rock band Rush and radio personality Howard Stern among them).[16] No doubt this list has not been vetted in the sense of its honorees having confirmed the designations. Nonetheless, it remains of some interest. The anonymous host of the website shares numerous of his essays, including those examining antisemitism among libertarians and others articulating a libertarian defense of Zionism.

These are merely biographical snippets, though nothing jumps out as definitively linking Jewish heritage and the development of or commitment to libertarian ideas. Nevertheless, the economist Steven Horwitz thinks there is something there:

> It is not a coincidence that among the leading libertarian thinkers of the 20th century, we have a large number of Jews, starting with Mises, Milton Friedman, Israel Kirzner, and Robert Nozick. And despite the ways in [which] both rejected their Judaism, we should not forget Ayn Rand and Murray Rothbard. They are only the tip of the iceberg of the disproportionate number of Jews who have been instrumental in forwarding the ideas of classical liberalism in the last century. It is no exaggeration to say that the modern libertarian movement would not exist were it not for these Jews.[17]

One of the problems, of course, with trying to detect a connection between Jews and libertarianism is that Jews have featured prominently in many different political movements across the spectrum, from Left to Right, and off this spectrum as well. Has there truly been a disproportionate presence of Jews among leading libertarian thinkers? And even if so, has such a presence been any more disproportionate among libertarians as compared with those from other schools of thought? In the United States, Jews have traditionally voted heavily in support of Democratic candidates at all levels of government. Although since the 1980s and the rise of Ronald Reagan there has been some shift among

Orthodox Jews towards the Republican Party, a majority of Jews still votes for Democratic candidates.

In the end, it is not at all clear one can link the libertarian leanings or ideas of Jewish libertarians to their Judaism or Jewishness. At least, we cannot find any connections here we could not easily find among Jews of other political orientations. And Horwitz does not necessarily disagree. Whatever the disproportionality of Jews in the libertarian world of ideas might be, Horwitz also notes the following: "I do not wish to argue that Jewish values should produce a libertarian politics, but it is true that many of the elements of Jewish thinking and practice are strongly consistent with some of the values of the broad liberal tradition." Our investigations here would appear to align with such an observation.

Standing on One Foot

We must consider one, last, rather tantalizing parallel between Jewish and libertarian thought, perhaps even between Jewish thinkers and libertarianism.

In one of the most well-known tales recorded in the Talmud, a man seeking to convert approaches the great teacher Hillel. Previously, this proselyte had approached Shammai, Hillel's rabbinic colleague and sparring partner of sorts. Hillel and Shammai each led a group of students, and over generations these groups—Beit Hillel and Beit Shammai, or the House of Hillel and the House of Shammai—frequently disagreed over how to rule in various questions and cases of Jewish law. With only a few exceptions, the tradition rules according to the opinion of Beit Hillel, though the opinions of both schools retain the status of *Divrei Elohim Chayim*, which can be translated—and this is fascinating—either as *the words of the living God* or as *the living words of God*. Both winning and losing opinions remain within the talmudic text.

In any case, on this particular day, our questioner first approaches Shammai, promising he would convert if he could teach him the entire Torah while he, the proselyte, stood on one foot. For those of us who have not achieved the poise of a yoga master, the time most of us can balance on one foot is hardly enough to learn much Torah, let alone its entirety. Shammai, perhaps to demonstrate the absurdity or foolishness of the request, pushes away the proselyte—maybe knocking him over while so precariously balanced.

After this rejection, the man approaches Hillel with the very same challenge. Hillel, by contrast, does not rebuff the questioner. The Talmud relates to us that Hillel first converted him and then provided a response:

דעלך סני לחברך לא תעביד זו היא כל התורה כולה ואידך פירושה הוא זיל גמור.

That which is hateful to you, to your friend do not do. This is all of the Torah, all of it. The rest is commentary, go and learn.[18]

For at least three reasons, this story figures importantly for our consideration of the compatibility of Judaism and libertarianism.

First of all, Hillel's encapsulation of Judaism into this single principle, not doing to others what one considers hateful is somewhat resonant of libertarianism's nonaggression axiom we discussed earlier: "No one has the right to initiate aggression against the person or property of anyone else."[19] Aggressive and hateful behavior might seem different, but to do something hateful to someone is in a sense to commit an aggression against her or him.

Secondly, both of these are negatively phrased principles in the sense that they *proscribe* rather than *prescribe*. They both expect us *not* to interfere with others in ways we would not want other people to interfere with our lives. Both principles also frown upon the initiation of harmful actions, but do not rule out self-defense or the pursuit of justice. Of note, Hillel's principle cannot be found in the Torah itself. It is clearly reminiscent of the mitzvah to love one's neighbor as oneself, yet flips it from prescription to proscription.

Finally, not only are these principles quite similar, but we find at least two prominent libertarian thinkers identifying the nonaggression principle as the single, foundational principle of libertarianism. (Gratitude and credit for suggesting this idea go to my cousin, Marc, the one who in my youth handed me the Jerome Tuccille book *It Usually Begins with Ayn Rand*.) Walter Block writes that "The foundation of libertarianism is the non-aggression axiom. This states that it is illicit to initiate or threaten invasive violence against a man or his legitimately owned property. Murray Rothbard characterized this as 'plumb line' libertarianism: follow this one principle, and you will be able to infer the libertarian position on all issues, without exception."[20] Rothbard himself comes across a bit more ambiguously. He does indeed claim that "The libertarian creed rests upon one central axiom: that no man or group of men may aggress against the person or property of anyone else. This may be called the 'nonaggression axiom.'"[21] Yet only a few pages later he writes that "The libertarian . . . concludes by adopting as his primary axiom the universal right of self-ownership, a right held by everyone by virtue of being a human being."[22] And then not so many pages later, Rothbard tells us the following: "These two axioms, the right of self-ownership and the right to 'homestead,' establish the complete set of principles of the libertarian system. The entire libertarian doctrine then becomes the spinning out and application of all the implications of this central doctrine."[23] The scholar John Tomasi states that for Rothbard, and for Robert Nozick as well, "self-ownership trips the first domino and makes the rest run."[24] Well, which is it, which is the central axiom, nonaggression or self-ownership? We might suggest a talmudic response: that perhaps these are two sides of the same coin, that they are in essence a single principle. After all, self-ownership cannot operate effectively without a prohibition on aggression. Rothbard's phrasing of "the spinning out" from the "central doctrine" perhaps echoes Hillel's "The rest is commentary."

Our brief consideration of Murray Rothbard's Jewishness showed little if any warmth and engagement. And although Walter Block has written that he sees religion as the natural enemy of his enemy—the state—and therefore an ally of sorts for which he bears no hostility, he does not identify himself as religious.[25] Despite these facts, is it not possible there exists some sort of link between the Jewish heritage and libertarian thoughts of these two individuals? When they wrote their words characterizing the nonaggression axiom as the basic notion of libertarianism, were they aware, consciously or not, of Hillel's encounter with the proselyte and Hillel's reduction of Judaism to this one principle? As my cousin summarizes the matter, "To them libertarianism consists of a single commandment—the Non-Aggression principle. Everything else is an interpretation or application—so their books and articles are like a libertarian Talmud."[26] Perhaps from this we can repeat the conclusion and directive of Hillel and say that the rest is commentary, now go and learn.

Epilogue

Just to be clear, I am *not* running for office.

Indeed, although I identify as a religiously observant Jew, I do not consider myself a libertarian (and I hope this lends credence to the notion that this book is a sincere investigation rather than something driven by an ideological agenda). As I explained in the Introduction, I did have that adolescent flirtation with Ayn Rand, or rather with her books and heroes, and I did for a brief time connect with a local Libertarian Party group, yet I have not identified as libertarian for over three decades. Well, at least not in the sense most libertarians would find sensible.

In another sense, then? In my view, libertarians ask important questions, ones which adherents across the political spectrum ought to take seriously and ask more frequently. Or maybe it would be more appropriate to say that libertarians tend to manifest a particular attitude which adherents across the political spectrum ought to consider adopting: a skepticism of government and government spending. As I have noted more than once in this book, there is an admirable consistency in libertarian critiques of government assistance programs, whether this takes the form of aid to those with few resources or the form of corporate welfare for those already rather quite well off.[1]

In this sense, perhaps, I retain something of a libertarian sensibility. I agree that government ought to be limited to that which only government can do—and do reasonably well. For some libertarians, this means anarchism, that government is always and altogether unnecessary. For nonanarchist libertarians of a minimalist bent, this means a government engaged in nothing more than providing for the defense of individual rights, whether abroad or close to home. In my take, government is best positioned to do considerably more than this. With my background in public health, I believe only government is in a position to protect the public health through sanitation and clean water systems and epidemic surveillance. And as we confront the coronavirus pandemic in the year 2020, I have difficulty imagining how a minimalist government or the private sector would have been able to mobilize effectively against this massive challenge—both the public health emergency and the accompanying financial crisis. I also find myself skeptical about libertarian approaches to the dire, global, existential threat of climate change, the corrupting influence of money on elections and political decision-making, and systemic racism as encoded in decades and centuries of law and policy.[2]

Now, just because my take is that a "minimalist" government ought to address such matters, this does not mean I think government ought to do anything and everything. We ought to take a skeptical stance at the outset on each issue before us. So, for example, maybe governments ought not to be in the business of solemnizing marriages? Maybe government should not decide that some things—such as home ownership or charitable giving—deserve tax deductions and that other things do not? Maybe government should not be in the business of promoting business in general and specific businesses with tax credits and other incentives? Is military spending far too high? Perhaps state and local police departments do not need military-grade equipment? And does it not seem likely the case that public safety does not require locking up so many people behind bars and for so long?

If, in some sense, I possess something of a libertarian attitude of skepticism, my definition of minimalist government would not pass muster with most members of any libertarian party or with most libertarian thinkers, so I will not be running for office as a libertarian. If any self-identifying libertarians wish, nevertheless, to welcome me into the club, that's up to them.

And although I imagine I would very much enjoy serving as a legislator, designing and debating and voting on laws, I would make for a miserable candidate and campaigner. So, unless someone wishes to appoint me to a vacated seat somewhere, I do not expect ever to hold office.

Whatever my own political and philosophical inclinations, I hope that the framing of this book—the question of whether or not a religiously observant Jew could run in good faith as a libertarian candidate for office—provides a useful means for investigating important questions of political philosophy. I also hope it facilitates seeing through and challenging some simplistic, stereotypical notions of both Jewish and libertarian thought—thereby leaving all of us with a somewhat richer understanding of both.

Finally, I wish to return to this book's title: *Running in Good Faith*. No doubt government and politics have never been pure, but today, a couple of decades into the twenty-first century, we would appear to have a large number of officeholders who have forgotten what it means to run and to serve in good faith. To serve in good faith means to act on principle and to abhor hypocrisy. To serve in good faith means to serve the public and not oneself or one's party. I mean good faith not only in the sense of faithfulness to one's theological or moral commitments, but also faithfulness to one's constituents, to the members of one's community, local and national. Such good faith is independent of one's particular political commitments.

Endnotes

Chapter 1

1   The one possible candidate for a book like this one would be Michael R. Paley, *Orthodox Judaism, Liberalism and Libertarianism: When Secularism Becomes a Religion* (Baltimore: PublishAmerica, 2006). Perhaps due to the fact that the author passed away at a young age during the very year of the book's publication, this title is unavailable anywhere for purchase, and not even a table of contents appears online. According to the summary at Google Books, the author argues for the consistency of libertarianism with Orthodox Judaism and the incompatibility of Orthodox Judaism with modern liberalism. Although Paley addresses a number of issues—taxation, charity, government coercion, and private property—considered in my book, it would appear he takes a more ideological position from the outset. Regardless, the book was published more than a decade ago and is now unavailable. WorldCat identifies a single copy residing at the Library of Congress.
One quite helpful and available book is Joseph Isaac Lifshitz, *Judaism, Law & the Free Market: An Analysis* (Grand Rapids: Acton Institute, 2012). Published by the Acton Institute (from the organization's website: "The Acton Institute is a think tank whose mission is to promote a free and virtuous society characterized by individual liberty and sustained by religious principles" (https://www.acton.org/), this slim but important volume originates from a strong ideological perspective, addressing in some detail economic issues concerning Judaism and libertarianism. These issues include property rights and social welfare, though the author does consider an important, though less well-known element of some libertarian thought, with origins in the work of F. A. Hayek and other economists: spontaneous order, the way the interactions of many individuals produce relationships and institutions, as contrasted with a more purposeful organization, as attempted by most governments. Lifshitz's book proved of value for chapter 6 of the present book, where I consider spontaneous order and voluntary communities.
Another book, Philip Z. Maymin, *Freedom and the Torah* (n.p.: CreateSpace Independent Publishing Platform, 2014), presents many short essays about the weekly Torah portion and a brief concluding essay, perhaps close to 2,000 words, addressing the compatibility of Judaism and libertarianism. As I discuss in chapter 5, Maymin suggests that the Torah, the five books of Moses, figures as "the quintessential Libertarian text" (135).

All in all, my book will be perhaps be the first of its type not committed to promoting a predetermined position.
2   Michael Satlow, *Creating Judaism: History, Tradition, Practice* (New York: Columbia University Press, 2006), 3–4. On Judaism not being monolithic and related issues, see also Daniel Boyarin, *Judaism: The Genealogy of a Modern Notion*, None ed. (New Brunswick: Rutgers University Press, 2018) and Aaron J. Hahn Tapper, *Judaisms: A Twenty-First-Century Introduction to Jews and Jewish Identities* (Oakland: University of California Press, 2016).
3   Ayn Rand, *The Fountainhead* (New York: Signet, 1996), 678.
4   Rand, *Fountainhead*, 23.
5   Jerome Tuccille, *It Usually Begins With Ayn Rand* (New York: Stein and Day, 1971), 13–15. I cite the copy of the book my cousin gave to me and still in my collection more than three decades later; however in 2012 a revised and expanded edition was issued, with twenty-nine chapters instead of the original sixteen; see Tuccille, *It Usually Begins With Ayn Rand* (Baltimore: WinklerMedia Publishing Group, 2012).
6   Douglas Brinkley, "Obama and the Road Ahead: The Rolling Stone Interview," *Rolling Stone*, November 8, 2012, http://www.rollingstone.com/politics/news/obama-and-the-road-ahead-the-rolling-stone-interview-20121025#ixzz3zJnOVUL1.
7   Though with a different meaning, more a philosophical than a political one, focused on free will as contrasted with determinism.
8   Dean Russell, "Who is a Libertarian?," *Ideas on Liberty*, Fee.org, May 1, 1955, https://fee.org/articles/who-is-a-libertarian/.
9   David Boaz, *The Libertarian Mind: A Manifesto for Freedom*, rev. ed. (New York: Simon & Schuster, 2015), 35.
10 From interview "Question Period: Noam Chomsky on Being Censored, CHRC Censorship, Ayn Rand, Robert Nozick and Libertarianism," interview by Peter Jaworski, *The Shotgun Blog*, December 8, 2008, https://westernstandard.blogs.com/shotgun/2008/12/question-period.html, and quoted at Brian Leitter, "Chomsky on Libertarianism and Its Meaning," *Leiter Reports: A Philosophy Blog* (Blog), August 11, 2009, https://leiterreports.typepad.com/blog/2009/08/chomsky-on-libertarianism-and-its-meaning.html.
11 For the 1972 *Libertarian Party Platform* and the Libertarian Party platforms adopted for every even numbered year since, see "National Platform," lpedia.org, accessed June 22, 2020, https://lpedia.org/wiki/National_Platform.
12 Despite the initial success of the Tea Party and its professed, libertarian-friendly goals of smaller government and lower taxes, most of its elected officials appear to have since abandoned any such principles in their often fawning support of their party's clearly nonlibertarian president.
13 See "Libertarian Party's 2019 State of the Union Address," lp.org, January 23, 2019, https://www.lp.org/libertarian-response-to-2019-state-of-the-union/.
14 Robert Draper, "Has the 'Libertarian Moment' Finally Arrived?" *New York Times*, August 7, 2014.
15 Nick Gillespie and Matt Welch, "The Libertarian Moment," *Reason*, November 25, 2008.
16 David Boaz et al, "Was the 'Libertarian Moment' Wishful Thinking?," cato.org, May/June 2016, https://www.cato.org/sites/cato.org/files/serials/files/policy-report/2016/5/cpr-v38n3-3.pdf, 9–11, 16.

17 Kevin D. Williamson, "The Passing of the Libertarian Moment," *Atlantic*, April 2, 2018, https://www.theatlantic.com/politics/archive/2018/04/defused/556934/.
18 See Amanda Becker, "Americans don't like big government—but like many programs: poll," reuters.com, last modified April 30, 2015, https://www.reuters.com/article/us-usa-election-libertarians/americans-dont-like-big-government-but-like-many-programs-poll-idUSKBN0NL15B20150430.
19 Jocelyn Kiley, *In search of Libertarians* (Washington, DC Pew Research Center, 2014), https://www.pewresearch.org/fact-tank/2014/08/25/in-search-of-libertarians/.
20 See Daniel Cox, Juhem Navarro-Rivera, and Robert P. Jones, *In Search of Libertarians in America* (Washington, DC, PRRI, October 29, 2013), http://www.prri.org/research/2013-american-values-survey/, accessed February 9, 2017.
21 According to the Pew Center, 2.2 percent of the US population consists of individuals who are Jewish by religion or were raised Jewish and still consider themselves Jewish, though not religiously so. See *A Portrait of Jewish Americans* (Washington DC, Pew Research Center, October 1, 2013), http://www.pewforum.org/2013/10/01/chapter-1-population-estimates/. The US Census Bureau put the figure at 2.1 percent in 2010; see *Statistical Abstract of the United States 2012*, Section 1, *Population* (Washington, DC, US Census Bureau, 2012), https://www.census.gov/prod/2011pubs/12statab/pop.pdf.
22 The following is anecdotal, and though not conclusive, it does have a ring of truth to it. Rabbi Berel Wein recounts a story I also recall hearing myself once from Rabbi Shlomo Carlebach:

> Shlomo Carlebach once said that when he performed on college campuses and asked a student who he or she was, the student would answer "I am Catholic." Carlebach said that then he knew that that person was Catholic. If another student told him he or she was Lutheran, he knew that that student was Lutheran. But if the student's answer was that he or she was a human being, then Carlebach knew that person was Jewish.

See Rabbi Berel Wein, "History," *Rabbi Wein.com* (Blog), accessed August 20, 2017, http://www.rabbiwein.com/blog/history-117.html.
23 GBAO Research and Strategy, *J Street: National Post-Election Survey* (Washington, DC: GBAO Research and Strategy, 2016), http://jstreet.org/wp-content/uploads/2016/11/2016-survey.pdf, for full results; see also "2016 Election Exit Polls," *The Washington Post*, November 29, 2016, https://www.washingtonpost.com/graphics/politics/2016-election/exit-polls/ (survey of 24,558 randomly selected voters through exit polling on election day and telephone polling of early and absentee voters, conducted by Edison Media Research for the *Washington Post*, the National Election Pool, and other organizations).
24 See https://www.ajc.org/news/ajc-survey-of-american-jewish-opinion-2016
25 Williamson, "Passing."
26 For any readers interested in the degree to which her or his own ideas fit within a libertarian framework, or how to categorize them, the Nolan Chart offers a characterization based upon answering a set of questions. David Nolan, a libertarian, designed the original quiz and chart, so this is less an unbiased, apolitical, social science instrument and more a tool to get one thinking about political ideas and beliefs. Versions of the quiz can be found at numerous websites, including the

following: http://www.polquiz.com/, https://www.nolanchart.com/survey-php, and http://freedomkeys.com/whoshould.htm.
27 My gratitude goes to Professor Moshe Koppel, founder and chairman of the Kohelet Policy Forum for sharing his understanding of the place of libertarians and libertarianism in the Israeli political landscape. The tagline of the Forum is "National sovereignty. Individual liberty." According to its website (www.en.kohelet.org.il), "The Kohelet Policy Forum strives to secure Israel's future as the nation state of the Jewish people, to strengthen representative democracy, and to broaden individual liberty and free market principles in Israel." Among other things, the organization conducts research, publishes policy papers, and engages in educational activities. For a libertarian defense of Israel's legal status, with a focus on private property rights, see the following over one-hundred-page article: Walter E. Block, Alan G. Futerman, and Rafi Farber, "The Legal Status of the State of Israel: A Libertarian Approach," *Indonesian Journal of International & Comparative Law* 3, no. 3 (July 2016): 435–553. See, also, the same authors' much briefer piece: Alan Futerman, Rafi Farber, and Walter E. Block, "The Libertarian Case for Israel," *Forward*, October 13, 2016, https://forward.com/scribe/351957/tk-tk/=.
28 The issues of freedom and of God's ownership of us both raise, at least implicitly, the matter of free will, yet this remains a massive philosophical and theological topic in its own right, one outside the scope of this book. Let us just say that one can discuss the first two matters without needing to make a determination as to the latter.
29 The 2018 platform was adopted at the party's July 2018 Convention, held in New Orleans, Louisiana. See Libertarian Party, *Libertarian Party Platform*, lp.org, accessed June 23, 2020, https://www.lp.org/wp-content/uploads/2018/09/Libertarian-Party-Platform-2018.pdf.
30 Jason Brennan, *Libertarianism: What Everyone Needs to Know* (Oxford: Oxford University Press, 2012), 5.
31 See, for example, Béla Kapossy, Isaac Nakhimovsky, and Richard Whatmore, eds., *Commerce and Peace in the Enlightenment* (Cambridge: Cambridge University Press, 2017), and Istvan Hont and Michael Ignatieff, eds., *Wealth and Virtue: The Shaping of Political Economy in the Scottish Enlightenment* (Cambridge: Cambridge University Press, 1986).
32 *Libertarian Party Platform*.
33 John Locke, *Locke: Two Treatises of Government*, 2 vols., ed. Peter Laslett, 3rd ed. (New York: Cambridge University Press, 1988), 269. For this and other citations of Locke, all references are to the second of the two treatises.
34 Ibid., 284.
35 Ludwig von Mises, *Liberty & Property*, Lrg ed. (n.p.: CreateSpace Independent Publishing Platform, 2009), 48.
36 Murray N. Rothbard, *For a New Liberty: The Libertarian Manifesto*, intro. Llewellyn H. Rockwell Jr. (n.p.: CreateSpace Independent Publishing Platform, 2006), 50.
37 Boaz, *Libertarian Mind*, 96.
38 Rose Wilder Lane, *The Discovery of Freedom: Man's Struggle Against Authority* (New York: The John Day Company, 1943), 149–150. Lane, along with Ayn Rand and Isabel Paterson, is considered by some as one of the three women who inspired the modern libertarian movement. In the single year of 1943, Lane published *The Discovery of Freedom*, Paterson *The God of the Machine*, and Rand *The Fountainhead*. On the three writers, their books, and their friendship, see Jim

Powell, "Rose Wilder Lane, Isabel Paterson, and Ayn Rand: Three Women Who Inspired the Modern Libertarian Movement | Jim Powell, Ayn Rand," fee.org, accessed June 21, 2020, https://fee.org/articles/rose-wilder-lane-isabel-paterson-and-ayn-rand-three-women-who-inspired-the-modern-libertarian-movement/; and Cato Institute, "Three Women Who Launched a Movement," Libertarianism.org, accessed June 19, 2020, https://www.libertarianism.org/publications/essays/three-women-who-launched-movement.

39 *Ha-Shem* translates literally as *the Name* and is a means of referencing God without saying a name of God, often or usually the Tetragrammaton, the unpronounceable four-letter name of God, the letter *yud* followed by the letter *he* followed by the letter *vav* followed be the letter *he*. The Tetragrammaton, which appears twice in the opening verse of the Shema, is often pronounced *Adonai*, which technically means my lord and is usually translated as *the Lord*.

40 *The Koren Pirkei Avot*, trans., Jonathan Sacks, commentary Rabbi Dr. Marc Angel, Blg Rep ed. (Jerusalem; New Milford: Koren Publishers Jerusalem, 2015), 64. Henceforth, referred to as *Pirkei Avot*.

41 Orthodox Jewish law obligates all adult Jews in prayer. Jewish males who have reached their thirteenth birthday and thereby the age of Bar Mitzvah, become obligated to pray three sets of prayers in the morning, afternoon, and evening. Women are welcome to engage in these same prayers, but have an obligation to pray once per day. Conservative Jewish law in principle also views daily prayer as obligatory, though not necessarily making distinctions based upon sex. By contrast, Reform Judaism operates according to a principle of individual choice, not obligating any particular practices. The reasons and justifications for differential prayer and other ritual obligations and status for men and women in Orthodox Jewish law and communities is a complicated topic and not a focus of this book. For our purposes, observant Judaism, whether Orthodox or not, considers prayer obligatory, not voluntary.

42 Joseph B. Soloveitchik, *And From There You Shall Seek* (Jersey City: KTAV Publishing House, 2009), 44, 35.

43 Aharon Lichtenstein, *By His Light: Character and Values in the Service of God* (Jersey City: KTAV Publishing House, 2002), 49, 55.

44 Levi Morrow, "God, Torah, Self: Accepting the Yoke of Heaven in the Writings of Rav Shagar," *Lehrhaus*, May 26, 2017, https://thelehrhaus.com/scholarship/god-torah-self-accepting-the-yoke-of-heaven-in-the-writings-of-rav-shagar/. In recent years, with the translation into English of his essays, Rav Shagar has become increasingly well known outside of Israel as someone who sought to integrate Orthodox Judaism and postmodernism.

45 Joshua Berman, *Created Equal: How the Bible Broke with Ancient Political Thought* (Oxford: Oxford University Press, 2011), 88.

46 From the Passover Haggadah passage citing the Babylonian Talmud Pesaḥim 116b, as well as Exodus 13:8 and Deuteronomy 6:23.

47 Morrow, "God, Torah."

48 See, for example, Alex S. Ozar, "Yeridah Le-Ẓorekh Aliyyah: Rabbi Joseph B. Soloveitchik on Autonomy and Submission," *The Torah U-Madda Journal* 17 (2016–2017): 150–173. See also Alexander Carlebach, "Autonomy, Heteronomy and Theonomy," *Tradition* 6, no. 1 (Fall 1963): 5–29.

49 Ezra Bick, "Prayer," etzion.org, accessed June 28, 2015, http://etzion.org.il/en/prayer-1.
50 Isaiah Berlin, "Two Concepts of Liberty," in *Liberty: Incorporating Four Essays on Liberty*, ed. Henry Hardy, 2nd ed. (Oxford: Oxford University Press, 2002), 166–217.
51 Brennan, *Libertarianism*, 28–29.
52 For one critic of Brennan, see George H. Smith, "Negative and Positive Liberty," Libertarianism.org, accessed December 19, 2017, https://www.libertarianism.org/publications/essays/negative-positive-liberty.
53 Abraham Joshua Heschel, *The Sabbath* (New York: Farrar Straus Giroux, 2005).
54 Nathan Lopes Cardozo, "Johann Sebastian Bach & Halacha," David Cardozo Academy, accessed June 25, 2017, https://www.cardozoacademy.org/thoughts-to-ponder/johann-sebastian-bach-halacha-ttp-35/.
55 *Pirkei Avot* 6:2, 56.
56 Locke, *Two Treatises*, 306.
57 Ibid.
58 Bick, "Prayer."
59 Joseph B. Soloveitchik, *Festival of Freedom: Essays on Pesah And the Haggadah*, ed. Joel B. Wolowelsky and Reuven Ziegler (Jersey City: KTAV Publishing House, 2006), 22–25.
60 Yeshayahu Leibowitz, *Judaism, Human Values, and the Jewish State*, ed. Eliezer Goldman, trans. Yoram Navon et al., rev. ed. (Cambridge, MA: Harvard University Press, 1995), 21–22.
61 For a number of additional explanations of Biblical slavery and attempts to reconcile it with modern sensibilities and ethics, see Gamliel Shmalo, "Orthodox Approaches to Biblical Slavery," *The Torah U-Madda Journal* 16 (2012–2013): 1–20.
62 In truth, human slavery, in the form of sex trafficking, remains widespread in the twenty-first century, with more humans effectively enslaved than at any time in history. The estimates exceed *forty million* enslaved human beings. For more information, see the website of the organization Anti-Slavery: https://www.antislavery.org/slavery-today/modern-slavery/, accessed June 23, 2020. See also this interactive guide from the Council on Foreign Relations: https://www.cfr.org/interactives/modern-slavery/#!/section1/item-1, accessed June 23, 2020. For the United States specifically, please visit the website of Polaris, an organization fighting slavery and human trafficking in the United States: www.polarisproject.org; for their typology of twenty-five kinds of slavery in the United States, see www.https://polarisproject.org/typology, accessed 23 June, 2020.
63 Berman, *Created*, 106, 103. Berman is an ordained Orthodox Rabbi as well as an academic scholar of the Bible and the ancient Near East.
64 B. Kiddushin, 20b.

Chapter 2

1 Locke, *Two Treatises*, 287.
2 Ibid., 287–288.
3 *Libertarian Party Platform*. Notably, the 1972 *Libertarian Party Platform* does not include any reference to the idea of self-ownership; indeed, this critical concept,

if implicit from the start, does not become explicit until the adoption of the 2014 platform; see https://lpedia.org/wiki/National_Platform.
4   Boaz, *Libertarian Mind*, 84, 85–86.
5   Rothbard, *New Liberty*, 35.
6   Ibid., 34–35.
7   Philosophers of libertarianism engage in extensive debates over self-ownership and particularly over the notion of *full* self-ownership. For the barest introduction to such debates, see *Stanford Encyclopedia of Philosophy*, s.v. "Libertarianism," Stanford University, accessed July 2, 2020, https://plato.stanford.edu/entries/libertarianism/: "If few libertarians endorse full self-ownership, even fewer endorse it as a foundational principle."
8   Rothbard, *New Liberty*, 33–34.
9   J. David Bleich, *Judaism and Healing: Halakhic Perspectives* (Jersey City: Ktav Pub Inc, 2002), 198.
10 Alfred Cohen, "Whose Body? Living with Pain," *Journal of Halacha and Contemporary Society* 32 (1996): 39–64.
11 Contrasted with passive euthanasia, not categorically rejected by Judaism.
12 Emanuel Rackman, *A Modern Orthodox Life: Sermons and Columns of Rabbi Emanuel Rackman* (Jersey City: KTAV Publishing House, 2008), 97.
13 Immanuel Jakobovits, "Some Modern Responsa on Medico-Moral Problems," *Assia: Jewish Medical Ethics* 1 (1998): 5–16. For his classic book, see Immanuel Jakobovits, *Jewish Medical Ethics*, box ed. (New York: Bloch Publishing Company, 1975).
14 Alan Jotkowitz, "The Intersection of Halakhah and Science in Medical Ethics: The Approach of Rabbi Eliezer Waldenberg, " *Ḥakirah: The Flatbush Journal of Jewish Law and Thought* 19 (Summer 2015): 103.
15 Daniel B. Sinclair, "Jewish Bioethics: The End of Life," in *The Oxford Handbook of Jewish Ethics and Morality*, ed. by Elliot N. Dorff and Jonathan K. Crane (Oxford, New York: Oxford University Press, 2016), 330–344. On the issue of Jewish bioethics and end of life care, see also Daniel Eisenberg, "Maintaining Compassion for the Suffering Terminal Patient While Preserving Life: An Orthodox Jewish Approach," *Perspectives in Biology and Medicine* 60, no. 2 (2017): 233–246. See p. 235 on the general notion of ownership of the body:

> Judaism approaches health from the perspective that humans function merely as stewards of their bodies, with true ownership rights retained by God. Like curators assigned the task of protecting delicate buildings, individuals are charged with guarding their bodies from preventable decay, destruction, and other imminent threats to their future, while mandated to use their bodies in a constructive way.

16 Shimon Finkelman, *Shabbos: The Sabbath, Its Essence and Significance* (Brooklyn: Artscroll, Mesorah Publications Ltd., 1994), 34.
17 I found this story in two different books, though neither cites the source of the original story or quotation. See Chaim Jachter, *Gray Matter*, vol. 3, *Exploring Contemporary Halakhic Challenges* (n.p.: Kol Torah Publications, 2008), 22. See also Shmuly Yankowitz, *The Soul of Jewish Social Justice* (Jerusalem: Urim Publications, 2014), 223.

18 Dena S. Davis, "Method in Jewish Bioethics: An Overview," *Journal of Contemporary Law* 20, no. 2 (1994): 329–330.
19 Elliot N. Dorff, "The Jewish Tradition," in *Caring and Curing: Health and Medicine in the Western Religious Traditions*, ed. by Ronald L. Numbers and Darrel W. Amundsen (Baltimore: Johns Hopkins University Press, 1998), 9.
20 Adam Goodkind, "Bodies on Loan: The Ethics of 'Renting' a Body," in *Jewish Choices, Jewish Voices: Body*, ed. Rabbi Elliot N. Dorff and Louis E. Newman (Philadelphia: Jewish Publication Society, 2008), 40.
21 Meir Dan-Cohen, *Harmful Thoughts: Essays on Law, Self, and Morality* (Princeton: Princeton University Press, 2002), 265.
22 Goodkind, "Bodies," 41.
23 Shlomo Zevin, "Mishpat Shylock" [Hebrew: The Case of Shylock], in *Le'Or Hahalacha* (Jerusalem: Beyt Hillel, 1946), 311–335. My gratitude goes to Rabbi Aryeh Klapper for introducing me to this debate and providing me with some materials and translations of the sources.
24 Shaul Yisraeli, "Tikrit Kivyeh l'or Ha-halacha," [Hebrew: The Incident at Kibye in the Light of Halakha], *Ha-Torah ve-ha-Medina* 5 (1953–1954): 71–113.
25 See letter of Nissan 26, 5772 (9April 14, 1969), accessed July 5, 2012, https://www.chabad.org/therebbe/letters/default_cdo/aid/1898676/jewish/Hebrew-Pronunciation-and-Organ-Donation.htm.
26 Avraham Steinberg, *Encyclopedia of Jewish Medical Ethics*, trans. Fred Rosner (Jerusalem; New York: Feldheim), 555.
27 Fred Rosner and Edward Reichman, "Payment for Organ Donation in Jewish Law," in *The Oxford Handbook of Judaism and Economics*, ed. Aaron Levine (Oxford: Oxford University Press, 2010), 328–329.
28 Steinberg, *Encyclopedia*, 555.
29 Although we have not quite stated it outright, self-ownership and the Lockean notion of having property in oneself suggest that in some sense we are property (objects) and not just persons (subjects). Some of us might find this idea troubling.
30 Pascal-Emmanuel Gobry, "The Libertarian Case for National Military Service," *Cato Unbound: A Journal of Debate*, September 9, 2013, https://www.cato-unbound.org/2013/09/09/pascal-emmanuel-gobry/libertarian-case-national-military-service.
31 *Libertarian Party Platform.*
32 Of course, in this matter as in others, I do not mean to provide Jewish legal advice; individuals seeking to make a decision about a particular situation would be advised to consult an appropriate religious authority. For the original Hebrew quoted in the text, see the following:
R. Eliezer Waldenberg, *Tzitz Eli'ezer* 9:51, chapter 3:

כשנשקפת סכנה לאשה בהמשכת ההריון יש להתיר הפלת העובר בשופי. גם כשמצב בריאותה של
האשה רופף מאד ולשם רפואתה או השקטת מכאוביה הגדולים דרוש לבצע הפלת העובר, אע"פ
שאין סכנה להתיר לעשות זאת, וכפי ראות עיני המורה המצב שלפניו

In regard to the specific case of Tay Sachs disease, Rabbi Waldenberg writes the following in *Tzitz Eli'ezer* 13:102, chapter 1:

Regarding the termination of pregnancy due to detection of Tay-Sachs in the fetus: After seriously examining all the facts concerning this serious question, in my humble opinion, based on what I have already clarified concerning the termination of pregnancy in my work Tzitz Eliezer Vol. 9:51 (section 3), it would be possible to permit performing an abortion up until the seventh month in this unique circumstance where the consequences of continuing the pregnancy are so severe. The abortion must be performed in a manner that there be no danger involved to the mother. From seven months and on the matter is much more severe.

הפסקת הריון בגלל המחלה הנקראת תייסקס כאשר מאבחנים את המחלה בעובר: והנה אחרי העיון
בדבר בכובד ראש בכל צדדי הנתונים שבבעיה האמורה, נלפענ"ד על יסוד הבירורים. הנרחבים
שכתבתי בדבר הפסקת הריון בספרי שו"ת צ"א חלק ט' סי' נ"א שער ג' על שלשת פרקיו
הארוכים. כי שבמקרה המיוחד הזה אשר תוצאות כה חמורות בכנפיו עם המשכת ההריון והלידה,
אפשר להתיר הפסקת הריון עד שבעה חדשים, ובאופן שבביצוע הפסקת ההריון לא יהא כרוך
בשום סכנה לאם. משבעה חדשים והלאה הדבר כבר יותר חמור.

These passages, including the English translations, can be found at https://www.sefaria.org/sheets/75444.31?lang=bi&with=all&lang2=en in the source sheet "Halachic Perspective on Abortion," assembled by Joshua Kotz, accessed December 1, 2019. The invaluable website https://www.sefaria.org provides access to many Jewish texts in Hebrew, and often in English translation, as well source sheets on a plethora of topics, source sheets assembled by individuals making use of the website and sharing what they produce.

For a broad and thorough examination of abortion in Jewish law, see Steinberg, *Encyclopedia*, 1–29.

33 Although in 2019 two prominent Orthodox organizations, the Rabbinical Council of America and Agudath Israel of America, criticized a new law in New York basically removing all restrictions on abortions prior to twenty-four weeks of gestation, both organizations "emphasized that they are not opposed to abortion in all cases, as Catholic and evangelical groups tend to be. Both said that Jewish law not only permits but in some cases requires abortion—for example, if the expectant mother's life is threatened. And both said abortion could be permitted in other cases as well—for example, if it would prevent serious psychological harm to the expectant mother." Another prominent organization, the Orthodox Union, did not even weigh in. See Ben Sales, "Orthodox rabbis compare abortion to murder—and Orthodox women are angry about it," *Jewish Telegraphic Agency*, January 31, 2019, https://www.jta.org/2019/01/31/culture/orthodox-groups-come-out-swinging-against-new-yorks-abortion-law.

34 Locke, *Two Treatises*, 271.

Chapter 3

1 *Libertarian Party Platform*.
2 Ibid.
3 Tom G. Palmer, *Realizing Freedom: Libertarian Theory, History, and Practice*, expanded ed. (Washington, DC: Cato Institute, 2014), 19.
4 See Locke, *Two Treatises*, 287–88.
5 Ibid., 290–291.

6   Ibid., 300–302.
7   Ibid., 360.
8   Ibid., 360–361; see also 362.
9   Brennan, *Libertarianism*, 111–112.
10 Boaz, *Libertarian Mind*, 87.
11 Ibid., 89–90.
12 Rothbard, *New Liberty*, 52.
13 John Hospers, *Libertarianism: A Political Philosophy for Tomorrow* (n.p.: CreateSpace Independent Publishing Platform, 2013), 29.
14 Ibid., 30.
15 Ibid., 31; Rothbard, *New Liberty*, 52–53.
16 Samson Raphael Hirsch, *The Nineteen Letters on Judaism* (Jerusalem: Feldheim Publishers, 1969), 87.
17 *Koren Talmud Bavli, Noé Edition*, vol. 1, *Berakhot*, commentary by Adin Even-Israel Steinsaltz, Hebrew/English ed. (Jerusalem: Koren Publishers, 2012), 240. From here referred to as bBer.
18 Here is the original text from the *Or ha-Chaim*:

תגנובו וגו

סמך מצות גניבה למצות פאת שדה. אולי שנתכוין על דרך מה שאמרו בתורת כהנים (כאן) וזה לשונם בן בג בג אומר לא תגנוב את שלך מהגנב שלא תראה כגונב ע"כ. וכאן נתכוין במה שסמך לא תגנובו לפאה, שבא עליה באזהרה לבל יגנוב אותה בחושבו כי שלו הוא לוקח

Torat Kohanim—although sometimes this refers to the book of Leviticus, here it refers to the *Sifra*, a talmudic-era midrashic commentary on the book of Leviticus; see *Sifra Kedoshim*, section 2.
Here is the relevant text from the *Sifra*:

[ב] "לא תגנובו" על מנת למיקט. "לא תגנובו" על מנת לשלם תשלומי כפל ולא על מנת לשלם תשלומי ארבעה וחמשה. בן בג בג אומר לא תגנוב את שלך מאחר הגנב שלא תראה גונב

2) "You shall not steal": (Even if only) to taunt the owner (thinking to return the theft afterwards). "You shall not steal": (Even to benefit the owner) thinking to pay (*kefel*) double (the amount of what you have stolen) or to pay "four and five" (times the amount of what you have stolen). Ben Bag Bag says: Do not steal what is yours from behind the thief, so that you yourself not appear to be a thief (but claim the object from him to his face).
The *Sifra* here presents a number of ways someone ought not to justify stealing: as a joke; as a means of finding a way to give money to someone (by having to pay the required penalty); or, as per Ben Bag Bag, by thinking oneself the owner. Stealing is a serious business and should not be carried out even for seemingly good or seemingly harmless reasons.
19 The Land of Israel generally refers to the areas allotted to the twelve tribes, following the Exodus. Its borders do not necessarily match exactly the borders of the modern State of Israel.
20 Rabbi Sacks reminds us that under Jewish law, not only does a person not work on the Sabbath, such a person does not employ others to do work on her or his behalf; see Jonathan Sacks, *Morals and Markets: Seventh Annual Hayek Memorial Lecture* (London: Institute of Economic Affairs, 1999), 20.

21 See Rashi to Leviticus 25:5–6.
22 See Sforno to Jeremiah 34:17.
23 Rabbi Dr Isaac Herzog, *The Main Institutions of Jewish Law*, vol. 1, *The Law of Property*, foreword by Professor M. Silberg (London; New York: The Soncino Press Limited, 1965), 71.
24 Ibid., 67.
25 Madeline Kochen, *Organ Donation and the Divine Lien in Talmudic Law* (New York: Cambridge University Press, 2014), 62.
26 Ibid., 76.
27 Hillel died in the year 10 of the Common Era, and according to tradition lived to the age of 120, the same as Moses. The Second Temple, in Jerusalem, was destroyed in 70 CE.
28 Moreshet Saul, "Shabbat Parashat Emor|5767," eretzhemdah.org, accessed May 28, 2018, http://www.eretzhemdah.org/newsletterArticle.asp?lang=en&pageid=48&cat=7&newsletter=96&article=300. Excerpted from pages 277–280 of *HaRabbanut v'HaMedina* by Rabbi Shaul Yisraeli.
29 Genesis 23.
30 *Pirkei Avot* 2:17, p. 50
31 Jonathan Sacks, "Re'eh (5771)—Making Poverty History," Rabbisacks.org, accessed August 27, 2011, http://rabbisacks.org/covenant-conversation-5771-reeh-making-poverty-history/.
32 Jonathan Sacks, "Judaism's Religious Vision and the Capitalist Ethic," Acton.org, accessed June 8, 2018, https://acton.org/pub/religion-liberty/volume-11-number-6/judaisms-religious-vision-and-capitalist-ethic.
33 Sacks, *Morals*, 16.
34 *Pirkei Avot* 2:2, p. 32.
35 See Rabbi Slifkin's blog *Rationalist Judaism* at www.rationalistjudaism.com.
36 *Koren Talmud Bavli, Noé Edition*, vol. 1, Berakhot, 241.
37 See, for example, the Tannaim, the Rosh, and Korban Nesanel. The accepted opinion of the tradition affirms its acceptability.
38 Isadore Twersky, ed., *A Maimonides Reader* (New York: Behrman House, Inc., 1972), 67–68.
39 See, in Maimonides, *Mishneh Torah*, book 1, Knowledge (Sefer ha-Madda), the section on the study of the Torah 3:10.
40 See Rabbi Dr. Natan Slifkin "The Chasam Sofer is Astounding!" *Rationalist Judaism* (Blog), June 24, 2020, http://www.rationalistjudaism.com/2014/03/this-chasam-sofer-is-astounding.html.
41 David Conway, "Judaism and Liberalism: Israel's Economic Problem with its Haredim," *Economic Affairs* 37, no. 2 (2017): 250, 240.
42 For a look at Jewish attitudes towards materialism in a very different context, that of nineteenth and early twentieth-century European and Zionist politics, see Eliyahu Stern, *Jewish Materialism: The Intellectual Revolution of the 1870s* (New Haven: Yale University Press, 2018).
43 Rabbi Jonathan Sacks, *To Heal a Fractured World: The Ethics of Responsibility* (New York: Schocken Books, 2005), 27.
44 For a persuasive essay arguing that the expression *l'taken 'olam* in the daily 'aleinu prayer is actually a scriptural or publishing error, see Mitchell First, "Aleinu: Obligation to Fix the World or the Text?," *Ḥakirah* 11 (2011): 187–97.

45 Sarah Yehudit (Susan) Schneider, *Eating as Tikun* (Jerusalem: A Still Small Voice, 1996), 11. Some write G-d instead of God, in order not to spell out unnecessarily a name of God, especially upon paper that might be disposed of in the trash. In terms of the notion of elevating the souls of animals by eating them, let us just say that not everyone finds such a notion plausible or laudable. I use the notion to characterize a Jewish mystical approach to the material world and not to endorse this particular case.
46 Italics added.
47 Sacks, *Morals*, 22.
48 Sacks, "Judaism's Religious Vision."
49 Saul Berman, "Jewish Environmental Values—The Dynamic Tension Between Nature and Human Needs," Jewishvirtuallibrary.org, accessed 24 June, 2020, https://www.jewishvirtuallibrary.org/jewish-environmental-values-the-dynamic-tension-between-nature-and-human-needs.
50 Berman, *Created*, 90–91.
51 Kochen, *Organ Donation*, 83: "There are also items that seem to be hybrid property with some kind of joint ownership."
52 Herzog, *Main Institutions*, 213–215.
53 In the nonmonetary realm of theology, the related principle of *shituf* has been employed since the twelfth century of the common era by some Jewish thinkers as a means of understanding Christianity as a monotheistic religion. With its Trinity, Christianity might be viewed as an idolatrous religion of three divinities, and therefore not a truly monotheistic religion, yet the notion of *shituf* has been used to explain the Trinity as three associated parts of a single God, a multiplicity in God. Indeed, in recent decades, at least, the same approach has been used to characterize Hinduism, with its seeming panoply of divinities, as an essentially monotheistic religion. see Alan Brill, *Judaism and Other Religions: Models of Understanding* (Basingstoke: Palgrave Macmillan, 2014), 176–180, and Alan Brill, *Judaism and World Religions: Encountering Christianity, Islam, and Eastern Traditions* (New York: Palgrave Macmillan, 2012), 229.
54 Kochen, *Organ Donation*, 65.
55 Ibid.
56 Ibid., 67.
57 Ibid.
58 Ibid., 68.
59 Ibid., 69. Kochen cites as foundational for her book a classic work in anthropology: Marcel Mauss, *The Gift: The Form and Reason for Exchange in Archaic Societies*, trans. W. D. Halls (New York, W. W. Norton & Company, 2000).
60 See the entirety of Kochen, *Organ Donation*, chapter 3, including page 101: "From their place within the broader rabbinic structure of mandatory gifts as conditions to initial or continuing ownership, other portions owed to the poor (leket – gleanings, peah – corner of the field, etc.) also share something in common with portions due to the priests. They are linked to the same divine lien, which under like circumstances operates in like manner – requiring the human donor to forfeit property in favor of another person as a condition of ownership."
61 J. David Bleich, "The Metaphysics of Property Interests in Jewish Law: An Analysis of Kinyan," *Tradition* 43, no. 2 (2010): 51.

62 J. David Bleich, *The Philosophical Quest: Of Philosophy, Ethics, Law and Halakhah* (Jerusalem: Koren Publishers, 2013), 328. Why, according to Rabbi Bleich, does a "meeting of minds" not serve as a sufficient condition for the transfer of property ownership? See page 326: "In Jewish law the concept of property reflects not rights but ontology. To be sure, there are rights that flow from the proprietor-property relationship, but those rights flow from . . . an ontological state." That is the existential status of the object itself is at issue and not merely which person has a right in the property of the object. He compares this to the institution of marriage, in which a metaphysical arrangement engenders certain rights and duties. So too with ownership, the metaphysical status matters.
63 This does not mean that in an actual case in the United States, with a signed contract and payment between a Jewish seller and buyer, that the seller would retain ownership of the spilled syrup. I present this example to illustrate the point, not as legal advice.
64 Kochen, *Organ Donation*, 73.
65 Ibid., 75–76. Also: "The lack of clarity is compounded by the fact that different combinations or hybrids of property ownership (divine and human) are possible" (Ibid., 73).
66 Ibid., 72.
67 Ibid., 107–108.
68 Ibid., 69.

Chapter 4

1   Rothbard, *New Liberty*, 28.
2   Palmer, *Realizing Freedom*, 499.
3   Rothbard, *New Liberty*, 29.
4   Ibid., 104–106.
5   Isabel Paterson, *The God in the Machine* (New Brunswick: Routledge, 1993), 246.
6   Robert Nozick, *Anarchy, State, and Utopia* (New York: Basic Books, 2013), 272.
7   Locke, *Two Treatises*, 361–362.
8   Ibid., 363.
9   *Libertarian Party Platform*, Section 2.4.
10 Boaz, *Libertarian Mind*, 283–284.
11 Hospers, *Libertarianism*, 216–217.
12 Ibid., 218.
13 See Aryeh Klapper, "Will the Messianic Monarchy be Limited or Unlimited?" an unpublished paper available for download at academia.edu, accessed August 25, 2019, https://www.academia.edu/16005359/Will_the_Messianic_Monarchy_be_Limited_or_Unlimited.
14 Moshe Halbertal and Stephen Holmes, *The Beginning of Politics: Power in the Biblical Book of Samuel* (Princeton: Princeton University Press, 2017), 5–7.
15 Meir Tamari, *With All Your Possessions: Jewish Ethics and Economic Life*, Kupietzky ed. (Jerusalem: Koren Publishers, 2014), 232.
16 Manuel L. Jose and Charles K. Moore, "The Development of Taxation in the Bible: Improvements in Counting, Measurement, and Computation in the Ancient Middle East," *The Accounting Historians Journal* 25, no. 2 (December 1998): 65–68.

17 Ibid., 64.
18 Robert A. Oden, Jr., "Taxation in Biblical Israel," *The Journal of Religious Ethics* 12, no. 2 (Fall 1984): 163; Elon, "Taxation," in Menachem Elon, ed., *The Principles of Jewish Law* (Jerusalem: Keter, 1975), 663.
19 Oden, "Taxation," 165–171.
20 Ibid., 164.
21 Ibid.; Oden quotes Salo Baron, *A Social and Religious History of the Jews*, vol. 1, 2nd ed. (New York: Columbia University Press, 1952), 76.
22 Tamari, *Possessions*, 233.
23 Lifshitz, *Judaism, Law*, 36.
24 Aaron Levine, *Economic Public Policy and Jewish Law* (Hoboken: KTAV Publishing House, 1993), 202; see also pages 23–24. The book deals with numerous fascinating topics, including the minimum wage, the goal of full employment, price setting, government regulation, and trading on insider information, though for the most part Rabbi Levine analyzes matters within the framework of Jewish law and not in terms of Jews living under the laws of a secular government. For more of his contributions and the contributions of others to these issues, see Aaron Levine, ed., *The Oxford Handbook of Judaism and Economics* (New York: Oxford University Press, 2010), as well as a number of other books he has authored.
25 Elisheva Carlebach, "The Early Modern Jewish Community and its Institutions," in *The Cambridge History of Judaism*, vol. 7, *The Early Modern World, 1500–1815*, ed. Jonathan Karp and Adam Sutcliffe (Cambridge: Cambridge University Press, 2018), 168.
26 Ibid., 181.
27 Ibid., 182.
28 Ibid.
29 Adam Chodorow, "Biblical Tax Systems and the Case for Progressive Taxation," *Journal of Law & Religion* 23, no. 1 (2007): 144.
30 *Arba-ah Turim*, section 247:

ואל יעלה בלבו עצה לומר איך אחסר ממוני ליתנו לעניים כי יש לו לדעת שאין הממון שלו אלא פקדון לעשות בו רצון המפקיד וזה רצונו שיחלק לעניים ממנו.

31 *Shulchan Arukh* 247:2:

לְעוֹלָם אֵין אָדָם מַעֲנִי מִן הַצְּדָקָה, וְלֹא דָבָר רַע וְלֹא הֶזֵּק מִתְגַּלְגֵּל עַל יָדָהּ, שֶׁנֶּאֱמַר: וְהָיָה מַעֲשֵׂה הַצְּדָקָה שָׁלוֹם. (יְשַׁעְיָה לב, יז)

32 Maimonides, *Mishneh Torah*, Laws of Gifts of the Poor, 10:1, quoted in Sperber, *On the Relationship of Mitzvot Between Man and His Neighbor and Man and His Maker* (Jerusalem: Urim Publications, 2014), 121; the translation, including the bracketed comments and formatting, come from Rabbi Sperber's book.
33 Noam Sachs Zion, *From Each According to One's Ability Duties to Poor People from the Bible to the Welfare State and Tikkun Olam* (Cleveland: Zion Holiday Publications, 2013), 459.
34 Kochen, *Organ Donation*, 79.
35 *Shulchan Arukh*, Yoreh Deah, 247:1 (emphasis added in translation):

מִצְוַת עֲשֵׂה לִתֵּן צְדָקָה כְּפִי הַשָּׂגַת יָד, וְכַמָּה פְּעָמִים נִצְטַוֵּינוּ בָּהּ בְּמִצְוַת עֲשֵׂה. וְיֵשׁ לֹא תַעֲשֶׂה בַּמַּעֲלִים עֵינָיו מִמֶּנָּה, שֶׁנֶּאֱמַר: לֹא תְאַמֵּץ אֶת לְבָבְךָ וְלֹא תִקְפֹּץ אֶת יָדְךָ (דְּבָרִים טו,ז). וְכָל הַמַּעֲלִים עֵינָיו מִמֶּנָּה נִקְרָא בְּלִיַּעַל, וּכְאִלּוּ עוֹבֵד עֲבוֹדַת כּוֹכָבִים. וּמְאֹד יֵשׁ לִזָּהֵר בָּהּ, כִּי אֶפְשָׁר שֶׁיָּבֹא לִידֵי שְׁפִיכוּת דָּמִים, שֶׁיָּמוּת הֶעָנִי הַמְבַקֵּשׁ אִם לֹא יִתֵּן לוֹ מִיָּד, כְּעוּבְדָּא דְנַחוּם אִישׁ גַּם זוֹ.

36 Feuer, *The Tzedakah Treasury*, 110.
37 *Shulchan Arukh*, Yoreh Deah, 247:3:

כָּל הַמְרַחֵם עַל הָעֲנִיִּים, הקב"ה מְרַחֵם עָלָיו. הַגָּה: וְיִתֵּן הָאָדָם עַל לִבּוֹ שֶׁהוּא מְבַקֵּשׁ כָּל שָׁעָה פַּרְנָסָתוֹ מֵהקב"ה, וּכְמוֹ שֶׁהוּא מְבַקֵּשׁ שֶׁהקב"ה יִשְׁמַע שַׁוְעָתוֹ כָּךְ הוּא יִשְׁמַע שַׁוְעַת עֲנִיִּים. גַּם יִתֵּן אֶל לִבּוֹ כִּי הוּא גַּלְגַּל הַחוֹזֵר בָּעוֹלָם, וְסוֹף הָאָדָם שֶׁיָּבֹא הוּא אוֹ בְּנוֹ אוֹ בֶּן בְּנוֹ לִידֵי מִדָּה זוֹ, וְכָל הַמְרַחֵם עַל אֲחֵרִים מְרַחֲמִין עָלָיו (מִלְּשׁוֹן הַטּוּר).

Translation is by the author. Alternatively, here is a translation from https://www.sefaria.org/texts/Halakhah/Shulchan%20Arukh:

> All the ones that are merciful to the poor, the Holy One Blessed Be He is merciful to them. RaMA Note: And the man should take it to heart that he should request every hour of his livelihood from the Holy One Blessed Be He, and like that he requests of this from the HKBH, so should he hear the pleas of poor men. Also he takes it to heart that what goes around comes around in the world, and end of the man that will come him or his son or his grandson are the ones in this state, and all the mercy he has shown to others, the Merciful one will have upon him." In this translation, the RaMA is Rabbi Moshe Isserles; HKBH means HaKodesh Baruch Hu, Hebrew for the Holy One, Blessed be He.

38 Personal conversation with Noam Zion.
39 Ayn Rand, *The Virtue of Selfishness* (New York: Signet, 1963), ix.
40 Ibid., 35.
41 There are actually, whether from a libertarian or liberal perspective, at least a couple of serious problems with tax deductions for charitable giving. The first is that when the government provides a deduction, it is foregoing revenue ordinarily due—and in this sense, all taxpayers are subsidizing the personal charitable giving of some taxpayers. Second of all, the law requires charitable foundations and trusts to give out only a small portion of the monies they hold, something on the order of 5 percent per year. This allows the building of endowments, but it also means that individuals receive tax deductions for charitable giving even though the money contributed may not reach recipients anytime soon, if ever. Some of the wealthiest philanthropists take credit for generosity while at the same time fighting to lower the taxes they pay.
42 Barbara Branden quoted in Rand, *Virtue*, 80.
43 Paterson, *God*, 246–247.
44 Palmer, *Realizing Freedom*, 383.
45 Zion, *From Each*, 446.
46 Ibid., 456.
47 Tamari, *Possessions*, 226–227.

48 Alex Robertson, "Welfare State and Welfare Society," *Social Policy & Administration* 22, no. 3 (December 1988): 222.
49 John J. Rodger, *From a Welfare State to a Welfare Society: The Changing Context of Social Policy in a Postmodern Era* (New York: Red Globe Press, 2000).
50 Zion, *From Each*, 519.
51 Ibid., 520. A *g'mach* is basically a collection of items, such as clothing, available for anyone to come and borrow (or services to use). Zion catalogs the resources available in the g'mach of one contemporary Israeli city: "Pacifiers; *t'fillin*; *mezuzas*; books; roadside help e.g., change of flat tires; spare parts; food and free accommodation for the Shabbat [Sabbath] for relatives of patients hospitalized; religious ritual artifacts; wigs and wedding dresses; clothes including maternity: [Purim] costumes; clothes drying in winter; challas; medicines; legal advice; real estate and job seeking agencies; dogs for the blind; eyeglasses; screws for eyeglasses frames; mother's milk; baby food; medicines; wheel chairs; inhalation equipment and hearing aids; baby furniture; babysitting; flowers with vases; suitcases."
52 Michael Satlow, "Poverty and its Relief," *Then and Now* (Blog), Dec 4, 2017, http://mlsatlow.com/2017/12/04/poverty-and-its-relief/, accessed December 25, 2018.
53 Tamari, *Possessions*, 227; italics added.
54 Zion, *From Each*, 519. For Levenson's original article, see Jon Levenson, "Poverty and the State in Biblical Thought," *Judaism* 25 (1976), 230ff.
55 Zion, *From Each*, 519.
56 Zion, *From Each*, 463.
57 Lifshitz, *Judaism, Law*, 44–45.
58 Zion, *From Each*, 446.
59 Lifshitz, *Judaism, Law*, 21, 33, 34, 54.
60 *Libertarian Party Platform*, Section 2.4.
61 Likhovski, "'Training in Citizenship': Tax Compliance and Modernity," *Law & Social Inquiry* 32, no. 3 (Summer 2007): 671.
62 Ibid., 678–679.
63 Tamari, *Possessions*, 244.
64 James L. Payne "The End of Taxation?" *The Public Interest* 111 (Summer 1993): 113–114.
65 Berman, *Created*, 92–93, 95, 97, 102, 108.

Chapter 5

1 *Pirkei Avot* 3:3, p. 58.
2 Ibid.
3 Although many Americans might not understand the difference, given that Iran sits in the Middle East and the majority of Iranians are Muslim, Iranians are not Arabs and Arabic is not their national or native tongue.
4 To see the text of the letter and learn more about the letter and the Touro synagogue in Newport, Rhode Island, see the synagogue's website, especially "George Washington and His Letter to the Jews of Newport," tourosynagogue.org, accessed December 14, 2019, https://www.tourosynagogue.org/history-learning/gw-letter.
5 *Pirkei Avot* 3:3, p. 61.

6   Haim Hillel Ben-Sasson, *A History of the Jewish People* (Cambridge, MA: Harvard University Press, 1985), 881–990.
7   Ibid., 881. Kiev, or Kyiv, is now the capital of Ukraine, but in the late nineteenth century the city was part of the Russian Empire.
8   Ibid., 656–657.
9   Ibid., 753.
10 See *Global Legal Research Center, Legal Restrictions on Religious Slaughter in Europe: March 2018* (Washington, DC: Global Legal Research Center, Law Library of Congress), https://www.loc.gov/law/help/religious-slaughter/religious-slaughter-europe.pdf; JTA and Cnaan Liphshiz, "Belgium's Flemish Region Bans Jewish and Muslim Methods of Ritual Animal Slaughter," *Haaretz*, Jan 02, 2019, https://www.haaretz.com/world-news/europe/belgium-s-flemish-region-bans-jewish-and-muslim-methods-of-ritual-animal-slaughter-1.6805896.
11 Walter Block, Geoffrey Brennan, and Kenneth Elzinga, eds., *Morality of the Market, Morality of the Market: Religious and Economic Perspectives* (Vancouver: The Fraser Institute, 1985), 403.
12 Ibid., 406.
13 Irving Kristol, "On the Political Stupidity of the Jews," *Azure* 8 (Autumn 1999): 48, 62.
14 Jerry Z. Muller, *Capitalism and the Jews* (Princeton: Princeton University Press, 2010), 2, 5. See also "The Jews and Capitalism: A love-hate enigma," chapter 6 of Walter E. Block, *Religion, Economics and Politics* (n.p.: The Educational Publisher/ Biblio Publishing, 2013).
15 Walter Block and Irving Hexham, eds., *Religion, Economics and Social Thought* (Vancouver: The Fraser Institute, 1986), 403.
16 Sacks, *Morals*, 14.
17 Aaron Rakeffet-Rothkoff, "Dina D'Malkhuta Dina—The Law of the Land in Halakhic Perspective," *Tradition: A Journal of Orthodox Jewish Thought* 13, no. 2 (1972): 6.
18 Rakeffet-Rothkoff argues that it does apply to the secular Israeli government. For an opposing perspective, see Leo Landman, "Dina D'Malkhuta Dina: Solely a Diaspora Concept," *Tradition: A Journal of Orthodox Jewish Thought* 15, no. 3 (1975): 89–96.
19 Herzog, *Main Institutions*, 24–25.
20 B. Gittin. 10b; B. Bava Kama 113a; B. Nedarim 28a; B. Bava Batra 54b. See Rakeffet-Rothkoff, "Dina": 21.
21 Ibid., 14.
22 Ibid., 6.
23 Ibid., 10.
24 Michael Walzer, *In God's Shadow: Politics in the Hebrew Bible* (New Haven: Yale University Press, 2012), 205–206.
25 Halbertal and Holmes, *Beginning*, 5–7.
26 Michael Walzer, Menachem Lorberbaum, and Noam J. Zohar et al, eds., *The Jewish Political Tradition*, vol. 1, *Authority* (New Haven: Yale University Press, 2000), 161–165.
27 See Aryeh Klapper, "Will the Messianic Monarchy be Limited or Unlimited," an unpublished paper available for download at academia.edu: https://www.academia.edu/16005359/Will_the_Messianic_Monarchy_be_Limited_or_Unlimited, accessed August 25, 2019.

28 Yoram Hazony, *The Philosophy of Hebrew Scripture* (New York: Cambridge University Press, 2012), 24, 149, 155, 160.
29 Maymin, *Freedom*, 128–135.
30 Berman critiques Walzer and others for framing the politics of the Bible in terms of modern consent theory rather than in terms of the treaties and context of the ancient Near East; see Berman, *Created*, 29. He also draws significant distinctions between modern and earlier societies. Whereas in the modern world we usually separate out such realms as the political and the theological, in the ancient world and up until the late modern age, religion and politics were integrated as part of a cosmic order: "To understand social and political thought in the ancient Near East, including Israel, we must bear in mind that within the land of Europe and the Near East from antiquity until the Renaissance, social and political orders were constructed and construed as serving some higher cosmic order and not merely the protection of individuals." See Berman, *Created*, 16.
31 Ibid., 87–88.
32 Ibid., 48–49.
33 See especially the introduction and first chapter of Berman, *Created*. One particularly interesting point of comparison is that vassal kings were often required to appear periodically before the superior king, paralleled in the Biblical requirement that Israelite men present themselves to God three times each year, a practice maintained during the period of the Temples in Jerusalem, when at least men would travel three times each year for the pilgrimage festivals of Passover, Shavout, and Sukkot; see Berman, *Created*, 42. On the matter of men and women as vassal kings in relationship to God, Berman acknowledges that the Pentateuch, the five books of Moses, "takes for granted women's subordination to men." See Berman, *Created*, 13.

Chapter 6

1 Rand, *Virtue*, 49.
2 Ayn Rand, *Atlas Shrugged*, 35th anniversary ed. (Dutton, 1992, 2005), 731.
3 Rand on members of the Libertarian Party:

> They're not defenders of capitalism. They're a group of publicity seekers who rush into politics prematurely, because they allegedly want to educate people through a political campaign, which can't be done. Further, their leadership consists of men of every persuasion, from religious conservatives to anarchists. Most of them are my enemies: they spend their time denouncing me, while plagiarizing my ideas. Now it's a bad sign for an allegedly pro-capitalist party to start by stealing ideas.

> From Robert Mayhew, ed., *Ayn Rand Answers: The Best of Her Q&A*, Details for this citation: (New York: Berkley, 2005) 73, cited at "What Was Ayn Rand's View of the Libertarian Movement," Aynrandlexicon.com, accessed 24 June, 2020, http://aynrandlexicon.com/ayn-rand-ideas/ayn-rand-q-on-a-on-libertarianism.html.

4 David Boaz, "Individualism and Community," May 23, 2011; https://www.cato.org/publications/commentary/individualism-community, accessed December 14, 2019.
5 Boaz, *Libertarian Mind*, 26.

6   David Boaz, ed., *The Libertarian Reader: Classic & Contemporary Writings from Lao-Tzu to Milton Friedman* (New York: Simon & Schuster, 2015), 60–61.
7   See, e.g., David Boaz, "Introduction to Libertarianism, Lecture Five: The Dignity of the Individual," libertarianism.org, accessed November 8, 2018, https://www.libertarianism.org/guides/lectures/dignity-individual.
8   John Stuart Mill, "Of Individuality," Boaz, *Libertarian Reader*, 123.
9   *Libertarian Party Platform.*
10 Joseph B. Soloveitchik, "The Community," *Tradition: A Journal of Orthodox Jewish Thought* 17, no. 2 (1978): 9.
11 Aryeh Kaplan, *The Handbook of Jewish Thought*, vol. 2 (New York: Moznaim Publishing Corporation, 1992), 136.
12 The difference between the Hebrew *ze la-ze* and *ze ba-ze* in the expression is perhaps subtle and probably not critical. The former translates as one *for* another, while the latter translates as one *in* another. All of Israel is (all Jews are) responsible one *for* another, or all of Israel is (all Jews are) responsible one in another. Perhaps there is something more intimate or connected with *ba* (or *in*), as in John Locke's language of having property in oneself or in something.
13 Jonathan Sacks, *Future Tense: Jews, Judaism, and Israel in the Twenty-first Century* (New York: Schocken, 2012), 42.
14 Kaplan, *Handbook*, 137.
15 Satlow, *Creating Judaism*, 80. For a detailed and fascinating discussion of the covenant between God and Israel and the ways it resembles other covenants of the region and time period, as well as the critically important ways it departs from those other covenants, see especially chapter 1 of Berman, *Created*.
16 The midrash plays off of Exodus 19:17, which states that the people stood under the mountain. More plausibly read as standing at the base of the mountain, the midrash imagines a situation in which the mountain is physically above the people.
17 The source of this interpretation—of the barrel as cutting off the people—now escapes my memory. Ideally, in Jewish tradition, one seeks to give credit where it is due.
18 For Orthodox Jews, a quorum consists of ten male Jews at or above the age of Bar Mitzvah. The non-Orthodox movements include women from the age of Bat Mitzvah in the ten required for a quorum. A discussion of this difference and of the inclusion of men only among the Orthodox is beyond the subject matter of this exploration of Judaism and libertarianism, but most authorities locate the limitation in a slight difference in Mitzvah-obligations between men and women. Given both traditional gender roles across the centuries and the weight of tradition, it is not surprising that many or most of the Orthodox today remain untroubled by all of this—or, if they feel troubled, accept it as part of a package deal and seek other ways to enhance the ritual and leadership roles of women in their synagogues and communities. Some "partnership" groups await the arrival of ten men and ten women for the quorum.
19 Nacha Cattan, "Conservative Head Calls Sabbath-Driving Rule a 'Mistake,'" *Forward*, November 7, 2003, https://forward.com/news/6998/conservative-head-calls-sabbath-driving-rule-a/.
20 Daniel Gordis, "Conservative Judaism: A Requiem," *Jewish Review of Books* (Winter 2014), https://jewishreviewofbooks.com/articles/566/requiem-for-a-movement/.
21 Steven M. Cohen, "Conservative Jewry's numbers plummeting, but core engagement steady," *Jewish Telegraphic Agency*, November 10, 2015, http://

www.jta.org/2015/11/10/news-opinion/united-states/op-ed-for-conservative-jews-smaller-numbers-but-steady-engagement.

22 Most likely, few adherents followed the ruling to the letter, at least not for long, and limited their Sabbath driving to traveling to and from synagogue. There certainly is a small, though not insubstantial, number of Conservative-identifying Jews who, like most of the Orthodox, do not drive at all on the Sabbath, but it is difficult to imagine there being many who drive only for the purposes of synagogue attendance. (One can also find so-called "Conservadox" Jews who seek, whether theologically or socially or both, to straddle any demarcation lines separating Conservative and Orthodox Judaism, and are likely to refrain from Sabbath driving.)
23 M. Sanhedrin 4:5.
24 B. Berakhot 61a.
25 M. Sanhedrin 4:5.
26 Likewise, in a sense, all Jews share a common origin in slavery and liberation from that situation. As Joshua Berman comments, "Indeed, no Israelite can lay claim to any greater status, because all emanate from the Exodus—a common seminal, liberating, and equalizing event." See Berman, *Created*, 88.
27 B. Baca Meẓi'a 58b.
28 See Sperber, *On the Relationship*, 102–114.
29 Jonathan Sacks, *Radical Then, Radical Now*, (New York: Continuum, 2004), 147.
30 See Jonathan Sacks, "A People that Dwells Alone (Balak 5778)," rabbisacks.org, accessed June 25, 2018, http://rabbisacks.org/people-dwells-alone-balak-5778/, accessed November 6, 2018.
31 See Yeshayahu Leibowitz, "The Individual and Society in Judaism," in Leibowitz, *Judaism, Human Values*, 88–91. See other essays in this volume of collected essays for additional and provocative insights on matters or religion and politics.
32 Some of Herbert's key writings were gathered in Auberon Herbert, *The Right and Wrong of Compulsion by the State, and Other Essays*, ed. Eric Mack (Indianapolis: Liberty Fund, 1978).
33 See Carl Watner, "Fundamentals of Voluntaryism," voluntaryist.com, accessed October 30, 2018, http://voluntaryist.com/fundamentals/fundamentals-of-voluntaryism/#.W9kNapNKhPY.
34 See the section "Some Reasons Why Voluntaryists Object to Compulsory Taxation in All Its Forms," from "Essay Ten. The Principles of Voluntaryism and Free Life," in Auberon Herbert, The *Right and Wrong of Compulsion by the State, and Other Essays* (Indianapolis: The Liberty Fund, 1978). The the full text is available at http://oll.libertyfund.org/titles/herbert-the-right-and-wrong-of-compulsion-by-the-state-and-other-essays-1978-ed, accessed October 30, 2018.
35 See "Essay Nine. A Plea for Voluntaryism" from Auberon Herbert, *The Voluntaryist Creed* (Oxford: Oxford University Press, 1908), and republished in Auberon Herbert, *Right and Wrong*; the full text is available at http://oll.libertyfund.org/pages/rc-herbert1?q=auberon#, accessed October 30, 2018.
36 See "Voluntaryism," *Wikipedia*, last modified June 17, 2020, https://en.wikipedia.org/wiki/Voluntaryism.
37 Palmer, *Realizing Freedom*, 48.
38 Although most libertarians would likely argue against mandatory union membership and dues, they would offer no objection to the voluntary organization of workers to advocate for their wages or salaries, other benefits, and working conditions.

39 Given this openness to diversity and the unlimited potential of human expression, it is perhaps something of a mystery why self-identifying libertarians and members of the Libertarian Party tend to be disproportionately white and male, and why the movement has not attracted a more diverse membership.
40 Palmer, *Realizing Freedom*, 43–44.
41 Rothbard, *New Liberty*, 33.
42 Palmer, *Realizing Freedom*, 47.
43 Rothbard, *New Liberty*, 45.
44 Ibid.
45 Bernard de Mandeville, *The Fable of the Bees: Or Private Vices, Publick Benefits* (London: Penguin Books, 1989).
46 Boaz, *Libertarian Mind*, 26.
47 Brennan, *Libertarianism*, 3.
48 Lifshitz, *Judaism, Law*, 91–94.
49 Ibid., 93, 103.
50 Berman, *Created*, 87.
51 Sacks, *Morals*, 14.
52 Matt Kibbe, *Don't Hurt People and Don't Take Their Stuff: A Libertarian Manifesto* (New York: William Morrow Paperbacks, 2015), 14.
53 Brennan, *Libertarianism*, 52–53.
54 See David Boaz "Individualism and Community," Cato.org, accessed November 12, 2018, https://www.cato.org/publications/commentary/individualism-community; this article also appeared on the Encyclopaedia Britannica Blog on May 23, 2011, http://blogs.britannica.com/2011/5/individualism-community.
55 The idea of the kibbutz as a voluntary community first occurred to me while listening to a speech by Ruth Wisse, the politically conservative scholar of Yiddish literature and Jewish history.

Conclusion

1 In both the United States and Israel, many Jewish and non-Jewish religious organizations seek the best of both worlds: government funding and preferential treatment without government interference. Others seek a greater separation of religion and state.
2 See chapter 13, "The State of Halakhah and the Halakhah of the State," in Chaim Saiman, *Halakhah: The Rabbinic Idea of Law* (Princeton: Princeton University Press, 2018), 213–241.
3 Arnold Heertje, "The Dutch and Portuguese-Jewish background of David Ricardo," *The European Journal of the History of Economic Thought* 11, no. 2 (Summer 2004): 289. On the appellation Ricardo the Jew, Heertje cites D. Weatherall, *David Ricardo: A Biography* (The Hague: Nijhoff, 1976), 58.
4 Heertje, "Dutch," 281.
5 Ibid., 289–290.
6 Ibid., 292.
7 From Ludwig von Mises, *Socialism* (Alabama: Ludwig on Mises Institute, 2011), 410; quoted In David Gordon, "Judaism, Capitalism, and Marx," part 1 of "Judaism and

Capitalism: Friends or Enemies?," The Lou Church Memorial Lecture in Religion and Economics, presented at the 2012 Austrian Scholars Conference; see https://mises.org/library/judaism-capitalism-and-marx, accessed July 2, 2020.
8 Ibid.
9 I find myself torn over whether even to mention that Rothbard has been accused of, in the last years of his life and in his support of right-wing populism and paleoconservatives, at least keeping the company of racists and antisemites, including expressing support for the former KKK leader David Duke. On the one hand, I do not wish to whitewash anything; on the other hand, I do not wish to publicize what might be guilt by association. As Rothbard alienated some allies, it is possible that the attacks on Rothbard arose out of internecine squabbles within the libertarian camp. In the end, I think the record is troubling enough that I will leave it to interested readers to follow up on such matters and judge for themselves. See, for example, John Ganz, "The Forgotten Man," *The Baffler*, December 15, 2017, https://thebaffler.com/latest/the-forgotten-man-ganz. See also Julian Sanchez and David Weigel, "Who Wrote Ron Paul's Newsletters?" *Reason*, January 16, 2008, https://reason.com/2008/01/16/who-wrote-ron-pauls-newsletter/.
10 Justin Raimondo, *An Enemy of the State: The Life of Murray N. Rothbard* (Amherst, NY: Prometheus, 2000), 67, 25.
11 Robert Asahina, "The Inquisitive Robert Nozick," *New York Times*, September 20, 1981, https://www.nytimes.com/1981/09/20/books/the-inquisitive-robert-nozick.html.
12 Anne C. Heller, *Ayn Rand and the World She Made* (New York: Nan A. Talese Doubleday, 2009), xiii.
13 Ibid., 102–103.
14 Ibid., 10.
15 See the full interview here: Kurt Keefner, "12 Questions for Anne Heller" *The Atlasphere*, April 2, 2010, http://www.theatlasphere.com/columns/100405-heller-interview.php.
16 See "Libertarianism: To Jews," chelm.freeyellow.com, accessed June 24, 2020, http://chelm.freeyellow.com/Jewish_index.html.
17 Steven Horwitz, "Libertarianism Rejects Anti-Semitism, fee.org, August 24, 2017, https://fee.org/articles/libertarianism-rejects-anti-semitism/.
18 bShab. 31a.
19 Boaz, *Libertarian Mind*, 96.
20 See the chapter "The Libertarian Axiom and Jonah Goldberg, Neo-Con" in Walter Block, *Toward a Libertarian Society* (Auburn, Alabama: Ludwig von Mises Institute, 2014), 163–165.
21 Rothbard, *New Liberty*, 27.
22 Ibid., 35.
23 Rothbard, *New Liberty*, 47–48, quoted (not quite correctly) in John Tomasi, *Free Market Fairness* (Princeton: Princeton University Press, 2013), 47.
24 Tomasi, *Free Market*, 47.
25 One might suggest a parallel between Judaism,, anti-idolatry and a libertarian critique of turning the state into an idol.
26 Personal communication.

Epilogue

1   That is, libertarians think *both* sorts of public assistance do not work or that they require an immoral redistribution of money or both. By contrast, many political conservatives tenaciously scrutinize aid to the poor, while expressing little concern over government payments to the wealthy and to large corporations. This is all caught up in ideas, with racist and sexist dimensions, of who among us are "deserving" of assistance.

2   At the same time that all of us face the coronavirus, many white Americans have been newly awoken to the systemic racism which has for centuries devalued Black lives and systematically stripped wealth and freedom from Black people. This is the true meaning of the expression *Black Lives Matter*, to counter the fact that to this day American society and law and policies and practices have treated Black lives as if they have less value and matter less than white ones. On the devaluing of Black lives, see (among dozens of others books) the following: Eddie S. Glaude Jr., *Democracy in Black: How Race Still Enslaves the American Soul* (New York: Broadway Books, 2017); Andre M. Perry, *Know Your Price: Valuing Black Lives and Property in America's Black Cities* (Washington, DC: Brookings Institution Press, 2020); Mehrsa Baradaran, *The Color of Money: Black Banks and the Racial Wealth Gap* (Cambridge, MA: The Belknap Press of Harvard University Press, 2019); Michelle Alexander, *The New Jim Crow: Mass Incarceration in the Age of Colorblindness*, anniversary ed. (New York: The New Press, 2020); Carol Anderson, *One Person, No Vote: How Voter Suppression Is Destroying Our Democracy* (London: Bloomsbury Publishing, 2019); and Ibram X. Kendi, *How to Be an Antiracist* (New York: One World, 2019). Even if a libertarian commonwealth were to make sense on an ideal, philosophical level, it is not clear to me how, from within a libertarian framework, one would even begin to transition from the messy here to the ideal there. Replacing generations of racist laws and policy with a minimalist libertarian government would not undo and reverse the structural disadvantages now in place. Though I should note that it is my understanding that at least some libertarians recognize the history of systemic racism and even support the notion of reparations, so maybe there is such a path.

Bibliography

Alexander, Michelle. *The New Jim Crow: Mass Incarceration in the Age of Colorblindness*. Anniversary ed. New York: The New Press, 2020.
Anderson, Carol, and Dick Durbin. *One Person, No Vote: How Voter Suppression Is Destroying Our Democracy*. London: Bloomsbury Publishing, 2019.
Angel, Marc, ed. *Koren Pirkei Avot*. Translated by Jonathan Sacks. Blg Rep ed. Jerusalem; New Milford: Koren Publishers Jerusalem, 2015.
Baradaran, Mehrsa. *The Color of Money: Black Banks and the Racial Wealth Gap*. Cambridge, MA: The Belknap Press of Harvard University Press, 2019.
Baron, Salo. *A Social and Religious History of the Jews*. Vol. 1. 2nd ed. New York: Columbia University Press, 1952.
Becker, Amanda. "Americans don't like big government—but like many programs: poll." Reuters. Last modified April 30, 2015. https://news.yahoo.com/americans-dont-big-government-many-programs-poll-101705188.html.
Ben-Sasson, Haim Hillel, ed. *A History of the Jewish People*. Cambridge, Mass: Harvard University Press, 1985.
Berlin, Isaiah. "Two Concepts of Liberty." In *Liberty: Incorporating Four Essays on Liberty*, edited by Henry Hardy, 166–217. 2nd ed. Oxford: Oxford University Press, 2002.
Berman, Joshua A. *Created Equal: How the Bible Broke with Ancient Political Thought*. New York: Oxford University Press, 2011.
Berman, Saul. "Jewish Environmental Values—The Dynamic Tension Between Nature and Human Needs." In *Human Values and the Environment*. Vol. Report 140. Madison: Institute for Environmental Studies, 1992. https://www.jewishvirtuallibrary.org/jewish-environmental-values-the-dynamic-tension-between-nature-and-human-needs.
Bick, Ezra. "Prayer." Etzion.org. Last modified November 10, 2015. http://etzion.org.il/en/prayer-1.
Bleich, J. David. *Judaism and Healing: Halakhic Perspectives*. Jersey City, NJ: Ktav Pub Inc, 2002.
———. "The Metaphysicis of Property Interests in Jewish Law: An Analysis of Kinyan." *Tradition* 43, no. 2 (2010): 49–67.

———. *The Philosophical Quest: Of Philosophy, Ethics, Law and Halakhah*. Koren Publishers Jerusalem, 2013.

Block, Walter. *Toward a Libertarian Society*. Auburn: Ludwig von Mises Institute, 2014.

Block, Walter, Geoffrey Brennan, and Kenneth Elzinga, eds. *Morality of the Market: Religious and Economic Perspectives*. Vancouver: The Fraser Institute, 1985.

Block, Walter E. *Religion, Economics, and Politics*. N.p.: The Educational Publisher / Biblio Publishing, 2013.

Block, Walter E., Alan G. Futerman, and Rafi Farber. "The Legal Status of the State of Israel: A Libertarian Approach." *Indonesian Journal of International & Comparative Law* III, no. 3 (July 2016): 435–553.

Block, Walter, and Irving Hexham, eds. *Religion, Economics and Social Thought*. Vancouver: The Fraser Institute, 1986.

Boaz, David. "Individualism and Community." Encylcopaedia Britannica Blog. Last modified May 23, 2011. http://blogs.britannica.com/2011/5/individualism-community.

———. *The Libertarian Mind: A Manifesto for Freedom*. Rev. ed. New York: Simon & Schuster, 2015.

———, ed. *The Libertarian Reader: Classic & Contemporary Writings from Lao-Tzu to Milton Friedman*. New York: Simon & Schuster, 2015.

Boyarin, Daniel. *Judaism: The Genealogy of a Modern Notion*. None ed. New Brunswick; London: Rutgers University Press, 2018.

Brennan, Jason. *Libertarianism: What Everyone Needs to Know*. Oxford: Oxford University Press, 2012.

Brill, Alan. *Judaism and Other Religions: Models of Understanding*. Basingstoke: Palgrave Macmillan, 2014.

———. *Judaism and World Religions: Encountering Christianity, Islam, and Eastern Traditions*. New York: Palgrave Macmillan, 2012.

Brinkley, Douglas. "Obama and the Road Ahead: The Rolling Stone Interview." *Rolling Stone*, November 8, 2012. https://www.rollingstone.com/politics/politics-news/obama-and-the-road-ahead-the-rolling-stone-interview-123468/.

Cardozo, Nathan Lopes. "Johann Sebastian Bach & Halacha." David Cardozo Academy. Accessed June 25, 2017. https://www.cardozoacademy.org/thoughts-to-ponder/johann-sebastian-bach-halacha-ttp-35/.

Carlebach, Alexander. "Autonomy, Heteronomy and Theonomy." *Tradition* 6, no. 1 (Fall 1963): 5–29. https://traditiononline.org/autonomy-heteronomy-and-theonomy/.

Carlebach, Elisheva. "The Early Modern Jewish Community and Its Institutions." In *The Cambridge History of Judaism*. Vol. 7, *The Early Modern World, 1500-1815*, edited by Jonathan Karp and Adam Sutcliffe, 168–98. Cambridge: Cambridge University Press, 2018.

Cato Institute. "Three Women Who Launched a Movement." Libertarianism.org. Last modified March 1, 2014. https://www.libertarianism.org/publications/essays/three-women-who-launched-movement.

Cato Institute. "Was the 'Libertarian Moment' Wishful Thinking?" Cato.org. Last modified May/June 2016. https://www.cato.org/policy-report/mayjune-2016/was-libertarian-moment-wishful-thinking.

Cattan, Nacha. "Conservative Head Calls Sabbath-Driving Rule a 'Mistake.'" *Forward*, November 7, 2003. https://forward.com/news/6998/conservative-head-calls-sabbath-driving-rule-a/.

Chodorow, Adam. "Biblical Tax Systems and the Case for Progressive Taxation." *Journal of Law & Religion* 23, no. 1 (2007): 101–45.

Coates, Ta-Nehisi. *Between the World and Me*. Melbourne: Text Publishing Co, 2015.

Cohen, Alfred. "Whose Body? Living with Pain." *Journal of Halacha and Contemporary Society* 32 (1996): 39–64.

Conway, David. "Judaism and Liberalism: Israel's Economic Problem with Its Haredim." *Economic Affairs* 37, no. 2 (2017): 240–53.

Dan-Cohen, Meir. *Harmful Thoughts: Essays on Law, Self, and Morality*. Princeton: Princeton University Press, 2002.

Davis, Dena S. "Method in Jewish Bioethics: An Overview." *Journal of Contemporary Law* 20, no. 2 (Summer 1994): 325–52.

Dorff, Elliot N. "The Jewish Tradition." In *Caring and Curing: Health and Medicine in the Western Religious Traditions*, edited by Ronald L. Numbers and Darrel W. Amundsen. Baltimore: Johns Hopkins University Press, 1997.

Dorff, Elliot N., and Jonathan K. Crane, eds. *The Oxford Handbook of Jewish Ethics and Morality*. Oxford; New York: Oxford University Press, 2016.

Draper, Robert. "Has the 'Libertarian Moment' Finally Arrived?" *The New York Times*, August 7, 2014. https://www.nytimes.com/2014/08/10/magazine/has-the-libertarian-moment-finally-arrived.html.

Eisenberg, Daniel. "Maintaining Compassion for the Suffering Terminal Patient While Preserving Life: An Orthodox Jewish Approach." *Perspectives in Biology and Medicine* 60, no. 2 (2017): 233–46. https://doi.org/10.1353/pbm.2017.0030.

Feuer, Avrohom Chaim. *The Tzedakah Treasury*. Brooklyn: Mesorah Publications Ltd., 2000.

Finkelman, Rabbi Shimon. *Shabbos: The Sabbath, Its Essence & Significance*. Brooklyn: Artscroll, Mesorah Publications Ltd, 1994.

First, Mitchell. "Aleinu: Obligation to Fix the World or the Text?" *Hakirah* 11 (2011): 187–97.

Freedman, Harry, and Maurice Simon, eds. *Midrash Rabbah*. 10 vols. London: Soncino Press, 1939. https://archive.org/stream/RabbaGenesis/midrashrabbahgen027557mbp_djvu.txt.

Futerman, Alan, Rafi Farber, and Walter E. Block. "The Libertarian Case for Israel." *Forward*, October 13, 2016. https://forward.com/scribe/351957/tk-tk/.

Ganz, John. "The Forgotten Man." *The Baffler*, December 15, 2017. https://thebaffler.com/latest/the-forgotten-man-ganz.

Gillespie, Nick, and Matt Welch. "The Libertarian Moment." *Reason*, November 25, 2008. http://reason.com/archives/2008/11/25/the-libertarian-moment.

Glaude Jr., Eddie S. *Democracy in Black: How Race Still Enslaves the American Soul*. New York: Broadway Books, 2017.

Gobry, Pascal-Emmanuel. "The Libertarian Case for National Military Service." *CATO Unbound: A Journal of Debate*, September 2013. https://www.cato-unbound.org/2013/09/09/pascal-emmanuel-gobry/libertarian-case-national-military-service.

Goodkind, Adam. "Bodies on Loan: The Ethics of 'Renting' a Body." In *Jewish Choices, Jewish Voices*, vol. 1, *Body*, edited by Elliot N. Dorff and Louis E. Newman, 40–45. Philadelphia: Jewish Publication Society, 2008.

Gordis, Daniel. "Conservative Judaism: A Requiem." *Jewish Review of Books*, Winter 2014. https://jewishreviewofbooks.com/articles/566/requiem-for-a-movement/.

Halbertal, Moshe, and Stephen Holmes. *The Beginning of Politics: Power in the Biblical Book of Samuel*. Princeton: Princeton University Press, 2017.

Hazony, Yoram. *The Philosophy of Hebrew Scripture*. New York: Cambridge University Press, 2012.

Heertje, Arnold. "The Dutch and Portuguese-Jewish Background of David Ricardo." *The European Journal of the History of Economic Thought* 11, no. 2 (Summer 2004): 281–94.

Heller, Anne Conover. *Ayn Rand and the World She Made*. New York: Nan A. Talese Doubleday, 2009.

Herbert, Auberon. *The Right and Wrong of Compulsion by the State*. Indianapolis: Liberty Fund Inc., 1978.

———. *The Voluntaryist Creed; Being the Herbert Spencer Lecture Delivered at Oxford June 7, 1906; And a Plea for Voluntaryism*. N.p.: HardPress Publishing, 2012.

Herzog, Rabbi Dr Isaac. *The Main Institutions of Jewish Law*. 2 vols. [Vol. 1, *The Law of Property*; vol. 2, *The Law of Obligations*]. London; New York: The Soncino Press Limited, 1965.

Heschel, Abraham Joshua, and Susannah Heschel. *The Sabbath*. New York: Farrar Straus Giroux, 2005.

Hirsch, Rabbi Samson Raphael. *The Nineteen Letters on Judaism*. Feldheim Publishers, 1969.

Hont, Istvan, and Michael Ignatieff, eds. *Wealth and Virtue: The Shaping of Political Economy in the Scottish Enlightenment*. Cambridge: Cambridge University Press, 1986.

Hospers, John. *Libertarianism: A Political Philosophy for Tomorrow*. N.p.: CreateSpace Independent Publishing Platform, 2013.

Jachter, Rabbi Chaim. *Gray Matter*. Vol 3, *Exploring Contemporary Halakhic Challenges*. n.p.: Kol Torah Publications, 2008.
Jakobovits, Immanuel. *Jewish Medical Ethics*. New York: Bloch Publishing Company, 1975.
―――. "Some Modern Responsa on Medico-Moral Problems." *Assia: Jewish Medical Ethics* 1 (1998): 5–16.
Jose, Manuel L., and Charles K. Moore. "The Development of Taxation in the Bible: Improvements in Counting, Measurement, and Computation in the Ancient Middle East." *The Accounting Historians Journal* 25, no. 2 (December 1998): 63–80.
Jotkowitz, Alan. "The Intersection of Halakhah and Science in Medical Ethics: The Approach of Rabbi Eliezer Waldenberg." *Ḥakirah* 19 (Summer 2015): 91–115.
Kaplan, Aryeh. *The Handbook of Jewish Thought*. Vol. 2. New York: Moznaim Publishing Corporation, 1992.
Kapossy, Béla, Isaac Nakhimovsky, and Richard Whatmore, eds. *Commerce and Peace in the Enlightenment*. Cambridge: Cambridge University Press, 2017.
Kendi, Ibram X. *How to Be an Antiracist*. New York: One World, 2019.
Kibbe, Matt. *Don't Hurt People and Don't Take Their Stuff: A Libertarian Manifesto*. New York: William Morrow Paperbacks, 2015.
Kiley, Jocelyn. "In search of libertarians." FACTTANK. Last modified August 25, 2014. https://www.pewresearch.org/fact-tank/2014/08/25/in-search-of-libertarians/.
Kochen, Madeline. *Organ Donation and the Divine Lien in Talmudic Law*. New York: Cambridge University Press, 2014.
Kotz, Joshua. "Halachic Perspective on Abortion." sefaria.org. Last Accessed July 7, 2020. https://www.sefaria.org/sheets/75444.31?lang=bi.
Kristol, Irving. "On the Political Stupidity of the Jews." *Azure*, no. 8 (Autumn 1999): 47–63.
Landman, Leo. "Dina D'Malkhuta Dina: Solely a Diaspora Concept." *Tradition: A Journal of Orthodox Jewish Thought* 15, no. 3 (1975): 89–96.
Lane, Rose Wilder. *The Discovery of Freedom: Man's Struggle Against Authority*. New York: The John Day Company, 1943.
Leibowitz, Yeshayahu. *Judaism, Human Values, and the Jewish State*. Edited by Eliezer Goldman. Translated by Yoram Navon, Zvi Jacobson, Gershon Levi, and Raphael Levy. Rev. ed. Cambridge, MA: Harvard University Press, 1995.
Levine, Aaron. *Economic Public Policy and Jewish Law*. Hoboken; New York: KTAV Publishing House, 1993.
―――, ed. *The Oxford Handbook of Judaism and Economics*. New York: Oxford University Press, 2010.
Libertarian Party. *Libertarian Party Platform* [2018]. lp.org. Accessed June 23, 2020. https://www.lp.org/wp-content/uploads/2018/09/Libertarian-Party-Platform-2018.pdf.

Lichtenstein, Aharon. *By His Light: Character and Values in the Service of God*. Jersey City: KTAV Publishing House, 2002.
Lifshitz, Joseph Isaac. *Judaism, Law & the Free Market: An Analysis*. Grand Rapids: Acton Institute, 2012.
Likhovski, Assaf. "'Training in Citizenship': Tax Compliance and Modernity." *Law & Social Inquiry* 32, no. 3 (2007): 665–700.
Locke, John. *Locke: Two Treatises of Government*. Edited by Peter Laslett. 3rd ed. Cambridge; New York: Cambridge University Press, 1988.
Lpedia. "National Platform." lpedia.org. Last modified November 6, 2019. http://blogs.britannica.com/2011/5/individualism-community.
Mandeville, Bernard, and Phillip Harth. *The Fable of the Bees: Or Private Vices, Publick Benefits*. Harmondsworth: Penguin Classics, 1989.
Mauss, Marcel. *The Gift: The Form and Reason for Exchange in Archaic Societies*. Translated by W. D. Halls. New York: W. W. Norton & Company, 2000.
Maymin, Philip Z. *Freedom and the Torah*. N.p.: CreateSpace Independent Publishing Platform, 2014.
Mises, Ludwig von. *Liberty & Property*. Lrg ed. N.p.: CreateSpace Independent Publishing Platform, 2009.
———. *Socialism: An Economic and Sociological Analysis*. Auburn: Ludwig von Mises Institute, 2011.
Morrow, Levi. "God, Torah, Self: Accepting the Yoke of Heaven in the Writings of Rav Shagar." *The Lehrhaus* (blog), May 26, 2017. https://thelehrhaus.com/scholarship/god-torah-self-accepting-the-yoke-of-heaven-in-the-writings-of-rav-shagar/.
Muller, Jerry Z. *Capitalism and the Jews*. Princeton: Princeton University Press, 2010.
Nozick, Robert. *Anarchy, State, and Utopia*. New York: Basic Books, 2013.
Oden Jr., Robert A. "Taxation in Biblical Israel." *The Journal of Religious Ethics* 12, no. 2 (Fall 1984): 162–81.
Ozar, Alex S. "Yeridah Le-Ẓorekh Aliyyah: Rabbi Joseph B. Soloveitchik on Autonomy and Submission." *The Torah U-Madda Journal* 17 (2016): 150–73.
Paley, Michael R. *Orthodox Judaism, Liberalism and Libertarianism: When Secularism Becomes a Religion*. Baltimore: PublishAmerica, 2006.
Palmer, Tom G. *Realizing Freedom: Libertarian Theory, History, and Practice*. Expanded ed. Washington, DC: Cato Institute, 2014.
Paterson, Isabel. *God of the Machine*. New Brunswick: Routledge, 1993.
Payne, James L. "The End of Taxation?" *The Public Interest*, no. 112 (Summer 1993): 110–18.
Pelcovitz, Raphael. *Sforno: Commentary on the Torah, Complete Volume*. Brooklyn: Mesorah Publications, 1997.
Perry, Andre M. *Know Your Price: Valuing Black Lives and Property in America's Black Cities*. Washington, DC: Brookings Institution Press, 2020.

Powell, Jim. "Rose Wilder Lane, Isabel Paterson, and Ayn Rand: Three Women Who Inspired the Modern Libertarian Movement | Jim Powell, Ayn Rand." fee.org. Last modified May 1, 1996. https://fee.org/articles/rose-wilder-lane-isabel-paterson-and-ayn-rand-three-women-who-inspired-the-modern-libertarian-movement/.

Rackman, Emanuel. *A Modern Orthodox Life: Sermons and Columns of Rabbi Emanuel Rackman*. Jersey City: KTAV Publishing House, 2008.

Raimondo, Justin. *An Enemy of the State: The Life of Murray N. Rothbard*. Amherst: Prometheus, 2000.

Rakeffet-Rothkoff, Aaron. "Dina D'Malkhuta Dina—The Law of the Land in Halakhic Perspective." *Tradition: A Journal of Orthodox Jewish Thought* 13, no. 2 (1972): 5–23.

Rand, Ayn. *Atlas Shrugged*. 35th Anniversary ed. New York: Dutton, 1992.

———. *The Virtue of Selfishness*. New York: Signet, 1963.

Rand, Ayn, and Leon Peikoff. *The Fountainhead*. Anniversary ed. New York: Signet, 1996.

Reuters. "Do you consider yourself a libertarian?" Reuters.com. Last modified 19 April, 2015. http://polling.reuters.com/#!response/TM547Y15/type/smallest/dates/20150410-20150424/collapsed/false.

Robertson, Alex. "Welfare State and Welfare Society." *Social Policy & Administration* 22, no. 3 (1988): 222–34. https://doi.org/10.1111/j.1467-9515.1988.tb00305.x.

Rodger, John J. *From a Welfare State to a Welfare Society: The Changing Context of Social Policy in a Postmodern Era*. Edited by Jo Campling. New York: Red Globe Press, 2000.

Rosner, Fred, and Edward Reichman. "Payment for Organ Donation in Jewish Law." In *The Oxford Handbook of Judaism and Economics*, edited by Aaron Levine, 324–39. New York: Oxford University Press, 2010.

Rothbard, Murray N., Murray Rothbard, and Llewellyn H. Rockwell Jr. *For a New Liberty: The Libertarian Manifesto*. N.p.: CreateSpace Independent Publishing Platform, 2006.

Russell, Dean. "Who Is a Libertarian?" fee.org. Accessed July 8, 2020. https://fee.org/articles/who-is-a-libertarian/.

Sacks, Jonathan. *Future Tense: Jews, Judaism, and Israel in the Twenty-First Century*. New York: Schocken, 2012.

———. *Radical Then, Radical Now*. New York; London: Continuum, 2004.

———. *To Heal a Fractured World: The Ethics of Responsibility*. New York: Schocken, 2007.

Sacks, Jonathan, Norman Barry, Robert Davidson, and Michael Novak. *Morals and Markets: Seventh Annual Hayek Memorial Lecture*. London: Institute of Economic Affairs, 1999.

Saiman, Chaim N. *Halakhah: The Rabbinic Idea of Law*. Princeton: Princeton University Press, 2018.

Sales, Ben. "Orthodox Rabbis Compare Abortion to Murder—and Orthodox Women Are Angry about It." *Jewish Telegraphic*

Agency, January 31, 2019. https://www.jta.org/2019/01/31/culture/orthodox-groups-come-out-swinging-against-new-yorks-abortion-law.

Sanchez, Julian, and David Weigel. "Who Wrote Ron Paul's Newsletters." *Reason*, January 16, 2008. https://reason.com/2008/01/16/who-wrote-ron-pauls-newsletter/.

Satlow, Michael. *Creating Judaism: History, Tradition, Practice*. New York: Columbia University Press, 2006.

Schneerson, Rabbi M.. Letter of 26 Nissan, 5729 [April 14, 1969] on "Hebrew Pronunciation on Organ Donation." chabbad.org. Accessed July 7, 2020. https://www.chabad.org/therebbe/letters/default_cdo/aid/1898676/jewish/Hebrew-Pronunciation-and-Organ-Donation.htm

Schneider, Susan. *Eating as Tikun*. Jerusalem: A Still Small Voice, 1996.

Sefaria Library. Brooklyn, NY. https://www.sefaria.org/texts.

Shmalo, Gamliel. "Orthodox Approaches to Biblical Slavery." *The Torah U-Madda Journal* 16 (2012): 1–20.

Sinclair, Daniel B. "Jewish Bioethics: The End of Life." In *The Oxford Handbook of Jewish Ethics and Morality*, edited by Elliot N. Dorff and Jonathan K. Crane, 330–44. Oxford; New York: Oxford University Press, 2016.

Smith, George H. "Negative and Positive Liberty." Libertarianism.org. Accessed December 19, 2017. https://www.libertarianism.org/publications/essays/negative-positive-liberty.

Soloveitchik, Joseph B. *Festival of Freedom: Essays on Pesah And the Haggadah*. Edited by Joel B. Wolowelsky and Reuven Ziegler. Jersey City: KTAV Publishing House, 2006.

———. "The Community." *Tradition: A Journal of Orthodox Jewish Thought* 17, no. 2 (1978): 7–24.

Soloveitchik, Joseph B., David Shatz, and Reuven Ziegler. *And from There You Shall Seek*. Translated by Naomi Goldblum. Jersey City: KTAV Publishing House, 2009.

Sperber, Daniel. *On the Relationship of Mitzvot Between Man and His Neighbor and Man and His Maker*. Jerusalem: Urim Publications, 2014.

Steinberg, Avraham. *Encyclopedia of Jewish Medical Ethics*. Translated by Fred Rosner. Box ed. Jerusalem; New York: Feldheim, 2003.

Steinsaltz, Adin Even-Israel. *Koren Talmud Bavli, Noé Edition*. Vol. 1, *Berakhot*. Commentary by Adin Even-Israel Steinsaltz. Hebrew/English ed. Jerusalem: Koren Publishers Jerusalem, 2012.

Stern, Eliyahu. *Jewish Materialism: The Intellectual Revolution of the 1870s*. New Haven: Yale University Press, 2018.

Tamari, Meir. *With All Your Possessions: Jewish Ethics and Economic Life*. Kupietzky ed. Jerusalem: Koren Publishers Jerusalem, 2014.

Tapper, Aaron J. Hahn. *Judaisms: A Twenty-First-Century Introduction to Jews and Jewish Identities*. Oakland: University of California Press, 2016.

Tomasi, John. *Free Market Fairness*. Princeton: Princeton University Press, 2013.

Tuccille, Jerome. *It Usually Begins With Ayn Rand*. New York: Stein and Day, 1971.
———. *It Usually Begins With Ayn Rand*. Baltimore: WinklerMedia, 2012.
Twersky, Isadore, ed. *A Maimonides Reader*. New York: Behrman House, Inc., 1972.
Walzer, Michael. *In God's Shadow: Politics in the Hebrew Bible*. New Haven: Yale University Press, 2012.
Walzer, Michael, Menachem Lorberbaum, and Noam J. Zohar, eds. *The Jewish Political Tradition: Authority Volume I: Authority*. New Haven: Yale University Press, 2000.
Weatherall, D. *David Ricardo, A Biography*. The Hague: Nijhoff, 1976.
Williamson, Kevin D. "The Passing of the Libertarian Moment." *The Atlantic*, April 2, 2018. https://www.theatlantic.com/politics/archive/2018/04/defused/556934/.
Yanklowitz, Rabbi Dr Shmuly. *The Soul of Jewish Social Justice*. Jerusalem: Urim Publications, 2014.
Yisraeli, Shaul. "Tikrit Kivyeh L'or Ha-Halacha." *Ha-Torah ve-Ha-Medina* 5 (1953/1954): 71–113.
Zevin, Rabbi Shlomo Yosef. "Mishpat Shylock." In *Le'Or Halakha*, 311–35. Jerusalem: Beyt Hillel, 1946.
Zion, Noam Sachs. *From Each According to One's Ability Duties to Poor People from the Bible to the Welfare State and Tikkun Olam*. Vol. 1, *Jewish Giving in Comparative Perspectives: Tzedakah, Greek Philanthropy, and Christian Charity*. Cleveland: Zion Holiday Publications, 2013.

Acknowledgements

I suspect that few people, Jews included, realize that the very word Judaism (in Hebrew, *Yahadut*) basically means *thankfulness*. Judaism is named after the tribe of Judah, and Judah/*Yehudah* was one of the sons of the patriarch Jacob and the matriarch Leah. When Leah gave birth to her fourth son, she exclaimed, "This time I will praise [*odeh*] Ha-Shem (The Lord); therefore she called his name *Yehudah*." (Gen. 29:35) In modern Hebrew, one says *ani modeh* or *ani modah*, I am thankful or I thank. For many Jews, this is the very first word we say upon arising each morning: *Modeh/modah ani lifanekha, Melekh chai v'kayam, she-hechezarta bi nishmati b'chemlah, rabbah emunatecha* (I am thankful before You, living and eternal King, that You have, with mercifulness, returned into me my soul, great is Your faithfulness). Going back to the Hebrew-language root system we discussed earlier, the root *yud-dalet-he* connotes thankfulness. And this essentially is the name of the religion. If libertarianism is an ideology centered on liberty, then we might say that Judaism is an ideology centered on gratitude.

With this awareness, I here offer my gratitude to all those who have supported me during the far too long of a period I have worked on this book. And I apologize for anyone I have inadvertently left out.

To my late father and to my mother, who brought me into this world. And to my late maternal grandmother, Eleanor Lincoln, who started something of a family tradition. It was her view that on one's birthday, a person should give a present to his or her mother—out of gratitude for bringing one into the world. The mother deserves the credit for the day of one's birth and should be celebrated, more so than the one who was born on that day. My father played his part as well, in my birth and life, and I very much miss him and my grandmother. In gratitude to my parents, Madelyn and Howard Krinsky, I dedicate this book to them.

To Udi Merioz, an artist with a gallery and shop in the Cardo in the Old City of Jerusalem (*Blue and White Art Gallery*, http://www.blueandwhiteart.com/wp/). We have met him only a few times over the last few years during trips to visit our children during their gap years between high school and college, and yet even during those few visits, Udi's kindness and generosity were absolutely clear. Not rushing us out of the shop, despite his need to close early to visit a family member in the hospital. Turning away the customers after us, but handing them a free print while doing so. Sending us a free print across the ocean after we purchased some others, because we admired the beautiful painting he was completing. I was so pleased we managed to identify a piece of his artwork suitable for the cover of this book.

Here is the artist's explanation of the painting and how it fits with the ideas of freedom and community discussed in this book: "This artwork has the seven species, the menorah and several other elements. To elaborate a little bit, the seven species represent the first commandment to the Children of Israel who were entering into Israel with Joshua. That was to plant a tree. The act of planting your own tree is very important in Judaism. It has to be done by yourself, a foreigner cannot do it for you. It is done by individuals, not the state. The Menorah is also based on the desert plant called Marva. It is to bring the fact that we have been a nation with no land wandering through the desert into the symbol of light into the Temple in Israel. The dove represents peace and the spiritual aspect. The painting itself is made from all the colors in the rainbow to remind us of the covenant between us and God."

To Alessandra Anzani, Editorial Director and my main contact at Academic Studies Press (ASP), who has encouraged me and stewarded this project to completion, and to Stuart Allen, Editorial Coordinator, who worked with me to usher the manuscript to the production team. To Kira Nemirovsky and the entire production team at ASP, and to Jenna Colozza and Matthew Charlton, the marketing and sales team, who saw promise in this book and, given its electoral theme, pushed to get it into print in conjunction with the 2020 elections in the United States. To the anonymous reviewers, who provided numerous suggestions helping improve the book; I am especially grateful to one reviewer for pointing me in the direction of Joshua Berman's wonderful book on ancient Judaism.

To Molly Oringer, my other editor, who read my manuscript carefully and provided excellent advice prior to my submission of the full manuscript to the publisher.

To the readers of this book, for considering what I have to share, I thank you and hope your investment of time proves worth it.

To my cousin, Marc Joffe, who both helped start me on this journey so many years ago with his gift to me of the Jerome Tuccille book—and who also has encouraged me throughout the writing and production of this book, reading selections and responding quickly to questions and putting me in touch with numerous individuals in the libertarian world, among them Walter Block. My thanks to Walter Block for a number of email exchanges and my thanks to others who have responded to my inquiries, if only to answer a single question.

To Rabbi Aryeh Klapper, who not only graciously agreed to write this book's foreword but has provided me with feedback and materials and insight, particularly concerning Rabbi Zevin's essay on Shylock and Rabbi Yisraeli's response. Rabbi Klapper is a great teacher, unafraid to take on difficult topics, and probably has thought more than all but a few people about the practical application of Jewish law to the modern state and world. I encourage readers to visit the website (http://torahleadership.org/) and blog (https://moderntoraleadership.wordpress.com/) of his organization, the Center for Modern Torah Leadership.

To Rabbi Marc Angel, who has published my writings on his *Jewish Ideas and Ideals* website and in his journal *Conversations*, and who has shared kind and supportive words with me over a number of years.

To Noam Zion, a teacher and writer, who welcomed me into his Jerusalem home to discuss tzedakah, one of his areas of expertise, and other matters. To Moshe Koppel, perhaps the leading libertarian thinker in Israel, for taking time to meet with me and discuss libertarianism and Judaism and Israel.

To Rabbi Shlomo Dov Rosen, leader of Yakar Jerusalem, for making time to talk with me during a visit to Israel, for a number of conversations during a brief visit; his genuine interest in and engagement with other people and what they are thinking and saying is admirable and too rare. I think of Yakar as a spiritual home—with its eclectic combination of serious intellectualism and soul-stirring song during prayer.

To friends who have read parts of this book or otherwise provided good advice, including Amy Strachman, David Strachman, and Michael Satlow. To Mayer Juni, who recommended to me Madeline Kochen's brilliant book on organ donation, a book which has had a great impact upon my understanding of ownership in Judaism. To Rabbi Barry Dolinger and Naomi Baine, at whose Sabbath table Mayer mentioned the book. Rabbi Dolinger has been our rabbi here in Providence, Rhode Island for nearly a decade now and I thank him for the many invigorating conversations—about Judaism, about politics, and about Judaism and politics—we have had, often while walking home Friday night after services at synagogue.

To the many dear friends and neighbors who belong to the various voluntary communities to which I too belong religious communities, political communities, and boardgaming communities.

To my colleagues at the Economic Progress Institute, where I managed, at the age of 50, to start what has felt like my real career, a period that has overlapped with the completion of the writing of this book and with its production. That my day job has been so rewarding and meaningful has given me additional strength to complete this book.

To my sister, Karen, and my brother-in-law, Chris. I am so happy that we invited Karen to stay with us in our new home of Rhode Island about two decades ago, and that she made it her home too. That we share our commitment to veganism and that she shares the ice cream from their shop, Like No Udder, makes it all that much sweeter, figuratively and literally.

To my wife and partner, Laura, and to our three children, Shira, Shalom, and Menucha. I am grateful both for the time we have spent together and the time they have allowed me to write. I do not know that they have always understand my compulsion to write, especially during those times when the writing seems frustrating. And as important as writing is to me and as happy as I am to complete this book and even as I start imagining another writing project, I hope they have never doubted that they are far more dear to me than anything I have ever written or will ever write.

I began by thanking my parents. Yet in Judaism there is a notion that there are three partners involved in an individual's creation: the mother, the father, and God. Not that I have any profound understanding of God or of God's role in our world or of the inequities and suffering in our world—the most I can do is repeat the words of Rabbi Jonathan Sacks, who in a lecture on faith delivered two decades ago (https://rabbisacks.org/faith-lectures-judaism-justice-and-tragedy-confronting-the-problem-of-evil/) explained that Judaism begins in a world where both God and evil exist, although one might have thought the existence of one necessarily excludes the other: "Judaism begins not in the conventional place where faith is thought to begin, namely in wonder that the world is. Judaism begins in the opposite, in the protest against a world that is not as it ought to be." So, I try to do something with my life to engage in such protest—and just as I express my gratitude to God each morning, here again I am grateful for the blessings I have received and the opportunity to protest against the world as it is, towards the world as it ought to be.

Index

A
Abel, xvii, 177, 178
abortion, 62, 63
Abraham, 84
absolute power, 101, 102
Adam, 160, 161
Agudath Israel of America, 200n33
altruism, 117
American law, 94, 95
Anarchy, State, and Utopia (Nozick), 102
Angel, R. Marc, 85, 133
autonomous Jewish community/autonomous communities, 111, 121, 122, 129
autonomy, 15, 24, 46, 64, 108, 148, vii, viii
arbitrary power, 101, 102
Atlantic, 8, 9
'avodah, 20, 157

B
Ba'al HaTurim. *See* ben Asher, Rabbi Jacob
Baron, Salo, 107
bar Yochai, Shimon, 86
The Beginning of Politics: Power in the Biblical Book of Samuel Book (Halbertal and Holmes), 105, 145
beit din/rabbinical court, 82, 83
ben Asher, Rabbi Jacob, 112
ben Isaac, Rabbi Solomon, 77
ben Maimon, Rabbi Moshe, 49
ben Nachman, Rabbi Moses, 30
Ben-Sasson, H. H., 137
Berlin, Isaiah, 24, 26
Berman, Joshua, 92, 130, 148, 149, 173, 209n30, 211n26
Bible, human slavery/servitude in, 37–38
Bick, Rabbi Ezra, 24, 35
Bleich, Rabbi J. David, 43, 94, 204n62
blessings, xii, xv, 50, 74, 75, 90, 94, 158, 228
Block, Walter, 184, 187
blood redeemer, 49–51
Boaz, David, 4, 8, 18, 40, 69–70, 103, 152, 153, 169, 173–174
body/bodies, 17, 18, 23, 33, 36, 38–66, 80, 90, 104, 110, 155, 165, 198n15
Brennan, Jason, 16, 28, 29, 69, 169, 173
b'tselem Elohim/divine image/image of God, 56, 72, 162

C
Cain, xvii, 177, 178
capitalism, 5, 67, 138–141, 183
capitation tax, 106
Cardozo, Rabbi Nathan Lopes, 32
Carlebach, Elisheva, 109, 110
Carlebach, Rabbi Shlomo, 194n22
Cato Institute, 4
Chabad-Lubavitch, 48, 53
Chaim, Chofetz, 46
Chajes, Rabbi Zvi Hirsch, 147
chametz, 81
charity, 117–121
    in Jewish thought, 111–117
children, 17, 19, 28, 31, 58, 59, 63, 84, 112, 124, 135, 152, 158, 183, 225, 227
Chodorow, Adam, 110
Chomsky, Noam, 4
Choshen Mishpat, 79
Christianity, 203n53
Classical Liberals, 4
coercion, 11, 13, 18, 19, 42, 58, 70, 100, 103, 125, 150, 153, 165, 166, 170, 192n1
Cohen, Rabbi Alfred, 43, 44
Cohen, Steven M., 159
common law, 168
communal leadership, 157
community, 179
    individualism *versus*, 151–174, 173–174
    Judaism and, 154–159
    libertarianism and, 163–171
communism, 138

conscription, 61, 104, 157
consent, ix, 55, 68, 69, 102, 105, 145, 157, 164, 170, 209n30
Conservative Judaism, 46, 158, 159, 196n41
Conway, David, 89
courts, ix, viii, 49, 51–53, 78, 79, 82–84, 103, 107, 142, 143, 148, 166, 167, 171, 172, 180
Created Equal: How the Bible Broke with Ancient Political Thought (Berman), 148

D
Dan-Cohen, Meir, 47
Danish Jews, 134–135
Davis, Dena S., 46
Democratic Party, xiii, 4-5, 133
Deuteronomy, 71, 104, 145
dina d'malkhuta dina, 141–144, 178
dignity of the individual/individual dignity, 13, 152, 153, 161–163
The Discovery of Freedom (Lane), 18
diversity, 162
discrimination, 28, 134
diversity, ixv, 15, 16, 162, 166, 179, 212n39
Divine Ownership Theory, 51, 56, 63
Don't Hurt People and Don't Take Their Stuff: A Libertarian Manifesto (Kibbe), 173–174
Dorff, Rabbi Elliott, 46
Douglass, Frederick, 153
Draper, Robert, 7, 8
drugs, 59, 60, 126

E
egalitarianism, 130, 148, 149
elections, xi, 5, 6, 8, 10, 11, 76, 136, 170, 190
Eliezer, Tzitz. *See* Waldenburg, Rabbi Eliezer
Elon, Menachem, 107
Enlightenment, 129, 140
Eve, 160
Exodus, ix, 12, 22, 24, 33, 35, 36, 86, 201n19, 210n16, 211n26

F
Feiglin, Moshe, 11
Feinstein, Rabbi Moshe, 45
Feuer, Rabbi Avrohom Chaim, 115

food, 27, 30, 59, 72–76, 79, 80, 90, 137, 138, 143, 207n51
Foundation for Economic Education, 3
The Fountainhead (Rand), 152
fraud, 15, 60, 61, 67, 70, 99, 132, 142, 143
freedom, 175–176
  different kinds of, 24–29
  Judaism and, 22–24
  libertarian understandings of, 16–19
  versus servitude, 15–38
Freedom and the Torah (Maymin), 192n1
Freedom Caucus, 5–6
free market, 4, 67, 138–141, 171-172, 195n27
Friedersdorf, Conor, 8
Friedman, Milton, 4, 138–141, 184
Friedman, Rose, 184
From a Welfare State to a Welfare Society (Rodger), 122

G
Genesis, 72, 73
Gillespie, Nick, 6, 7
Gobry, Pascal-Emmanuel, 61
God, Judaism and service of, viii, 15 19–22, 35, 175
The God of the Machine (Paterson), 101
Goldberg, Rabbi Zalman Nechemia, 55
Goodkind, Adam, 46
Gordon, David, 183
government, 178–179
government persecution, of Jews, 136–138
government protection
  government tyranny *versus*, 132–150
  of Jews, 133–135
government regulation, 60, 61, 205n24
government spending
  in Jewish thought, 121–127
  libertarianism, charity, the welfare state and critique of, 117–121
government tyranny, *versus* government protection, 132–150

H
Haggadah, 23
Halbertal, Moshe, 105, 145, 147
Hanina, Rabbi, 133, 136
Hatam Sofer. *See* Sofer, R. Moses
Hayek, F. A., 192n1
Hazony, Yoram, 147
Hebrew, 20, 72, 78, 84

Hebrew scriptures, 58, 84, 107, 147, 173, 176
   politics of, 144–150
Heertje, Arnold, 181
hefker, 80
Heller, Anne C., 184
Herbert, Auberon, 164, 165
Heritage Foundation, 7
Herzog, R. Isaac, 78, 92, 142
Heschel, Rabbi Abraham Joshua, 31
Hillel, 82, 186, 187
Hirsch, Rabbi Samson Raphael, 73, 90
A History of the Jewish People (Ben-Sasson), 137
Holmes, Stephen, 105, 145, 147
Horwitz, Steven, 185, 186
Hospers, John, 70, 71, 103
Hutner, Rabbi Yitzchok, 184

I
ibn Attar, Rabbi Chaim, 76
ibn Migash, Joseph ben Meir HaLevi, 50
ibn Zimra, David ben Solomon, 51
income tax, 106
Index of Economic Freedom, 7
indirect taxes, 106
individualism, vii, xiv, 5, 8, 18, 179, 181
   versus community, 151–174
   Judaism and, 160–163
   libertarianism and, 151–174
individual liberty, 195n27
infants, 17, 58, 87
In God's Shadow: Politics in the Hebrew Bible (Walzer), 145
Internet, 7
Israel, 51, 61, 74, 75, 77, 78, 84-89, 92, 105-107, 112-113, 127, 129, 134, 140, 142, 145,148, 154-156, 162-163, 172, 180, 184, 195n27, 196n44, 201n19, 209n30, 210n12n15, 212n1
   particularities of, 11–12
Israel (modern state), 105, 122, 142, 180, 201n19
Isserles, Rabbi Moshe, 115
It Usually Begins With Ayn Rand (Tuccille), 1

J
Jakobovits, Rabbi Immanuel, 44
Jefferson, Thomas, 153

Jeremiah (prophet), 78
Jewish attitudes, towards labor, 85–90
Jewish community, 111, 120, 131, 136, 155
Jewish ideas
   favoring property ownership, 78–85
   against property ownership, 71–78
Jewish law, 53, 57, 63, 78–79, 95, 143, 162, 180, 186
Jewish libertarians, 141, 181, 185-186
Jewish Medical Ethics (Jakobovits), 44
Jewish mysticism, 89
The Jewish Political Tradition (Walzer, Zohar and Lorberbaum), 145, 146
Jewish property law, 85
Jewish spontaneous order, 171–173
Jewish taxation, 121
Jewish Theological Seminary, 158
Jewish thought
   government spending and the welfare state in, 121–127
   ownership and stewardship of body in, 43–48
   taxation in, 104–111
   tzedakah versus charity in, 111–117
Jews, 10, 20–21, 87, 184, 185
   capitalism, the free market and, 138–141
   and government, 150
   government persecution and neglect of, 136–138
   government protection of, 133–135
   history of, 134
   and libertarianism, 150, 181–186
   in North Africa, 134
   in United States, 135
Johnson, Gary, 5, 10
Jose, Manuel L., 105, 106
Jotkowitz, Alan, 45
Jubilee/*Yovel*, 77, 96, 97, 107, 125
Judaism, 12, 15, 99, 104, 180, 198n15
   and community, 154–159
   and freedom, 22–24
   and individualism, 160–163
   and service of God, 19–22
   and spontaneous order, 171–173
Judaism and Healing: Halakhic Perspectives (Bleich), 43
Judaism, Law & the Free Market: An Analysis (Lifshitz), 171
Judaism values community, 157

K
Kagan, Rabbi Yisrael Meir, 45
Kaplan, Rabbi Aryeh, 155
Karo, Rabbi Yosef, 79, 112, 114-115
Khmelnitski, Bogdan, 137
Kibbe, Matt, 173-174
kinyan, 49, 50, 95
Kirzner, Israel, 184-185
Klapper, Rabbi Aryeh, 48, 57, 104, 146, 147
Kochen, Madeleine, 80, 81, 93-95, 113
Kohelet Policy Forum, 195n27
Koppel, Moshe, 195n27
Kristol, Irving, 140
kuppa, 120

L
labor, Jewish attitudes towards, 85-90
Lane, Rose Wilder, 18, 19
Law of Nature, 17
law of the land, 141-144
Leibowitz, Yeshayahu, 36, 162, 163
leket, 74, 75, 80, 94, 108, 116, 203n60
Levine, Aaron, 108
Levine, Rabbi Aaron, 205n24
Levi, Rabbi, 74
Leviticus, 76
libertarianism, *passim*
    from Ayn Rand to, 1-14
    and community, 163-171
    and government, 150
    and individualism, 151-174
    Jews and, 150, 181-186
    philosophers of, 198n7
Libertarianism: A Political Philosophy for Tomorrow (Hospers), 70, 103
Libertarianism: What Everyone Needs to Know (Brennan), 28
The Libertarian Mind (Boaz), 40
Libertarian Moment, 5-12
Libertarian Party, 5, 6, 8, 11, 170, 212n39
Libertarian Party of the United States, 127
Libertarian Party Platform, 16, 17, 40, 58, 62, 64, 67, 83, 100, 102, 154, 163-164, 170, 171, 176
libertarian socialism, 4
libertarian thought, self-ownership in, 40-43, 58-63
liberty, exclusive/overlapping ideas of, 38
Lichtenstein, Rabbi Aharon, 21, 22

Lifshitz, Joseph Isaac, 108, 125-127, 171, 172
Likhovski, Assaf, 127, 128
Locke, John, 17, 33-34, 39-41, 64, 68-70, 101-102, 124, 153
Lorberbaum, Menachem, 146, 147

M
Maimonides, 37, 49, 50-53, 88, 105, 112, 147,
Mandeville, Bernard, 168
marriage, 8, 27, 28, 34, 79, 87, 180, 190, 204n62
Marxism, 140
Marx, Karl, 183
materialism, 89, 202n42
Maymin, Philip Z., 148, 192n1
"Me Decade," 7
medical ethics, 43-46
midat S'dom, 83
Mill, John Stuart, 153
Mishnah, 47, 78, 79
mitzvah, 19-21, 32, 34, 75, 76, 80, 81, 88, 90, 93, 111,112, 114-115, 174, 180, 187, 210n18
Modern Hebrew, 50
Moore, Charles K., 105, 106
morality, 13, 29, 117, 125, 126, 133
mortgage/property lien, 91, 92, 95, 96
Moses, 20, 22, 24, 30, 33, 47, 57, 71, 88, 89, 144, 149, 156, 192n1, 209n33
Mount Sinai, 156
Muller, Jerry Z., 138, 140
Muslim, 136-138

N
National Review, 8
nefesh, 49, 52-54
Negative Liberty, 24-29, 33, 38
neglect, of Jews, 136-138
neshama, 54
Nicholas II, Tsar, 136-137
Nolan, David, 194n26
nonaggression axiom, 18, 26, 42, 59, 165, 187, 188
Nozick, Robert, 4, 102, 184, 188

O
Obama, Barack, 2-3
Objectivism, 1, 152

obligation, vii, xi, xii, xvii, 21, 23, 26, 27, 30, 31, 41, 44, 45, 46, 50, 52, 54, 56, 59, 60, 74, 75, 78, 80, 81, 87, 88, 93, 99, 108, 109, 111, 113, 114, 116, 125–127, 129, 157, 158, 161, 163, 166, 180, 196n41
Oden, Robert A., Jr., 107
Oral Torah, 48
Organ Donation and the Divine Lien in Talmudic Law (Kochen), 81, 93
Or ha-Chaim, 76, 115, 201n18
Orthodox Jewish law, 196n41
Orthodox Jews, 46, 186, 192n1, 210n18
Orthodox organizations, 200n33
Ottoman Empire, 137
ownership
   in Jewish thought, 43–48
   versus possession, 90–97
   versus stewardship, 39–65, 66–97, 98–131

P
Paine, Thomas, 153
Paley, Michael R., 192n1
Palmer, Tom G., 67–68, 120, 165–166
Paschal sacrifice, 36
Passover Seder, 22
Paterson, Isabel, 101
Paul, Ron, 8
Payne, James L., 129
peace, 15, 16, 19, 67, 68, 112, 113, 165, 225
pe-ah, 74, 75, 76, 80, 93, 94, 108, 116
Persian Jews, 134
Pesach/Passover, 22, 23, 33, 34, 36, 81, 196n46, 209n33
Pew Research Center, 9, 159
Philosophy of Objectivism (Rand), 1
Pirkei Avot/Chapters of the Fathers/Ethics of the Fathers, xvii, 19, 33, 85, 86, 133, 136, 196n40
pluralism, 162
police, 60, 103, 130, 132, 190
politics, 146
Ponnuru, Ramesh, 8
Portuguese Synagogue, 181, 182
Positive Liberty, 24–29, 38
possession, ownership *versus*, 90–97
poverty, 25, 85, 86, 109, 111, 112, 115, 116, 123, 124, 148

prayer, 19, 20, 22, 37, 50, 79, 86, 113, 157, 158, 182, 196n41, 202n44
private property, 66–97, 176
product labeling, 86
property ownership
   Jewish ideas against, 71–78
   Jewish ideas favoring, 78–85
   libertarian notions of, 67–71
property rights, 67–71
property tax, 106
prosperity, 7, 15, 16, 19, 61, 66–68, 135, 140
prozbul, 82, 83
Public Religion Research Institute (PRRI), 10

R
Rabban Gamliel, 86
Rabbinical Council of America, 200n33
Rabbinic Assembly, 158
race/racism, 6, 153, 155, 190, 214n2
Rackman, Rabbi Emanuel, 44
Raimondo, Justin, 183
Rakefet-Rothkoff, Rabbi Aaron, 141
Rand, Ayn, 1–5, 117–118, 151, 152, 163, 177, 181, 184, 185, 189, 195n38, 209n3
Rashi. *See* ben Isaac, Rabbi Solomon
Read, Leonard, 3
Reason magazine, 6
Republican Party, xiii–xiv, 4–6, 8–9, 11, 186
Ricardo, David, 181, 182
rights, xi, xii, 4, 13, 15, 18, 22, 28, 29, 34, 38–44, 55–58, 61, 62, 64, 66, 67, 69–73, 83, 91, 92, 96, 107, 122, 124, 126, 127, 132, 135, 148, 153, 154, 166, 167, 171, 189, 192n1, 195n27, 198n15, 204n62
Ri Migash. *See* ibn Migash, Joseph ben Meir HaLevi
Robertson, Alex, 122
Rodger, John J., 122
Rolling Stone interview, 2
Rosenbaum, Alissa Zinovievna, 181, 184
Rosenberg, Rabbi Shimon Gershon, 22
Rosh HaShanah, 19, 83, 113
Rothbard, Murray, 18, 41–43, 70, 71, 100, 166–168, 183, 188, 213n9
Russell, Dean, 3
Ryan, Paul, 5

S

Sabbath, 31-32, 45, 51, 73, 77, 79, 80, 90, 144, 148, 158, 161, 207n51, 211n22
Sacks, Rabbi Jonathan, 85, 89, 91, 141, 162, 201n20
safety net, 119, 124
Saiman, Chaim, 180
Satlow, Michael, 123, 124, 156, 193n2
Schneerson, Rabbi Menachem Mendel, 53
Schorsch, Rabbi Ismar, 158
Scottish Enlightenment, 16
self-defense, 57
self-injury/self-harm, 56
selfishness, 117
self-ownership, 55-57, 176, 199n29
  of body in libertarian thought, 40-43, 58-63
  theory of, 64
servitude, freedom *versus*, 15-38
Shagar, Rav. *See* Rosenberg, Rabbi Shimon Gershon
Shammai, 186-187
shared ownership, 52, 55, 63, 97, 176
Shemittah, 77, 82, 83
Shmuel, Mar, 142
Shneur Zalman of Liadi, 48, 54
Shulchan Arukh, 79
shuttafut/partnership, 55, 75, 92, 93, 176, 210n18
Shylock's pound of flesh, 48-55
Sifra, 201n18
Sinai, Mount, 156
Sinclair, Daniel, 45
slavery, 17-19, 22-24, 35, 37-38, 41, 42, 58, 101, 148, 154, 157, 165, 175, 197n61, 197n62, 211n26
Slifkin, Rabbi Natan, 86, 88
Smith, Adam, 16, 168, 181
socialism, 140, 141
Sofer, R. Moses, 88
Soloveitchik, Rabbi Joseph B., 21, 24, 36, 155
special assessment tax, 106
speech/free speech, 9, 26, 67, 71, 126, 212n55, xv
Sperber, Rabbi Daniel, 112, 161
spontaneous order, 168, 169, 171-173, 192n1
state of Israel, 11, 105, 134, 142, 180, 201n19
Steinberg, Rabbi Avraham, 55

stewardship
  in Jewish thought, 43-48
  ownership *versus*, 39-65, 66-97, 98-131
suicide, 42, 43, 46, 51, 52, 56-58, 64, 156
Sukkot, 80, 81

T

Talmud, 30, 33, 79, 84, 94, 142, 161, 172
  human slavery/servitude in, 37-38
  key passages in, 86
  rabbis of, 96
  recitation of blessing food items, 74
Tamari, Meir, 105, 108, 121, 124, 129
taxation, 98, 176-177
  in Jewish thought and practice, 104-111
  theft, 99-104
tax culture, 129
Temple tax, 110
Ten Commandments, 21
Tetragrammaton, 184, 196n39
tikkun 'olam, 31, 89
Tomasi, John, 188
Torah, xiii, 19-21, 24, 30, 33, 37, 47-48, 51, 75, 77-78, 82, 86-89, 148-149, 154-156, 158, 171-172, 182, 186-187
Torat Kohanim, 201n18
Tuccille, Jerome, 1, 2, 187, 193n5
Two Treatises of Government (Locke), 39
tzedakah, 177
  in Jewish thought, 111-117

U

United States, Jews in, 135
United States Congress, 6
United States House of Representatives, 6

V

vaccination, 58-59
The Virtue of Selfishness (Rand), 151
voluntary charity, 98, 99
voluntaryism, 164-165
The Voluntaryist Creed (Herbert), 164
voluntary associations, 36, 151, 164, 165, 169, 170, 173, 174
voluntary taxation, 127-131
von Mises, Ludwig, 17, 182

W

Waldenburg, Rabbi Eliezer, 44-45
Walter, David, 103

Walzer, Michael, 145, 146, 147, 209n30
Washington, George, 135
Watner, Carl, 164
Welch, Matt, 6, 7, 8
Weld, William, 5, 10
welfare, 177–178
welfare state, 13, 117–121, 131, 133, 139, 141, 178
   in Jewish thought, 121–127
Williamson, Kevin D., 9, 11
Wollstonecraft, Mary, 153

Y
Yehoshua, 84
Yishmael, Rabbi, 86

Yisraeli, R. Shaul, 51–54, 82–83
yoke of mitzvot, 20
yoke of the Kingdom of Heaven, 19, 20
yoke of Torah, 19, 20, 34
Yom Kippur, 79, 113
Yose, Rabbi, 85
Yovel, 77

Z
Zalman, Rabbi Shneur, 49, 53
Zevin, Rabbi Shlomo Yosef, 48, 50, 52, 54
Ziglar, Zig, 21
Zion, Noam, 113, 118, 120, 122, 124, 125
Zionism, 185
Zohar, Noam J., 146

www.ingramcontent.com/pod-product-compliance
Lightning Source LLC
Chambersburg PA
CBHW051120160426
43195CB00014B/2282